J.R.

# J.R.

## THE FAST, CRAZY LIFE OF HOCKEY'S MOST OUTSPOKEN & MOST COLOURFUL PERSONALITY

## JEREMY ROENICK

WITH KEVIN ALLEN

 HARPERCOLLINS PUBLISHERS LTD

*J.R.*
Copyright © 2012 by Jeremy Roenick.

Published by HarperCollins Publishers Ltd

First Edition

HarperCollins books may be purchased for educational, business,
or sales promotional use through our Special Markets Department.

HarperCollins Publishers Ltd
2 Bloor Street East, 20th Floor
Toronto, Ontario, Canada
M4W 1A8

*www.harpercollins.ca*

Library and Archives Canada Cataloguing in Publication
information is available upon request

ISBN 978-1-44340-679-6

Printed and bound in the United States
RRD 9 8 7 6 5 4 3 2 1

*For Tracy*

# Contents

# Introduction

In 2007, I was watching Pittsburgh Penguins star Sidney Crosby being interviewed live by NBC analyst Pierre McGuire before an NHL playoff game, and I wanted to reach through the television and grab Crosby by the fucking throat.

McGuire asked Crosby what the Penguins needed to do to beat Ottawa, and Crosby was prattling on about how the Penguins needed "consistency" and to have every Pittsburgh player step up.

It was the wrong fucking answer. It was a bullshit answer. When McGuire asked Crosby that question, Crosby should have stared into the eye of the camera and said, "We are going to win this game because I'm going to be the best motherfucking player on the ice."

If you want to inspire your teammates, those are the words that get the job done.

That's what I would have said. Maybe I would have sanitized my language for television, or maybe not. It would not have been the first—or last—time I said something I should not have said on live television.

Crosby should have taken that moment in 2007 to announce to himself and his teammates that failure was not an option. Don't give us that "We are going to try our best" line. Mark Messier isn't remembered for saying his team needed to be consistent against the New Jersey Devils in the 1995 playoffs. He's remembered for guaranteeing a victory against New Jersey. Patrick Roy didn't stand up in the Montreal dressing room and tell his teammates he was going to play "consistently." Roy told his teammates that if they scored two goals, they were going to be Stanley Cup champions because he wouldn't give up more than one goal.

In 1996, I pissed off Team USA general manager Lou Lamoriello because I predicted the Americans were going to win the fucking World Cup of Hockey. I hadn't even been named to the team yet, and I ended up not playing because I didn't have an NHL contract. But I wanted to fire up my teammates, and maybe rile up the Canadians, with my words.

When I was playing for the Chicago Blackhawks in 1992, captain Dirk Graham told us, "You will see me play the best game I've ever played tonight." Then he went out and scored a hat trick.

We were in awe of him after that effort.

When you are an athlete and someone asks you what you intend to do to win a game, you need to challenge yourself. You need to announce to the world that you intend to do whatever it takes to win. You need to show some balls. That's the way I played. That's the way I think.

The modern athlete has become too worried about saying anything that is going to rile up the other team. Modern stars worry too much about being diplomatic.

Fuck diplomacy. Leave polite competition for church-league softball players, or athletes who let fear be an obstacle to realizing their full potential.

Fear of failure can paralyze your inner drive. Fear can become the roadblock to your success. Fear can prevent you from achieving your objective. Fear can overwhelm you to the point of smothering your dreams and ambition.

But you can look at fear another way. Fear can also be the world's greatest motivator. Former NHL coach Mike Keenan taught me to use fear to fuel my energy. When I became terrified by the consequences of failure, that's when I played my best hockey. The thought that Keenan could bury me on the bench, or kill my career, scared the shit out of me. It also motivated me to play the game as if my career depended upon my next shift. If I wasn't an NHL player, who was I? Was I going to be a garbageman? Was I going to be a fireman? I didn't know. I just knew that the idea of not playing hockey was fucking frightful.

I wasn't a physical player before I played for Keenan. Fear of Keenan motivated me to become a top NHL player. That fear drove me for two decades in the NHL. No one influenced my career more than Keenan, but there were two other events prior to my meeting Keenan that had an impact.

When I was seven years old, I went to a Hartford Whalers game, and Gordie Howe was playing for them. A bunch of us would lean over the glass to get a better look as players skated in the pre-game warmup. During one of his laps around his zone, Mr. Hockey scooped up some ice shavings and dumped them on my head as he skated by. I thought it was the coolest thing I had ever seen—until a couple of seconds later, when Howe looked back and winked at me.

For three seconds, it was just me and Gordie Howe connecting. That moment changed my life. I felt like Gordie had given me a gift, and I wanted to pay it back. When I arrived in the NHL, I made sure I connected with fans the way Gordie had taught me to do.

The other event that changed me was watching the U.S. team defeat the Soviets on television in 1980. It was that moment that I knew I wanted to be an elite-level hockey player. It was not Mike Eruzione's goal that excited me as much as the celebration that followed the victory. I wanted to know what it would be like to celebrate with teammates the way the Americans did at Lake Placid. Like many other American players, I carried some of that confidence with me as I continued along my path toward an NHL career.

What links together the Howe, Keenan and Eruzione moments is that they each made me emotional and fuelled my passion. Flying around the ice with my jersey flapping behind was the key to my success. Certainly, talent is crucial, but you won't be respected at the NHL level unless you play with overflowing desire. Aren't passion and emotion what life is about? I really don't want to do anything that doesn't stir my passion. Life is short. Why bother with anything that doesn't excite you?

When I started this book project, my stated objective was to produce an honest, raw, emotional book that gives the reader a peek at what happens to players when the curtains are drawn. I'm hoping this work elicits a strong emotional response from you. When you read this book, I hope it makes you angry. I hope it makes you curious. I hope it makes you laugh. I hope it makes you think. Mostly, I hope it makes you wonder, "What the fuck was Roenick thinking?"

If I get that response from you, then you and I are on the same page.

# CHAPTER 1

# Please Come to Boston

When I was an 11-year-old playing peewee hockey in the Washington, D.C., area, I remember backing down from an encounter with an opponent and hearing a voice from the crowd yell, "Get off the ice, you pussy."

Looking into the stands, I realized it was my mother.

In the 1980s, the Roenicks were not like the model American families depicted on a television situation comedy. We were not like *Leave It to Beaver*, *The Cosby Show* or *Family Ties*. There was nothing typical about our American family. The Roenicks would have been a better fit for one of today's reality shows. We could have produced the level of swearing, screaming, angst, drama and unusual storylines necessary to bring viewers back every week. They would have tuned in just to see how many miles we were driving, or how many mountains the Roenicks would be willing to move, to make sure I could play in a good hockey game.

If we were on reality television, directors could have built an entire episode around the time my father, Wally, booted me out of the car and made me walk three miles home in winter conditions because my effort wasn't as strong as it should have been in a hockey game. My family's overzealous pursuit of hockey success for their oldest son probably would have had viewers shaking their heads about the nutty lifestyle we lived to support my ability to play elite-level hockey. We were such a hockey family that my dad tells the story of driving away from our house in Connecticut after it was sold and realizing that one side of the house was black from pucks striking it over and over and over again.

Certainly, there were people around us who considered it bizarre, or maybe even insane, that my mom and dad built their lives around my sports activities. At age 13, I was living in Fairfax, Virginia, and commuting 250 miles each way on weekends to play for a hockey team in Totowa, New Jersey. Every Friday during the hockey season, I had a 3 p.m. reservation on People Express Airlines to fly from Dulles Airport in Virginia to Newark for the weekend. Even with People Express's special fares of $79 or $99 one way, my dad estimated that it cost about $25,000 in total for me to play for the New Jersey Rockets that season. He always joked that my NHL travel schedule was like a walk in the park compared to the miles we logged in my youth hockey days.

"Tough travel is when you are 14 and you get home from a road trip at five in the morning," my dad said. But, as he points out, at least I was able to fly to New Jersey. "The idiots had to drive," he said.

He was referring, of course, to himself and my mother, Jo, who would drive from Virginia to New Jersey. At the time, my dad was an executive for Mobil Oil and he travelled around the country for his work. It was standard procedure for him to land in Virginia after a lengthy work trip and then jump into a car for a drive to New Jersey. Sometimes he would take a red-eye flight directly from the west coast to Newark. As busy as my dad was, he usually found a way to attend my games.

To get an invitation to play for the New Jersey Rockets was an honour for a bantam-age hockey player in that era. The Rockets organization has been around since the 1970s. Joey Mullen, the first American player to reach 500 goals at the NHL level, played for the Rockets. They prided themselves on bringing together the best players from Long Island, New Jersey, Connecticut and the Washington, D.C., area. They recruited me after I had scored 203 goals and produced 485 points for the Washington Metros in my final season of peewee hockey. If it is possible for an 11-year-old to have a hockey reputation, I had one. The NHL is full of players whose first international notice came from the Quebec peewee tournament. I was one of those guys. In one tournament game, I netted eight goals. The tournament record was nine goals, set by some kid named Wayne Gretzky.

The Rockets also recruited my Metros linemate Matt Mallgrave. When my family moved us to Northern Virginia when I was 10, all I heard was that Mallgrave was the best player in the area. I don't know who I was expecting to meet, but I sure didn't expect to meet a player sporting a Mohawk haircut. I remember thinking, "This freak is the best player in the area?" Meanwhile, he told me later that he kept hearing I was going to come into Washington and be the new best player. He was unimpressed when he saw me in street clothes and realized that I weighed 15 pounds less than everyone else. He told me later he was thinking, "This little shit is the guy everyone is talking about?"

Despite our first impressions, we ended up becoming lifelong buddies. Although I didn't recall this, Matt remembers that he was matched up against me in our first scrimmage and I scored six goals against him. He said he knew then that the hockey in Washington, D.C., wasn't quite as strong as the hockey we were playing on the east coast. But Matt was unquestionably a quality player, netting more than 100 goals for the Metros one season. He was also one of the top players for the Rockets.

When Mallgrave decided to play for the Rockets, his father secured a townhouse in New Jersey. The Mallgraves would pick me up at the airport when I landed there on Friday afternoons. My dad would join us later when he drove in from home, or flew in from his latest business trip.

In my youth hockey days, my dad was heavily invested in my career. My playing style in those days came from the many talks I had with him about how the game should be played. He believed in teamwork, and if he thought I was selfish on the ice, he would holler at me on the car ride home.

The impression that everyone had in those days was that my dad was more intense than I was. Most of my teammates considered me laid-back. What everyone also remembers about my dad was that he was a chain smoker. When he coached my peewee team, the kids thought it was hilarious when smoke would come out of his mouth when he was barking instructions at us.

In looking back at our weekends in New Jersey, Mallgrave always recalls my dad with a cigarette in his hand. "Over a weekend, I swear he must have smoked 170 cigarettes," Mallgrave recalls.

The Rockets won back-to-back U.S. national bantam championships when Matt and I played for them in 1983 and 1984. In my first season with the Rockets, the only team we couldn't beat consistently was the Chicago Young Americans, a team that boasted

Justin Duberman, who ended up playing college hockey at North Dakota, plus a few games for the Pittsburgh Penguins; Joe Suk, who would become a quality scorer in the Quebec Major Junior Hockey League; and Rick Olczyk, who is an assistant general manager of the Edmonton Oilers. He is also the brother of former NHL standout Eddie Olczyk, who is also an NBC analyst. The Rockets always ended up playing against Chicago in the finals of tournaments, and I believe we only beat them twice all season. But one of our wins came in a 3–2 quadruple-overtime national championship game in Buffalo. I played in that game with a separated shoulder, courtesy of a check by Duberman in our preliminary loss to the Young Americans. In the title contest, I exacted my revenge with two goals and an assist.

Mike Ross, who went on to be a top college player at Brown University, scored the game winner after a giveaway by Olczyk. In 1996–97, Ross scored 50 goals for the East Coast Hockey League's South Carolina Stingrays. He was a smooth, smart fucking player in the style of Craig Janney. He was probably faster than Janney.

Interesting, Duberman ended up playing with the Rockets the following year. We went all the way to the finals again—this time in Madison, Wisconsin, where we downed Detroit Compuware 3 2. Future NHL player Denny Felsner played on that team, as did Mike Boback. At that time, some people argued that Boback was the top American player in our age group.

At the peewee and bantam age, it's impossible to project who has NHL potential and who has not. But even when I was a peewee, everyone in the hockey world knew who the best players in the country were. Mike Modano was in Detroit's Little Caesars organization, and my rivalry with him started when we were 10 or

11 years old. At every tournament over the next few years, I measured myself against what Modano was accomplishing. That didn't stop when we reached the NHL.

The funny thing is that many in the hockey world thought Boback—who, like Modano, was from Michigan—was Modano's equal. Boback seemed to be more physically mature than Modano. Both of them seemed like they were extra large.

Boback was a quality college player at Providence and a solid minor-league player. But he never made the NHL. In my era, Michigan had another top player in Neil Carnes, who ended up playing in the Quebec Major Junior Hockey League when I was there. But he was killed in a motorcycle accident. Rick Olczyk played for Brown University but never played professional hockey. If there was one story that has defined the Roenick family during my childhood, it is my father's decision to take a significant demotion—and a dramatic cut in pay—from Mobil Oil to move the family from Virginia to Massachusetts when I was ready to enter high school. My dad has said the move was about "quality of life" as well as hockey. "But hockey was a big part of it," he says.

My dad worked 40 years for Mobil and says his career chart looks like "the point of an arrow." He had a steep rise to the top and then a quick fall after he moved to Massachusetts. He was a marketing projects manager when we lived in Northern Virginia; he was an entry-level territory manager after going to Massachusetts. My dad won't say how much money he lost in the change of venue, but it has been my impression that his pay was cut in half.

The backstory behind our move to Massachusetts was my parents' weariness and concern about all of the moving the family had endured until that point. Because of my dad's position, we had moved

10 times in 15 years. If my dad had continued on his career path as a projects manager, he knew he would continue to move every couple of years. He noted that other executives moving that often had children who were in trouble. He didn't want that to happen to his two sons. Based on where my dad knew his career was heading, he expected that his next move could be to Florida, or Los Angeles, Dallas or Louisiana. This was the mid-1980s and those areas didn't have the hockey presence they have today. Because hockey was a big part of our life, he didn't want to risk going someplace where we couldn't find quality competition. My parents wanted to put down roots in Massachusetts and stay there.

We were a dedicated hockey family. Thanksgiving tradition for us meant having a turkey dinner at four o'clock on Wednesday and then my mom and younger brother, Trevor, climbing into the car for a drive to Buffalo for a tournament. When they arrived there, they would call my dad to make sure he knew they'd arrived safely. And then my father and I would board a plane for Detroit, where I had a tournament. The family would be reunited at nine o'clock Sunday night to resume our lives. When I was a peewee, we would have Christmas dinner and then we would pick up Mallgrave and his father and drive all night from Maryland to Ottawa, Ontario, for a tournament.

Perhaps the best aspect of my move to Massachusetts was my decision to play at Thayer Academy, where I met my wife, Tracy, and my lifelong friend Tony Amonte. Tony and I lit it up at Thayer in terms of offensive production. Our game was built on speed, and there weren't many defences that could keep up with us.

It is anybody's guess whether Tony or I was the faster skater, but I'm going to say it was Tony because of the bizarre story of his broken leg. As a Thayer freshman, he had broken his leg during a game. The break was severe enough that there was concern about whether he would still be the same player. It was broken badly enough that he missed a month and a half of school. People wondered whether his skating would be the same. It wasn't; it was better. After the injury, he became an amazing skater. He was a powerful strider. No one should have been surprised because he was such a hard worker.

It was costly to attend Thayer Academy, and Tony and his brother Rocco had their own landscaping business to raise their own money. When Tony wasn't playing hockey, he was working. Rocco also played college hockey at Lowell. Tony wasn't the best athlete in the Amonte family. His sister Kelly was an unbelievable lacrosse player, and today she coaches at Northwestern.

On the ice, Tony and I had great fucking chemistry. As a sophomore, I played 24 games and had 31 goals and 34 assists for 65 points. Tony had 57 points on 25 goals and 32 assists. As a junior, I played 24 games and had 34 goals and 50 assists for 84 points. Tony had 68 points on 30 goals and 38 assists. The third man on our line was Danny Green, a quality high school player who is now an attorney.

But what I remember most about our days at Thayer is how much fun we had *off* the ice. Tony and I had our version of mild hazing for the rookie players when we were there. We held naked cookie races. In the dressing room, the freshmen had to place a cookie between their ass cheeks and scoot across the floor without dropping the cookie. The loser had to eat the cookies. It was a lot more fun than it sounds in writing.

Today, I'm a guy who thinks he has a fashion sense. But

when I was in high school, I was the worst fucking dresser in Massachusetts. I regularly wore this ugly pink, fuzzy sweater that looked like something Dr. Huxtable would have worn on *The Cosby Show*. The sweater had threads hanging off it like split ends. Mallgrave attended St. Paul's Academy, and he was always razzing me that my entire wardrobe came from the Sears catalogue. Everyone always kidded me about my sweater.

One day at practice, Tony was using a blowtorch to work on his hockey stick. He turned to talk to me as I entered the room, and the flame of his blowtorch reached the threads of my sweater, and suddenly they were on fire. The flames climbed up my sweater and singed my eyebrows before they fucking leaped over my head and evaporated. The threads were like wicks, and the flames went out as soon as they burned down.

Although it seems like a scary situation, the two of us just fucking laughed hysterically for a very long time.

Tony has the most infectious laugh you will ever witness. When he laughs, it seems as if he is out of control. His laughter makes *you* laugh. Our laughfest over my singed eyebrows didn't come close to matching Tony's greatest cascade of laughter. That would occur a few years later, when we were teammates on the Chicago Blackhawks. We decided to see the movie *Dumb and Dumber*. Early in that flick, Tony started laughing and couldn't stop. His laughter became so outrageously loud and funny that everyone in the theatre was laughing at him, instead of at the movie. I was in stitches.

Tony was also with me when I got my first tattoo, of the Tasmanian Devil holding a hockey stick. We were 16 at the time, way too young for me to be getting ink on my body.

Although Mallgrave and I went to different schools, we remained friends because he would stay with us in the summer—we played hockey together in the summer leagues. He would play on a line with Amonte and me. One of our favourite memories is of the time I tried to fix up Mallgrave with Tracy Vazza, the woman who would eventually become my wife. I've known Tracy since I was about 14, but I initially didn't view her as a potential soulmate. At the time, she seemed out of my league. I wasn't the most confident person on the planet when I was in prep school. She was a grade ahead of me, and she was far more socially active than I was. She was into fashion, and the only fashion I was concerned about was how I looked in a hockey jersey.

At the time, I was trying to date Tracy's friend, Martine Sifakis. It seemed it would be in my best interest if I could get Tracy and Matt together.

We were driving on Route 3 in Massachusetts en route to the arena for a game, and I told him, "Matt, I'm going to hook you up with this hot, awesome girl named Tracy." Just as I said this, a Porsche flew past us at about 90 miles per hour, coming back from Cape Cod. It was Tracy, behind the wheel of her mom's car. "That's her," I said as the sports car zoomed ahead.

We laughed then, and we still laugh about it today.

Tracy has always said that it didn't make any sense to her when she was introduced to me as Thayer's new hockey star. She didn't know much about the sport, but her brothers had both played at Thayer. Based on her brothers, Rick and Stephen, and their teammates, Tracy's impression was that all hockey players were rough and tumble and aggressive. I didn't fit that description. She considered me shy. When she tells that story to people who know me now, they find it amazingly funny.

"My brothers would fight someone on the street," Tracy has told me, "and you seemed like a wimp. I wondered, 'Who is this kid?'"

Anyone who knew us both would have said that Tracy was rebellious and I was straitlaced. Tracy dated a guy who wasn't from Thayer, someone her parents didn't like. She liked to host parties and attend parties; I was the kid who stayed home on a Friday night because I wanted to be well rested for a hockey tournament.

Tracy always says our relationship happened because she pursued it. We were friends for a couple of years before we started to date. We were always around each other. Amonte was actually dating Tracy's close friend Laurie Pfeffer, who is now Tony's wife. Laurie's parents and Tracy's parents were close friends. Laurie and Tracy used to take baths together when they were toddlers. Then, one day, Tracy and I became a couple. It just kind of happened. One minute we were talking after a hockey game, and the next we were making out at a party. Now, 25 years later, we are still together, married for almost two decades, with two great children, Brandi and Brett.

If you ask Tracy why she decided to make the first move, she will say "because Jeremy was just so flipping nice." I hope people still say that about me, because that has always been my objective. I've always tried to treat people with respect, and I try to be courteous to people I meet. What I liked about Tracy, besides the fact that she was hot, was the fact that she is a very smart, strong woman. That would become increasingly important to me as we started to navigate through life as adults.

Initially, Richard Vazza, Tracy's dad, had doubts about whether I was the right fit for his daughter. Mr. Vazza was a highly successful real estate developer who lived in style and comfort with his wife and five children. He placed a high value on ambition and education, and he wondered whether I would have either of those items when I was an adult.

Tracy still didn't know much about professional hockey at that point in our relationship, and when I told her that I thought I would be drafted early in the 1988 NHL draft, she didn't know what to think about it. When she mentioned to her dad my expectation of being drafted, he told her not to become too excited.

"Every kid wants to get drafted into the NHL, and few actually do," he said. Although Mr. Vazza had never seen me play, I'm sure he looked at my scrawny physique and figured I was confusing my daydreams with reality.

One evening, I was eating with the Vazza clan at a family dinner when the subject of college came up.

"I'm not sure that I'm going to end up in college," I said.

"What do you mean?" Tracy's mom asked.

"I think I can make it in the NHL," I answered.

Tracy's dad looked across the table at me as if I had just committed a felony in his presence. "Son," he said, "you had better think about an education, because the chances of you making the NHL probably aren't as good as you think they are."

Later that night, Tracy told me that when I was in the bathroom, her dad asked where our relationship was going.

"We are 17, Dad," Tracy had said. "We aren't getting married tomorrow."

But he still wanted to make it clear that he was concerned about what kind of potential mate I would make for his daughter. Tracy was an accomplished equestrian rider with Olympic aspirations, and her dad had just spent $250,000 on a quality horse for her.

"The boy is going nowhere," Mr. Vazza told Tracy. "He is never going to be able to afford another horse for you."

I wondered why it was deathly quiet when I returned from the bathroom.

Marrying Tracy was the best decision I ever made, and the second-best decision was hiring attorney Neil Abbott as my agent. Like my wife, Neil was with me through richer and poorer, and through sickness and health, during my NHL career.

At a time when many agents were knocking at my door, Neil seemed like the right fit for me. He knew the game because he was a former player, having played college hockey at Colgate from 1971 to 1975. Mike Milbury was his teammate there. As a lawyer, he knew the law. Because he was also working with NFL players, he knew the ins and outs of negotiating and injuries. He knew how to deal with American prep school players because he had represented Brian Lawton when he was the NHL's first-overall pick in 1984.

More importantly, Neil had a sincerity about him that convinced my family that his objective would always be to do what was in my best interest.

As it turned out, we were right in our assessment. Neil took care of my contract issues, my legal issues, and often some of my personal issues. He seemed more like a friend, or an older brother, than an agent. He was never the kind of agent who tells clients only what they want to hear. His opinions were always well reasoned, and his advice was always straight to the point. If he believed I was making a mistake, he told me. He didn't varnish his words to make me feel better. I've always respected him for that approach. When you are taking a cut of an athlete's salary, I think it is human nature to not want to rock the boat with that athlete. Neil would tip my boat over if he felt I needed it.

He had formed a partnership with Gus Badali, who at the time represented Wayne Gretzky, Mario Lemieux and Steve Yzerman.

Neil was always well versed in injuries and public relations; throughout my career, if I was hurt, Neil always knew who should be called. If I created a messy situation with my mouth, he served as the cleanup crew. Neil could contain the contamination before it spread too far.

"Neil is too smart for the business he is in," Duberman always says. "This business is not rocket science, and Neil could have been a rocket scientist. He is very intelligent and weird at the same time. He is an abstract thinker."

The bottom line for me is that Neil always had my back, through bad times and good ones.

In 1982, Neil represented Normand Léveillé, who received his full contract and benefits after he was stricken and paralyzed while playing for the Bruins in October 1982. In 1989, Neil was co-counsel when Glen Seabrooke sued the Philadelphia Flyers doctor for malpractice over treatment he received. Former first-round pick Seabrooke was awarded more than $5 million in damages. It may still be the largest sports injury case ever.

It was at Thayer that I met coach Arthur Valicenti, who helped ready me to play for Mike Keenan. When I met Keenan for the first time, his ability to intimidate reminded me of Valicenti. He was tough, and he looked like a fucking Mafia crime boss. Maybe that's why I didn't like looking him in the eye when he was yelling at me.

Valicenti also coached football, and I begged him to let me play wide receiver on his team. But he would only let me serve as the placekicker because he was afraid I might get hurt for hockey season. The following season, Amonte replaced me as the kicker.

During my freshman year at Thayer Academy, I was still playing part time for the New Jersey Rockets. I essentially played before and after my prep school tournament, but Coach Valicenti and our family had a disagreement about one tournament in which the Rockets wanted me to play in North Bay, Ontario.

The disagreement was simple: Coach Valicenti said I couldn't play in that tournament, and we decided to go anyway and not tell him. Remember, this was before the Internet. This was before every breath a young premium draws is recorded on YouTube. This was before players were committing to colleges at age 15.

Our trip to North Bay was scheduled carefully to make sure we could fly from Boston to Ottawa to North Bay and back again in time for me to be at school Monday morning. Even planning for the Rockets to make the tournament final, we felt like it would be no problem getting home on time.

Our mistake was that we didn't count on a winter storm that forced our flight from North Bay to Ottawa to be cancelled. Undaunted, my dad rented a car and we drove through ice and snow. The trip should have taken four and a half hours. Instead, it required 10 hours of scary driving. But we made our connection in Ottawa, and I was in school the next morning and at practice on time, comfortable in my belief that Coach Valicenti would never know.

But when I showed up at practice, Valicenti knew every detail from the tournament.

"About 15 scouts called me about you," Valicenti said. We realized then that it was no longer possible for me to hide at a tournament.

Despite my gaudy numbers and the attention I was receiving, it wasn't really until after my freshman season at Thayer Academy that it seemed reasonable to dream about being an NHL player. Before then, my family believed I was a better soccer player than a hockey player. On many weekends, I would head home from New Jersey and then go directly to a soccer game.

In Virginia, I had played AAA travel soccer, and I had a knack for finding space on the soccer field. I actually took some of the tactics that worked for me on the pitch and applied them to hockey. Soccer is about anticipating where the seams of the defensive coverage are going to be and sliding into those areas to receive a pass. My father is a very analytical man, and he and I would talk constantly about understanding where I needed to be in order to be successful.

There was truthfully not much discussion about me playing in the NHL until Thayer Academy played undefeated Avon Old Farms for the New England Prep School Championships in my freshman year. It was estimated that there were about 300 NHL scouts, major junior scouts and college coaches there, mostly to look at Brian Leetch, who was Avon Old Farms' best player. Leetch had 94 points that season, and Avon Old Farms was heavily favoured. But when the game was over, we had won, and Amonte and I had two goals and two assists each.

After that game, my life changed dramatically. My father was surrounded by scouts and coaches. "It was like I was standing in

Best Buy at five o'clock in the morning on Black Friday," my dad recalled about that day. "I was surrounded."

I was the hot item, and it seemed like every junior team in Canada called me. One call I did take was from then-Edmonton Oilers star Wayne Gretzky, who owned the Hull Olympiques of the Quebec Major Junior Hockey League. His general manager, Charlie Henry, reached out first and said Gretzky wanted to talk with us about the possibility of me playing in Hull. He met my family for breakfast when the Oilers were in Boston and brought us down to the dressing room in the Boston Garden. Gretzky was quite persuasive about the benefits of playing junior hockey, but the bottom line was that Wally and Jo Roenick were concerned that if I went off to play junior hockey, I would pay no attention to my high school studies. They probably were correct in that assessment.

The interest the NHL had in me was mind-boggling. In my second year at Thayer, I was playing in a summer pro-amateur league and had games on Monday, Wednesday and Thursday. On Tuesday, my dad gave me money to go to the movies. Ten minutes after he dropped me off, the phone rang and it was a Pittsburgh Penguins official saying that Pittsburgh general manager Eddie Johnston was in town to see me play that night.

My dad told him that I wasn't scheduled to play that night, and the Penguins official was insistent that I needed to come down and play. My gear was thrown in the car, and my dad pulled me out of the movie. I showed up five minutes before game time and scored three goals with Johnston watching. When I was playing for the San Jose Sharks two decades later, my family was in Pittsburgh the night before I played there, and Johnston strolled into the restaurant where we were eating. His first words to us were, "Do you remember when I came to Boston and you left the movies so I could see you play?"

In the NHL, I played an aggressive, gritty style. I viewed myself as a pit bull. Heavy hitting was part of my game. Probably everyone who watched me play in high school would be surprised by my transformation. In high school, I was strictly a finesse player. Mallgrave would joke that I was a "wimpy" player. I was never known for being overly tough. I didn't particularly like to be checked, and I would whine when I was hacked. One night, while playing in the Hockey Night in Boston tournament, I was incensed that I was getting hacked all night. In my rage, I punched a door and broke my hand.

When I was younger, I would be the player who lay on the ice after a collision. It got to the point that my dad wouldn't even come out. But I was never a perimeter player. I went where I needed to go to score goals. And I was definitely not a weakling. Although I barely weighed 150 pounds when I was a junior in high school, I always felt like I was the strongest player on the ice. I never touched a weight in high school, but the strength of my forearms and wrists always seemed to be an advantage.

Mallgrave started lifting weights when he was 15. He weighed 185 pounds and could bench 185 pounds. He outweighed me by more than 30 pounds, and my training consisted only of hockey and golf. But he could never defeat me in a wrestling match. He kept increasing his weightlifting and training. "I'm going to beat you this time," he would say. But no matter how strong he was, the outcome never changed. I would roll him over and pin his ass every time. NHL scouts certainly suspected how strong I was, but they didn't know for sure because prospects aren't tested like they are today.

I was somewhat worried about my weight, a worry shared by my agent. When I attended my first sports festival through USA Hockey, NHL officials came in to weigh us. I tucked a 10-pound weight under my towel just to pad my numbers a bit. I was 16 then, and I barely weighed 140 pounds.

Although I certainly didn't play a rough game in high school, I believed I did demonstrate a determination to score goals. In describing me as a young player, Duberman said, "You were like the dog that you have to shoot to get away from you."

Considering my brother, Trevor, and I were four years apart, I believe I can say we had a great relationship, as long as you can give me a pass on the fact that I terrorized him when I was nine and he was five. Isn't that what older brothers are supposed to do with younger brothers? I was always trying to scare him, and I was successful to the point that he slept about two years on the floor of my parents' bedroom because he didn't want to be alone in the dark.

Fuck, I was mean to him.

One time, I was teasing him mercilessly and he become infuriated to the point that he snapped. My five-year-old brother made a fist and landed a roundhouse right to my face that would have made Muhammad Ali proud. In all of the years I played hockey, I never suffered a black eye more hideous than the one Trevor gave me in 1979.

I can still see him laughing his ass off every time he looked at my black eye.

Undoubtedly, I deserved the shot because I regularly took pleasure in Trevor's discomfort. At the Roenick dinner table, vegetables were always served. And my mother made us eat all of our vegetables before we could be excused from the table to continue our day.

One day, my mom's vegetable of choice was lima beans, which Trevor detested with unwavering commitment. But my mother wouldn't compromise on her house rules. Trevor had to finish those beans, and I took special delight in sitting at the table, watching him trying to force down lima beans. He would put one bean in his mouth, and then his gag reflex would kick in. His eyes would water and he would sound like he was going to throw up. I would be howling with laughter. I sat there for 90 minutes, watching him being tortured by lima beans. By the end, he was hitting me, throwing kitchen utensils at me and crying uncontrollably. I thought it was the funniest scene I had ever seen, and I still feel that today.

Trevor and I were vastly different as hockey players and people. He was slightly overweight as a child, and he wasn't a great skater. But he competed like a son of a bitch. He started to blossom in high school. Our personalities were different as well. He was earthy, retro, almost flower child–like. He owned a 1969 yellow Volkswagen beetle automobile he named Otis. Twice, he drove that beastly car across the country with no money and no place to stay. He just slept in his car. I don't even like driving across the state, and I sure as hell wouldn't sleep in my car.

My parents were tough on Trevor and me. When I say that, I don't mean they abused us. What I mean is that they believed in tough love. Always, we had to say please and thank you. If we didn't use those words, there were consequences. Look someone in the eye when you talk to them. Treat people the way you would want to be treated. I heard those phrases many times.

One of my most vivid early childhood memories involves a trip to the bank with my mother and a lollipop given to me by a teller.

"What do you say?" my mom asked as I took the lollipop in my hand.

Don't know why, but I didn't say anything

"What do you say?" she repeated.

Again, I said nothing.

She ripped that lollipop from my grasp and handed it back to the teller.

"He will not be having a lollipop today," my mother said.

I was bawling as she dragged me out of the bank. My parents insisted upon strict adherence to their rules under their roof, from the time I was a toddler through my days as a teenager. My parents' take was that if I was going to commit to being a hockey player, then I was going to fully commit. They made sure I had my proper rest. I didn't skip practices. I didn't go to parties. My parents made sure I was fully invested in hockey.

My dad pushed me all of the time to be the best I could be.

Overbearing? Maybe. But as a parent myself, I can now look back and see that my parents were fully supportive. We were constantly on the road. Today, as a parent, I enjoy the moments I have when I have no commitments. My parents didn't have any of those times. They didn't go to dinner by themselves. They didn't travel unless it was for hockey. My parents didn't have free time. They were committed to placing us in the best possible environment to succeed as athletes and people. Yes, they were strict. But they were trying to do what they believed was in their children's best interest.

More than 30 years later, they still have my back. I bought a golf course, the Pembroke Country Club, in Massachusetts. They saved my ass by agreeing to manage it for me. The golf course was in a shambles when I first bought it, and now I'm proud to own it.

In retrospect, I didn't have a childhood as much as I had a career from about the age of 10 or 11. My life was a fucking road trip. Hockey was all-consuming. In high school, Amonte or Tracy would often try to convince me to come to a party, but I would stay home because it was the night before a game. While other kids were busy growing up, I was busy worrying about whether my shot was hard enough for the NHL. Unquestionably, my parents sheltered me at a time when my peers were learning about life through trial and error. When I signed my first NHL contract and was earning more than a hundred grand per season, I didn't even know how to use a chequebook.

My hockey-dominated childhood hurt me once I reached the NHL. As I now understand, I missed the trial-and-error period of adolescence when you learn who should be trusted and who shouldn't. Too busy playing hockey, I skipped the stage when you learn those lessons. When I arrived in the NHL, I had the skills necessary to play the sport but not the social maturity needed to make proper decisions away from the arena. My initial impulse was to trust everyone, a trait that didn't serve me well away from the rink.

I realize now that I resented my parents for sheltering me when I was in high school. When they were no longer watching over me, I raged, making up for all of the parties I didn't attend when I was at Thayer. Never did I find myself in any major trouble. But I made bad choices, particularly with regard to friends and hobbies. I could have been, should have been, a better husband for Tracy. It was tough on her when I was busy exploring the perks of being an NHL superstar. In the early years of my NHL career, Tracy tried to warn me that I was losing perspective on what was important and what was not. I didn't listen for the longest time.

What should have been done to better prepare me for adulthood? I don't have an answer for that. We were too harried, moving from rink to rink, to analyze whether I was socially prepared for the road ahead. Truthfully, what I see when I look back is a family that made major sacrifices to accommodate my career. Trevor probably was shortchanged because sacrifices were routinely made to support my career. He has the right to complain. However, he carved out his own path, earning a scholarship to play at the University of Maine. He also played some pro hockey, although he didn't make it to the NHL.

In hindsight, I wish somehow I could have been better prepared for the fame I would know before my 21st birthday. I wish I would have owned the wisdom to understand that new friends don't always have your best interests at heart. I wish I would have realized that Tracy had a far better understanding of what was happening to me than I did.

But it would be a lie for me to say that I would want a fucking do-over of my childhood. I played almost two decades in the NHL, earning almost $60 million. I scored more than 500 goals. I own a golf course. In those early years, the Roenicks must have done something right.

# CHAPTER 2

# Weighing My Odds

When my agent, Neil Abbott, prepared me for my team interviews before the 1988 NHL draft, it was as if he was providing me my Miranda rights. He told me that everything I say can and will be used against me. It was like receiving your attorney's instructions on how to testify in a trial. Neil predicted what questions would be asked, offered sample answers and gave me specific instructions on what I should avoid discussing.

To Neil, the taboo subject was my weight—or lack thereof. He told me to plead the Fifth Amendment about it because he was reasonably sure that revealing how much I weighed would scare off some potential suitors. In June of 1988, I weighed 155 pounds. But no one knew that because Neil made sure my weight was the biggest mystery of that year's draft.

Under no circumstance, Neil told me on several occasions, should I accept any team's request to step on a scale.

"The scale," Neil told me, "is not your friend."

This was an era in NHL history when teams wanted forwards to be as big as lumberjacks. The two highest-rated centres in the 1988 draft pool were American Mike Modano, who was six foot three and 212 pounds, and Canadian Trevor Linden, who was six foot four, 210 pounds. It seemed as if all of the top prospects outweighed me by more than 50 pounds.

Neil was convinced that it would hurt my draft status if anyone learned I still weighed less than 160 pounds, despite my efforts to gain weight. A few months before the draft, I was competing for Thayer Academy in a tournament when I decided to step out of our hot, cramped, smelly dressing room just to find some fresh air. The problem, as Neil saw it, was that I had ventured in public without my shirt. As soon as he saw me, Neil ran down the stairs of the bleachers as if he were fleeing a raging fire.

"Get back in that dressing room and don't walk out here again unless you have gear on," he said. He didn't want the hockey world to know that the potential first-round pick from the Boston area had skinny arms, a sunken chest and no discernible muscle mass.

My draft year came before the Internet explosion. Today, there are a handful of websites that rank potential draft picks and many that provide an overload of information about each prospect. But in my draft year, information was based on what scouts witnessed at the rink and what they heard through the grapevine. Scouts made it clear that they liked my speed, my hands and my heart, but we also heard that NHL teams were concerned about my size. That was reinforced when the *Hockey News*'s draft preview issue was published in the spring. The magazine's assessment of my potential was primarily positive, and I was ranked 11th. However, my evaluation stated there were "question marks" about my potential. Those concerns clearly centred on whether I was big enough to survive in the NHL jungle.

"How big is he going to get?" asked one scout in the article. "He is not that tall and he's light, too. That's not a good mix." Another scout called me "skinny."

*The Hockey News* also stated that I was five foot ten and a half and that I weighed 158 pounds. It didn't help my cause that every player ranked in the magazine's first round was heavier than me. The only other small players considered top prospects that year were fifth-ranked Martin Gélinas, who was my height but almost 40 pounds heavier, and Reggie Savage, who was an inch shorter than me but more than 20 pounds heavier.

As soon as the *Hockey News* article brought more attention to my weight, Neil got his propaganda machine running effectively. We never said how much I weighed, but we did say that *The Hockey News*'s number wasn't accurate. Most scouts seemed to assume that I had grown a bit and *The Hockey News*'s data was simply out of date. They assumed I weighed more, and we just let everyone believe that. We even had our own "expert witness," a chiropractor who had examined me and projected that I would grow to six foot one and 195 pounds.

The other worry we had was that I was an American playing prep school hockey. Scouts celebrated Modano because he had gone to the Western Hockey League to prove himself, and they questioned me because I had stayed in prep school. Even though I had produced 34 goals and 50 assists in 24 games in my junior year, scouts wanted to discount my statistics on the basis that they had been achieved against what they considered inferior competition.

Although NHL general managers had become far more open-minded about drafting Americans, they still preferred players trained in the Canadian Hockey League. The year before, at the 1987 draft, all 21 picks in the first round were Canadians. The success of the 1980 U.S. Olympic Team coached by Herb Brooks in Lake Placid had opened doors for Americans in the NHL, but eight years after that event, only 19 Americans had ever been taken in the first round of the NHL draft.

Some Americans were performing at a high level in the NHL. But Brian Lawton had been a first-overall pick in 1983 out of Mount Charles High School in Rhode Island. In my draft year, Lawton, then 23 years old, registered 17 goals and 41 points for the Minnesota North Stars. It didn't seem as if he was going to develop into the superstar the North Stars had hoped he would be. That didn't work in my favour. It also didn't help my case that I was a junior in high school. Scouts had worries about what I planned to do the following season. The possibility that I might play another season of prep school hockey didn't appeal to the scouting community.

Against that backdrop, Abbott was steadfast in his belief that I needed to exercise my right to remain silent when it came to my weight. But I was nervous about that plan, because I didn't know if I would have the courage to say no if a team asked me to get on a scale. Wouldn't a refusal signal that there was a problem with my weight? That's what I was thinking.

"What if they hold that against me?" I asked.

"They won't have a problem with it," Abbott insisted.

I wasn't convinced, and I spent plenty of time thinking about what I would say when they asked.

Going into the draft, we had a general idea of which general managers were thinking about taking me. We felt there was an outside chance that the Quebec Nordiques might take me with the fifth pick. If the Nordiques passed, Neil figured I could go eighth to Chicago, or 11th to Hartford or 12th to New Jersey. Although there had been some speculation about the Toronto Maple Leafs, with the sixth pick, being interested, Neil believed they wouldn't take an American high school player over a Canadian Hockey League player.

I thought there was a very good chance I would end up with the Devils. New Jersey general manager Lou Lamoriello knew me well because I had attended his hockey camps when I was younger. The Devils had brought me to New Jersey for an interview and had tested me there along with Michigan State player Rod Brind'Amour.

The Nordiques owned both the third and fifth picks, the latter coming from the New York Rangers as compensation for their signing Michel Bergeron as coach in 1987. Frankly, I had no desire to play in Quebec, although I never said that to anyone. I wasn't concerned about the prospect of playing in a French-speaking community. I was concerned that Quebec was a weak team and didn't seem to be on a path toward success.

We were sure Quebec wouldn't select me with the third pick, but we weren't positive general manager Maurice Filion wouldn't take me at number five. With two first-round picks, the Nordiques could have decided to take a risk on the skinny American with the raw speed. And the Nordiques did interview me in Montreal.

As it turned out, only the Blackhawks asked me to step on a scale.

I refused.

"Did you ever see a scale score a goal?" I asked.

There were six or seven members of the Chicago staff in the

room at the time, and most of them laughed. Maybe some of them thought I was a brat. Maybe some of them just thought I was cocky. But hopefully, they all understood that I had a personality.

The Blackhawks' interview group included Mike Keenan. The team had made headlines two days before when they signed Keenan to be their coach, replacing Bob Murdoch. Having led the Philadelphia Flyers to the Stanley Cup final 12 months before, Keenan was considered one of the NHL's best young coaches. He was only 38 years old at the time. But the Flyers had fired him essentially because they thought he was too tough. Keenan was viewed as a young Scotty Bowman, and the idea of bringing in a tough guy had appealed greatly to Chicago owner Bill Wirtz, who knew a little something about ruling with an iron fist.

I don't recall Keenan saying much in my interview. I'm sure the Blackhawks did other interviews, and maybe all of the young prospects started to look the same after a while, because he wasn't sure he recognized me the next time he saw me.

Our second encounter came the night before the draft, when I found myself standing next to him at the urinals in a restaurant in Old Montreal.

"Hello, Mr. Keenan," I said.

He nodded first, and then, after a pause, said, "You're Jeremy, aren't you?"

"Yes sir," I said. "I hope you draft me tomorrow."

"If we draft you, will you play hard for me?" Keenan said.

"Yes, I will," I said.

"Do you have big balls, kid?" he asked.

"I do, and considering we are standing here at a urinal, I can show them to you if you like," I joked.

Keenan laughed, and we still laugh about that meeting to this day.

The next morning, I had no idea whether the Blackhawks would take me, nor did I have any true idea who was thinking about drafting me. The draft unfolded as expected, with Minnesota taking Modano, and then Vancouver grabbing Trevor Linden and the Nordiques taking Curtis Leschyshyn of the Saskatoon Blades. Then the Pittsburgh Penguins took Darrin Shannon of the Windsor Spitfires, and then it was Quebec's turn.

We were both relieved and shocked when the Nordiques took six-foot, three-inch forward Daniel Doré with the number-five pick. Doré was much more of a tough guy than he was a player. Who takes a fighter with the number-five pick in the draft? We were told that the Nordiques felt an obligation to take a French-Canadian with their second pick in the first round. Today, that pick is considered one of the worst in NHL draft history.

Once the Nordiques passed, we figured our best chance for the selection was the Blackhawks. As Abbott predicted, the Maple Leafs passed on me to take Scott Pearson at number six, and then the Los Angeles Kings took Martin Gélinas at number seven. The Blackhawks then called a timeout, and general manager Bob Pulford spent some time talking to Buffalo general manager Gerry Meehan before going to the podium to announce they were taking me with the eighth pick.

In the next day's *Chicago Tribune*, sportswriter Mike Kiley revealed that Pulford believed he had a trade made with the Sabres that would have involved Chicago moving from number eight to number 13.

"I was really mad and disappointed the deal wasn't made," Pulford told Kiley.

Kiley's analysis was that the Blackhawks were willing to give up a veteran player and flop picks for either centre John Tucker or Adam Creighton. Pulford told Kiley that Meehan had changed his mind because he believed he could get the prospect he wanted with the number-13 pick. "And he didn't get that kid," Pulford told Kiley.

The best guess would be that the Sabres wanted to take either Brind'Amour, who went ninth to St. Louis, or Teemu Selanne, who was drafted 10th by Winnipeg. The Sabres picked Savage, who ended up playing just three NHL games.

After the draft, it came out that, had the Blackhawks made that trade, they would not have been able to draft me because the Devils were planning to take me with the 12th pick.

Based on his quotes to the media at the draft, you could tell that Pulford wasn't completely sold on me.

"He can skate like Denis Savard, but the risk is he's played high school hockey and never played at a higher competition level," Pulford told Kiley.

Jack Davison was Chicago's assistant general manager. He pushed for me to be the team's eighth selection, and through the years I've been told that he said he would quit if they didn't select me. He had watched me play at the World Junior Championship in Moscow six months before and apparently liked what he saw. "The first two games in Moscow, he was right there on a par with Mike Modano," Davison told Kiley. Davison told the media he thought I had an outside chance to make the Blackhawks next season if I signed. "He looks like a quick learner. A few players have made that jump from high school, players like Bobby Carpenter."

Abbott had prepared me to deal with the media. What I wanted to say was that I wanted to play in Chicago the following season. What I told the media was "I'll do whatever the Blackhawks want. I have scholarship offers from Boston College and Boston University, and I'll go to one of those schools if they want, or I'll go play in major juniors if they want."

One of the funniest aspects of the *Tribune* story is that Kiley said I weighed 179 pounds. Another story about the draft stated I weighed 170. Clearly, Neil's propaganda campaign had worked to perfection. I think it's fair to say that no one in the hockey world had any idea how much I weighed. The CIA could not have done a better job of covering up my weight than Neil did.

When the Blackhawks indicated they wanted to sign me right away, I was far more excited than Neil was. But Neil felt strongly about education and really wanted me to consider going to college. He had represented Lawton, and he wondered whether Lawton would have been better served by going to college rather than jumping from high school to the NHL. He believed the money would be there if I waited, and he thought there might even be more money if I waited. Plus, I would have more time to grow and get stronger.

Neil's first objective was to get me out of high school. Remember, I was a junior when I was drafted. We met with the headmaster at Thayer and worked out a plan for me to finish my high school course work by taking summer classes at Boston College. No one was more ready to leave high school than I was. Tony Amonte had been drafted by the New York Rangers 68th overall, and he planned to play college hockey. But he didn't try to expedite his high school exodus.

Although Neil wanted me to play college hockey, the Blackhawks didn't love that plan. Even in 1988, there were NHL teams that believed that college hockey didn't help quality prospects. But that didn't mean Pulford was going to open the vault to pay me. We found out very early in my career that Pulford was a stubborn negotiator. He offered me a three-year contract paying $90,000 the first year, $95,000 the second and $100,000 the third. There would also be a $50,000 signing bonus. Neil believed that to be an average offer, which further convinced him I should play college hockey.

I followed his advice. I had a drawer full of college offers, and there probably wasn't a college team that didn't want me. But I enrolled at Boston College, mostly because it was close to home and because the Eagles were a quality team.

After I moved into the dorm, before classes started, it really seemed as if I had made the proper decision. I hung my Cheryl Tiegs and Bobby Orr posters on the wall and attended a few parties. It felt as if I would fully enjoy life as a college student.

Then, right before school started, Boston College coach Len Ceglarski asked me to stop by his office. When I showed up, he sat me down and told me he had a problem that he needed me to help him fix. He said he had more quality recruits than he had scholarships. "And we want to take care of everybody," he said.

He explained to me that the solution he had come up with was to ask the football team to give me a scholarship as a placekicker. The idea was that I would practise with the hockey team, and then on Saturdays I would kick for the football team if I could win the job. At Thayer, I had been the kicker for the football team. In practice, I could boot 45-yard field goals.

Initially, I was flattered by the Ceglarski plan. Then, as I was discussing it with Tracy, I began to feel insulted that I was now technically a walk-on for the hockey team. But there wasn't time to think about it too much because classes started the next morning. My course work was starting with a math class at eight o'clock in the morning in a large lecture hall. Arriving 10 minutes early, I found a seat in the middle section. I had a bag full of books that I had already purchased for all of my classes.

The room filled quickly, and the professor didn't waste time as he walked in and started handing out papers to be passed down the aisles.

"This," the professor said, "is your syllabus."

I was totally confused. I had no idea what he was talking about. I had never heard of a fucking syllabus. I didn't know what the word meant.

"Are we getting tested?" I asked the girl next to me.

"No, the syllabus is the course outline," she said.

When the professor's syllabus arrived at my seat, it was several pages in length. It had the weight of a short novel. Looking down, I could see a class schedule that read: "Quiz. Quiz. Test. Oral. Paper. Quiz. Mid-Term. Test. Quiz. Quiz. Quiz. Test . . ." The workload seemed to go on fucking forever.

That professor's syllabus blew me away. Since then, I have actually hated the word "syllabus." Five minutes into my college education, I stood up, handed the syllabus to the girl next to me and asked her to return it to the professor.

"Have a nice time in this class," I told her as I hustled down the stairs.

I just left them in the classroom. I ran out of the room, bolted out the door, ran across the quad and found a pay phone. I dropped a quarter into the slot and called Neil.

"Neil, have you talked to the Blackhawks today?" I asked.

"Yes," Neil said. "There is no change in their offer. They aren't budging."

"Neil, let's take their offer," I said.

"But Jeremy, we said no to this contract the entire summer," Neil protested.

"Yes," I said, "but this entire summer I had never heard of the word 'syllabus.' Now I've seen a syllabus and I've got to get the fuck out of here because this school shit isn't for me. I'm not a student. I'm a fucking hockey player."

As I recall, Neil squeezed an extra $5,000 per season out of the Blackhawks, meaning I would be paid $95,000 in the first season, then $100,000 and later $105,000. The signing bonus was still $50,000.

At the time, my dad was making $90,000 working for Mobil Oil, and I remember thinking I must be doing pretty well if I'm making more than my father.

That night, Neil and I were on a plane from Boston to Chicago. The Blackhawks' training camp had already started, and Neil prepared me as if he were readying me for a championship fight. He told me to be the aggressor.

"You have to demand respect," he told me. "If someone fucks with you, you fuck with them."

That was the language he used. Neil had put fear into me like I had never known before. It felt like I was going off to war.

When I entered the Chicago dressing room for the first time, it was like a scene from a World War II movie where the young recruit is trying to fit into a platoon of combat-hardened veterans. Everyone in that room looked like they had seen plenty of action. I had never had a stitch or broken bone in my life, and many of the Chicago players seemed to have scars all over their bodies, plus several missing teeth. To a kid who was an 11th-grader four months before, the Chicago players seemed like old men. Denis Savard and Steve Thomas were sharing a cigarette in the corner of the room. With his receding hairline, Bob Murray looked old enough to be my grandfather. My grandfather had more hair than Murray had. Daniel Vincelette looked like the NHL's version of Sasquatch. He was the hairiest fucking man I had ever seen.

It was intimidating for me to dress in the same locker room with these guys. I was shaving every couple of months, and these guys looked like they needed to shave every three hours. The only hair on my body was on the top of my head. There was no need for manscaping at that point in my life. I went into the shower room with my clothes on and was mostly dressed before I came out.

Weightlifting was starting to catch on in those days, and some of the Blackhawks had chiselled bodies. Keith Brown was in impressive shape. Vincelette was fucking ripped. I had tried to add some weight over the summer, but going from 155 to 158 pounds was the best I could do. I still had no guns or definition on my body.

As I stepped onto the ice for my first scrimmage, I wondered what I had gotten myself into. Then, I saw Neil in the stands, waving wildly at me. As I skated closer, I could hear him yelling: "Get the shield off. Get the shield off."

Then I realized I was the only one on the ice wearing a face mask and the only one who had a mouthguard. I immediately skated to the bench, removed my cage, spit out my mouthguard and asked someone to fetch me another helmet.

When I started that game, I was scared to death I was going to get hit in the face by a puck. I soon discovered that flying pucks were the least of my concerns. Early in the scrimmage, I lifted Rick Vaive's stick and stole the puck. His response was a slash across my leg. Remembering what Neil told me, I answered with a retaliatory slash across his body. It was like a baseball swing at his arm and torso. Vaive was so startled by my reaction that he didn't do anything. He was a former 50-goal scorer with the Toronto Maple Leafs, and he certainly didn't expect an 18-year-old punk to be swinging at him as if he were a piñata. Later, in the dressing room, Vaive got in my face and told me never to fucking slash him again. I apologized profusely, but I didn't regret it. Neil had been right. After I went crazy on Vaive, no one bothered me again in a scrimmage.

After my first scrimmage, Neil and I had a meeting with owner Bill Wirtz and Pulford. We received the cheque for $50,000. Then I had to go through the battery of tests that the other players had been subjected to on their first day of camp. When I was finished, Neil and I talked about how I should handle myself in training camp. Time got away from us, and there wasn't a soul around when we exited Chicago Stadium at Gate 3½. That was a mistake, because the area around Chicago Stadium wasn't a friendly environment in those years. It was considered dangerous to the point that taxis wouldn't come to that part of town. It felt like a fucking war zone.

As soon as we were standing on Madison Street, Neil looked worried. We were both dressed in suits, and Neil was carrying a briefcase containing my cheque for $50,000. We ducked into a convenience store, and a clerk behind thick bulletproof glass stared at us as if we were aliens that had just walked through his front door. Neil was just trying to figure out if there was a way we could call a taxi, but the clerk just shook his head and laughed.

At that point, we began talking about trying to hoof it back to our hotel. No one was paying much attention to us. But then a younger man approached us. He kept eyeing Neil's briefcase.

"You are two crazy fucking white boys being out here right now," he said, laughing. "If I didn't have somewhere to be, I would be stealing that briefcase."

As he started to walk away, he added: "But see the guy coming toward you down there? He is going to knife your ass and steal everything you have."

Neil's eyes popped almost out of his fucking head. Neil is a very skittish and worrisome man. He has always been very protective of me. He may have soiled his pants at that moment. But he acted in a big way. Seeing a CTA bus coming down West Madison, he ran into the middle of the street and held up his arms in front of it. The bus came to a screeching halt. My memory of Neil stopping that bus is similar to the photo of that man in front of the tank in China's Tiananmen Square. The doors opened, and the driver started screaming to Neil, "You crazy, man—you could have been killed."

Meanwhile, Neil was motioning for me to climb onto the bus. When we were on the bus, he told the driver that if she turned it around and took us back to our hotel inside the Loop, he would give her $100. In less than a minute, the bus was headed in the direction Neil wanted it to go. There was one passenger on the bus, an elderly woman, and Neil handed her a hundred-dollar bill for her trouble.

That night, Neil reminded me again that I had a long way to go to prove I was an NHL player. Although I had made a statement to my teammates through my encounter with Vaive, I had a long way to go to earn Keenan's respect. The baseline for my relationship with Keenan was established in my second NHL preseason game, against the Minnesota North Stars in Kalamazoo, Michigan, when Keenan literally came close to strangling me on the bench.

As a prep school player, I had helped my team with my offensive ability. At that point in my development, hockey, to me, seemed to be about speed and skating. Because I was fast, my high school opponents couldn't catch me. I had never concerned myself with the physical side of the game. It didn't seem like trying to run someone over was an effective use of my energy. If I was chasing an opponent with the puck, and he moved it before I reached him, I would spin around without ever finishing that check.

What I learned in Kalamazoo was that my habit constituted sinful behaviour as far as Keenan was concerned.

On one of my early shifts, I was chasing a defenceman in the neutral zone, and when he moved the puck I peeled off and chased it back into my zone. Within seconds of my leaving the ice, Keenan had come down the bench, reached around me and dug his hands into my neck, pulling me back so his face could be directly in front of mine.

"If you pass by one more fucking hit in this fucking game, you will never play another fucking game in this league," Keenan screamed at me.

He may actually have been even more profane than that.

"Do you understand me?" he asked, as he pushed his face in even closer to mine.

"Yes, sir," I said. Came close to bawling right there on the bench. Tears definitely welled up in my eyes.

Probably, a U.S. marine could relate to this story, because having Keenan screaming at me in the middle of an exhibition game would probably be like having your sergeant yelling at you while you are trying to crawl through an obstacle course.

That encounter with Keenan was probably one of the defining moments of my career, because it steered me toward embracing a style of play that would allow me to play two decades in the NHL. At that point, I was afraid of Keenan, and afraid that my hockey career was going to be dead before it began. On my next shift, I threw my 158 pounds at every opponent I could reach. I tried to crush opponents who were 50 pounds heavier than me because I feared Keenan more than I feared injury. What I quickly discovered is that I was born to play hockey like I was a human battering ram. Each time I hit someone, I became more convinced I could survive, even thrive, playing that style even if I wasn't the biggest player on the roster. Playing like the Tasmanian Devil on the ice gave me confidence and earned me respect around the NHL. Chicago fans loved that style, and that high-energy output instantly became my trademark.

But I also learned that just playing with energy wasn't enough to earn you a place on an NHL team's roster. After making the Blackhawks coming out of training camp in 1988–89, I went pointless in my first three regular-season games. Keenan called me into his office and told me that I wasn't ready yet to play in the NHL.

At the time, I was devastated. Keenan made an effort to be compassionate, noting that he felt I was close to being ready. But he said he believed I would benefit from playing with players closer to my age. I had been drafted by both Sault Ste. Marie in the Ontario Hockey League and Hull in the Quebec Major Junior Hockey

League, and it was decided I would play in Quebec because it would be easier for my parents to come and see me.

It was the right call on Keenan's part, because my confidence grew and my game improved playing in the Quebec League. Alain Vigneault, now behind the bench for the Vancouver Canucks, was my coach in Hull. I liked him because he was like Keenan—tough and direct. I had 34 goals and 36 assists for 70 points in 28 games for Hull. I went off to the World Junior Championship and played well for the USA.

The Hull team had an exceptionally fun group of guys, including Stéphane Matteau, who remains one of my close friends. Cam Russell was on that team, and he and I ended up being buddies. Jason Glickman was the goalie. When I was with the New Jersey Rockets and we beat the Chicago Young Americans for the bantam national championship, they had a top player in Joe Suk, and he was on the Hull team. Future NHL defenceman Karl Dykhuis, who had come up through the junior ranks in Quebec, was on the team. Speedy Martin Gélinas, who went on to have a lengthy NHL career, was my winger. These guys knew how to have fun, and they knew how to play practical jokes on rookies.

The team's longest bus trip was an 11-hour excursion to Chicoutimi. When we were almost there, Vigneault told the bus driver to pull over. He stood up and told all of the rookies to gather at the front of the bus, because the assistant coach had forgotten the necessary paperwork for the rookies to travel through a park area. I can't remember exactly what their explanation was for why we needed papers to travel within Canada, but the gobbledygook the coach fed us seemed realistic enough to be believed. His bullshit fooled me.

"What are we going to do?" I said, concerned that I had made an 11-hour bus ride for nothing.

"We are going to sneak you guys in under the bus," Vigneault told us.

So we got out of the bus, and the three rookies climbed into the storage compartment, and then the bags were stacked around us. I don't remember what the temperature was, but it felt arctic under there.

We then drove a couple of miles, and then the bus stopped and we could hear voices outside. Someone said they were going to search the luggage compartment under the bus. "Hide," I whispered. "Get under the bags. Everyone get as low as you can."

The door was opened, and the three of us were holding our breath, trying to stay as still as possible. Then we peeked through the bags and saw Vigneault and all of the boys laughing their asses off at the naive rookies. That was Hull's method of initiating players onto the team.

The season I played in Hull, it was mandatory to use a facemask and a neck guard. Once, Gélinas and another player forgot their neck guards for a game at Three Rivers. They weren't allowed to play, and we lost the game. We headed back home that night like we always did, but when we pulled into our parking lot at two in the morning, Vigneault ordered everyone into the dressing room. He set up a video camera, and he ordered every player to put on his freezing equipment and go in front of the camera and count off. We had to put our equipment on, and take it off, 20 times while counting each time for the camera. Vigneault was going to make sure that no one ever forgot his equipment again.

The only negative of my Quebec season was injuring my knee in my first game back with Hull after the World Junior Championship.

Once you were sent to junior hockey, you had to remind yourself you would be there for the season, because the only way the parent club could recall a junior player at that time was as an emergency injury replacement. Imagine my surprise to be at practice on Valentine's Day in 1989 when I was told the Blackhawks were calling me up. I was stunned. Although I was skating again, I hadn't played since the beginning of January because of my knee injury.

The issue was that the Blackhawks had three forwards on the injured list, including Denis Savard. Since they had already summoned two players from the minors, they were able to recall me from Hull. My then-girlfriend, Tracy, had just arrived in town for a visit. I hurried home and told her the Blackhawks wanted me to travel to Bloomington, Minnesota, in time to skate with the team the next morning and then play with Chicago against the North Stars that night.

The catch was that, in order to make the morning skate, I had to be at the airport in an hour and fifteen minutes to board a flight in time to make a connection in Toronto.

There was no way I was going to miss that flight. With Tracy in tow, I flew to the airport in my Chevy Blazer. Worried about missing my flight, I was driving too fast and ran a stop sign. My Blazer slammed into a car driven by a woman who panicked upon impact and propelled her car into a house. When I exited my truck, I could see the woman's car parked in someone's living room.

A Hull police officer, a major hockey fan, showed up and recognized me immediately. I told him the story, explaining that I had just been called up by the Blackhawks. "Get out of here," he said suddenly. "Go play in the NHL. I will take care of everything here. We will get in touch with you."

The officer clearly gave me a break, because I never heard another word about that accident.

My car wasn't damaged at all, and Tracy and I climbed back in and made it to the airport in time for my flight. But when I landed in Toronto, I found out that my connecting flight to Minneapolis had been cancelled because of a snowstorm. I couldn't get out of Toronto until the next morning. I arrived at the rink in Bloomington near the end of the morning skate. It was a whirlwind day as I checked into the hotel and tried to get some rest. I was too excited to get a quality nap.

Because the call-up had not been planned, there was no sweater with my name on it hanging from a stall when I arrived in the dressing room. The equipment manager handed me number 51, with no nameplate on the back. It turned out to be the only game I played for Chicago where I didn't wear number 27.

The game started badly for the 'Hawks. Denis Savard, playing again after nine games on the disabled list with an ankle ligament injury, was reinjured less than six minutes into the game when Minnesota defenceman Shawn Chambers kicked the same ankle. With Savard gone, there was more playing time for me, and 23 seconds into the second period, I scored my first NHL goal, against Finnish goalie Kari Takko. My pass to Brian Noonan hit his stick and then caromed off the back boards into the crease, where Takko couldn't find it to get his glove on it. I flew into the crease to punch the loose puck into the net to give Chicago a 1–0 lead. It seems appropriate that Noonan was involved in the goal, because he was from the Boston area and we had been linemates many times in summer-league play.

The Blackhawks ended up winning that game 4–2, and Mario Doyon, playing his first NHL game, also scored. At the time, the Blackhawks were scraping for a playoff spot, and that victory was the team's seventh win in 10 games.

The next day, Pulford told the media: "Jeremy could stay here indefinitely. He can provide some offence for us."

It became clear that they wanted to keep me the rest of the season. They even kept some injured players on the disabled list longer than they would have just to ensure there would be no issue.

After netting no points in my first three games in Chicago in October, I had 9 goals and 9 assists for 18 points in 17 games after I returned in February. Although I was starting to establish myself with my teammates in the regular season, I probably didn't truly prove myself until a playoff game against St. Louis in April.

In the first period, I was battling in the corner, got knocked to the ice, and was on my hands and knees when Steve Larmer's skate came up and sliced my nose. It took 15 stitches to close the wound, the first stitches I had ever received. I remember thinking how close the cut was to my eyes. It didn't take long until I was back in the game, a fact that seemed to earn me respect from my teammates. Then, in the second period, with St. Louis up 1–0, I became entangled behind the net with Glen Featherstone. He gave me a fucking shot. I gave him a fucking shot. And then he came back and cross-checked me in the mouth.

It's the most sickening, disgustingly eerie sensation to feel your teeth disintegrate. I believe I would rather experience the pain of a knee injury over that feeling.

After Featherstone whacked me, I was in such shock that I didn't even spit out my teeth. The pieces were still floating around my mouth as I returned to the bench. I was telling my teammates what happened when Keenan hurried over and yelled: "Don't tell *them*. Tell the referee." Keenan summoned referee Kerry Fraser, and when I opened my mouth to tell him what happened, my four bloody Chiclets, as players call them, tumbled out. Four teeth! There one minute and gone the next. I could feel the nerve endings dangling as I entered the box to serve my two minutes for roughing. Featherstone received a major penalty, meaning we would have a power play when I left the penalty box.

My battle with Featherstone seemed to give us a lift, because we scored two goals eight seconds apart to take a 2–1 lead. Later, on another power play, Steve Thomas had the puck, and Greg Millen made the save. But I swatted in the rebound for what ended up being the game-winning goal.

My teammates were impressed by my willingness to keep playing after I had been cut up and lost teeth. Right before I finished this book, former teammate Greg Gilbert told me that the St. Louis game had proven to everyone what I was all about. And I vividly remember Dirk Graham coming up after the game and telling me it was a job well done. "That," he said, "is being a Blackhawk."

I could feel the acceptance because guys were joking with me about how bad I looked. The general themes of the jokes were that I was ugly before, and my encounter with Featherstone had made me uglier. Chicago defenceman Bob McGill had a face that looked like he had seen combat. He surveyed my purplish stitch wound, missing teeth and swollen lips and said, "Kid, you are starting to look more and more like me."

CHAPTER 3

# Knowing My Creator

Playing for coach Mike Keenan in Chicago was like camping on the side of an active volcano. You had to accept the reality that he erupted regularly and that there was always a danger of being caught in his lava flow. He was a tyrant, a schoolyard bully, an old-school coach who tried to motivate players through intimidation, belittlement and fear.

The truth is that Keenan scared me into being a better NHL player. I was 18 when I began to play for Iron Mike, and I was afraid of him. As a rookie, I felt as if my future depended on pleasing Keenan. I believed he was capable of murdering my career before it began. I believed he could do that with no sense of remorse. Before Keenan threatened me in my second NHL exhibition game, I didn't view myself as a physical player. Within a short period of time, he had bullied me into becoming one.

The veterans on the team didn't fear Keenan; they merely despised him, and I believe Mike liked it that way. He was always hard on players, like a drill sergeant trying to ready recruits for the dangers ahead. Dealing with Mike's rants was one of the job requirements for being a Blackhawk. One night, the Blackhawks were playing in St. Louis, and Keenan became enraged about our effort to the point that he ripped out seven ceiling tiles in the visitors' dressing room.

Keenan was a screamer who thought nothing of singling out one of his players for a personal attack, just to let the team know how upset he was with how the team was performing. Over the course of the season, Keenan had accused most of his players of being "chickenshit" or "an embarrassment to your family."

"You don't deserve to be in the fuckin' league," Keenan would often scream at you. "You should be ashamed of the way you are playing."

Mercy was not usually on the table when Keenan had a lock on a player. Some of Iron Mike's most memorable tirades came against Dave Manson, a defenceman who played for the Blackhawks early in my career. Manson was a skilled player with a heavy slapshot and a combative personality. Once teammates realized how quickly Manson's temper could boil over, they started calling him "Charlie Manson," in reference to the convicted murderer Charles Manson, who had those scary, crazed-looking eyes. When Dave Manson lost control, he looked as if he might kill you.

Dave was a tough competitor who had amassed 352 penalty minutes in my first season with the Blackhawks in 1988–89. During one game, Keenan had determined that Manson was responsible for everything wrong with the Blackhawks that night.

"You're fucking brutal," Keenan screamed at Manson between periods. "You are the reason we're losing this game."

Manson had his skates unlaced and his jersey off when Keenan began unloading on him with this verbal barrage. Initially, Manson took his medicine, like we all did at various times. But during

Keenan's rant, Manson snapped. He stood, yanked off his shoulder pads and flung them across the locker room, just missing Keenan as he ducked out of the way. That was merely the first salvo of Manson's attack. As the pads were launched, Manson began running, in his skates, directly at Keenan.

Keenan fled out the door with Manson on his tail. We all scurried to the door to witness the outcome. You can imagine how fucking comical it was to see Keenan sprinting down a hallway, in the bowels of Chicago Stadium, with Manson in determined pursuit. As he chased Keenan, sparks were leaping off Manson's skates as the blades scraped across the cement. If Manson hadn't lost his balance while trying to run on skates, he might have pummelled Keenan.

It wasn't their only hot-tempered confrontation. During a playoff series against Edmonton, Manson once pushed Keenan up against a wall by his collar before players intervened.

The strangest aspect of the repeated Keenan–Manson confrontations was the truth that Keenan liked Manson. He liked Manson's toughness and his aggressiveness. He was big, he was strong, and he had a mean streak. Keenan would have loved to have a roster full of players with Manson's ability. Keenan pushed on Manson because he believed Manson had more to give. Manson had licence to scream at Keenan, to chase him down the hallway, even to physically assault Keenan because Keenan liked his potential. In always hollering at Manson, Keenan's objective was to make him play every game at his highest level to prove that Keenan was wrong about him.

If you couldn't cope with adversity, the Chicago dressing room was not for you in those days. Keenan blow-ups were a regular occurrence, and they often involved some item being thrown or kicked. Another time in St. Louis, Keenan broke some toes kicking what he thought was an empty plastic ice chest. He was yelling at us between periods, and apparently he didn't realize the chests had been filled with Gatorade just before his arrival. When his foot struck the ice chest, it stopped like a car slamming into a brick wall. The players all knew immediately that Keenan was in pain, and you could see players with their heads down, trying to stifle their laughter. But Keenan continued his rampage, and he walked out of the dressing room without a limp. No way was he going to acknowledge he was in pain.

Later, we were told by stadium personnel that Keenan fell to the floor in agony after he shut the door behind him.

There was another time when we had gone through a very bad week, had lost three in a row, and the players knew Keenan was going to skate us until we were ready to puke. We came out for practice that morning and the lights were off. So we just started to skate around the rink. Five minutes passed, and no coaches appeared. Ten minutes passed, and still no coaches to be found. We just kept skating around the rink in the dark. Soon, 20 minutes had passed, and then 30 minutes.

Finally, Keenan came on the ice, carrying a chair that he parked at centre ice. Sitting down in the chair, he commanded half the players to line up at the goal line and the other half to line up along the side boards.

A whistle emerged from his pocket. He pointed to those of us on the goal line and told us to skate up and back. He blew the whistle. We skated up and back. Then he pointed to the players along the side boards and blew the whistle, and they skated across and back.

When those players returned to the side boards, he pointed to us again and blew the whistle. We did this for 15 minutes, and then he rotated the players along the side boards to the goal line and vice versa. Fifteen more minutes of up and back and across and back, and then we switched again.

After more than 45 minutes of this, we were all dog tired, and defenceman Trent Yawney was in the goal-line group going up and back. On the return trip, he stopped at the blue line. Keenan watched Yawney coast the final 35 feet and yelled, "Trent Yawney, go again."

Yawney went again, and for the second time, he started to apply the brakes at the blue line instead of the goal line.

"Trent Yawney, go again," Keenan bellowed.

Now we were all lined up watching Yawney being skated by himself, some of us thankful that Yawney's misfortune has allowed the rest of us to catch our breath. Don't recall how many times Yawney went up and back, but I'm clear on my memory that on one of his trips up the ice, he skated as fast as he could and caught Keenan with his shoulder. Keenan was knocked rudely from his chair, spilling hard onto the ice.

We were all stunned, petrified at the prospect of what Keenan might do.

What Keenan did was get up, sweep the ice off his pants, and scream: "It's about fucking time you hit somebody, Yawney. Everyone off the ice."

As we were all leaving the ice, our captain, Denis Savard, never a Keenan favourite, said, "If I knew that's all we had to do to get off the ice, I would have hit the motherfucker on the first fucking shift."

Singling out one player to blame always seemed central to Keenan's strategy. Maybe he just knew that shredding one player was far more uncomfortable for players than the ripping of an entire squad. It angered us. Probably, that was his objective.

Sometimes, if a player wasn't working hard enough in skating drills, Keenan would punish him by forcing him to watch all of his teammates being punished.

"So, you don't want to work today," Keenan would say to the offending player. "That's okay, because you have teammates that will work for you. You just rest." Then Keenan would have that player stand there while he skated us up and down the ice.

"You can thank your buddy for this skate," Keenan would say.

Of course, we would then be screaming at the teammate who forced us to be punished. Keenan seemed to like to have his dressing room filled with tension. He believed his team performed at a higher level if they were on edge. He liked to push his players to that edge any way he could. He clearly seemed to believe that keeping his players shoulder-deep in adversity at all times kept them sharp.

He was constantly benching players or criticizing them for some reason or another. Goalie Darren Pang played 35 games in net for Keenan in 1988–89, and Keenan pulled him 13 times. That's 37 percent of the time. Keenan once pulled Pang 28 seconds into a game against Pittsburgh when he was beaten on breakaways by future Hall of Famers Mario Lemieux and Paul Coffey.

"If you had a bad warmup, Mike might pull you," Pang once said.

When Ed Belfour was in the net, Keenan was just as willing to pull him. He would grab Belfour by the mask sometimes when he was yelling at him.

Belfour, the pride of Carman, Manitoba, and I were rookies at the same time, and he was the person who showed me that goalies could be temperamental, eccentric personalities. It was common for him to stay after a game until one in the morning, trying to sharpen his skates the way he liked them. Not wanting to stay that long, the Chicago equipment guy would leave the road skate sharpener out for Eddie so he could stay as late as he wanted. Eddie was crazy about many aspects of his game preparation. If he came off the ice and his chewing gum, water or tape wasn't where it was supposed to be, he would start throwing items and yelling at the trainers.

The two most volatile players on the team were Belfour and Manson, and they often clashed verbally and even physically. Eddie didn't like his tower buzzed with high shots in practice. One time, Manson fired a shot off Eddie's head in practice, and we all knew Eddie wasn't going to let that go.

A few minutes later, Keenan had us doing a drill where the player swings across the centre of the ice and takes a pass before heading into the offensive zone and shooting. As soon as Manson took off to receive his pass, Belfour charged out of his crease. When Manson made his turn and looked back for his pass, Eddie was there to crush him with a booming hit. They were both travelling at high speed. It was like a car wreck. Then, Belfour whipped off his mask and the two men fought toe to toe in one of the most intense fights you will ever see.

Eddie was an exceptional goaltender, but he was a little bit off his rocker at times. His emotions could blow up. Russian great Vladislav Tretiak was Chicago's goaltending coach when Keenan was there. Our goalies one season were Belfour and Dominik

Hasek, and Keenan said that Tretiak, who would put the pads on in practice, was more technically sound.

One day, Keenan watched Tretiak and then turned to Eddie and said: "You have just lost your job. I'm playing Tretiak tonight."

When it came to Keenan, it was difficult to know whether he was kidding or not.

In that first season with Keenan, even the Chicago veterans felt like rookies as they tried to figure out how to cope with the psychological games Keenan was playing with them. Most coaches coach from behind the bench, but Keenan wanted to coach from inside your head. When he arrived from Philadelphia, he brought along his team psychologist, Cal Botterill. Keenan was always looking for a motivational edge. He even put a jukebox in the weight room, believing the music would fire up his players during circuit training. He removed the ashtrays, which was another message.

Playing in Chicago Stadium, we already had a built-in advantage because the crowd noise was intimidating to the opposing team. Keenan believed devoutly in the power of intimidation. Our practice jerseys were black, because Keenan believed we looked meaner in black. The Oakland Raiders of the National Football League had turned black into an intimidating sports colour.

Today, we are debating whether equipment should be downsized because bigger, harder shoulder pads are now hurting as many players as they are protecting. Shoulder pads have become weaponized. You can point to Keenan as one of those who helped increase the size of the equipment. One day in my rookie season, players arrived in the dressing room to find oversized shoulder pads made by Donzi in their stalls. Keenan had thrown everyone's regular pads in the trash. Keenan liked bigger players, and if you weren't big, he wanted you to play big and look big.

"We are getting too many shoulder injuries, and I want everyone to wear these pads," Keenan said. Not everyone would wear the enlarged pads. By then, Chris Chelios was playing for us. His shoulder pads looked like rags held together with tape and paper clips. But he looked at the *Robocop*-style pads and said, "I'm not wearing this shit."

I did try them because I felt like I had no choice. If Keenan had asked me to play in a dress and a blond wig, I would have done it.

After we all tried them once, most of us went over to the trash can and reclaimed our old pads.

The coach's office was on the other side of our changing room in the Blackhawks' dressing room, and you could hear the fireworks when Keenan was ripping into a player.

Probably the first player to yell back at Keenan in one of those sessions was Yawney. That seemed to quiet Keenan a bit and gave teammates licence to also return fire on Keenan. Insubordination was part of your routine when you were coached by Keenan. Soon, we realized that Keenan seemed to respect you if you stood up to him. Troy Murray was a quiet man and didn't say much, and Keenan made him pay a price for his quiet nature. He was often a Keenan target.

Before Keenan promoted me from the Quebec Major Junior

League, the Blackhawks were playing in Boston Garden and were losing by a couple of goals when Keenan ordered Murray and Steve Larmer to remove their equipment after the first period because they weren't playing anymore. As they were undressing, I was told, defenceman Keith Brown stood up and said, "Coach, if they aren't playing, then none of us are playing. We are either all in it together, or we are all going to the showers."

Keenan turned around and said, "That's what I wanted to see here: someone to step up and pull this fucking team together."

Was that Keenan's plan all along? Or is that what Keenan said just to avoid a showdown with players? You can be the judge, because we will never know.

Once, I asked Keenan why he was always so confrontational with his players, and he said, "Because negative energy is better than no energy at all."

If Keenan felt he needed to embarrass you, or demean you, or anger you to inspire you to perform, he had no qualms about doing that. When he arrived from Philadelphia, he had decided that the Blackhawks didn't have a winning attitude, and he was determined to change that by any means necessary. Knowing he couldn't change every player immediately, Keenan's mission seemed to be to topple the team's entrenched leaders. He didn't seem to appreciate my first roommate, Doug Wilson. But Savard, one of the most popular players in Chicago history, seemed to be Keenan's primary target. Keenan and Savard were constantly bickering or yelling at each other on the bench during games.

Once, during a game, Keenan was giving Savard an earful, and Savard subtly drove his elbow into Keenan's groin—as he explained later, "just to shut him up."

Keenan and Savard didn't like each other, and that relationship was a constant source of tension. One time, Keenan was skating the Blackhawks hard as punishment, and Savard tried to leave the ice. He had had enough. Savard was popular with his teammates, and Wilson and Brown convinced him to stay. Watching the Savard-vs.-Keenan sideshow was part of being a Blackhawk.

Keenan liked to chew on ice during the game, and before every period, Savard would skate to the bench and knock over Keenan's cup of ice just to irritate him. During the 1990 playoffs, Keenan kicked Savard out of the dressing room and said he would only return if the players wanted him back. When we came into the dressing room one morning, we had to vote yes or no on a piece of paper on the question of whether Savard should return. Savard won that vote by a landslide. I think Keenan believed we would throw Savard overboard. He underestimated Savard's popularity. Personally, Savvy was one of my favourite people. He treated me well from the moment I walked into the dressing room. We played cards together.

Savard's vote of confidence from the players was only a temporary reprieve. Keenan didn't believe in democracy in NHL dressing rooms, and the following summer he dealt Savard to Montreal for Chris Chelios. As much as he didn't like Savard, I think Keenan also wanted to make the deal to show his players he was fully in charge of our lives.

To Keenan's credit, he could take abuse in addition to giving it out. Every season, he would come into the dressing room in full gear and say, "All right, you motherfuckers; this is your chance to take a shot at me." Keenan would play 30 minutes for each team, and he would take a beating.

Manson couldn't wait to get his shot at Keenan. Once, he hit Keenan so hard it looked like he almost fucking decapitated him.

Once, we were on a western road trip, and Keenan decided to scrimmage with us at the Kings' old practice facility in Culver City. Mike Eagles and Bob Bassen went after him with vengeance.

Keenan wasn't the prettiest of players, but he had played college hockey at St. Lawrence University. He could skate, and when he took to the ice against us in practice, he went to war. Everyone knew this was our time to go after Keenan, but we also knew that there would be no free shots. Keenan was a fucking stick hack, and when you got near him he would chop you up.

It wasn't always serious drama on the Chicago bench. We had some ridiculously funny moments, such as the time I had to explain to Keenan that I needed to leave a game in Vancouver, in the third period, because I had soiled my drawers. Maybe I didn't need to tell him, because everyone on the bench could smell the problem.

Having felt ill all day, I went into the corner and got checked hard. At impact, my bowels did an unexpected evacuation. When I returned to the bench to sit down, my odor caught everyone's attention.

"Who shit themselves?" Blackhawks trainer Mike Gapski asked.

He was undoubtedly joking, not knowing that I had done exactly that. I was so uncomfortable that I had to inform Keenan I was leaving the bench with 15 minutes left in the third period. I missed five or six minutes of the game because I had to change my underwear. It was the most embarrassing moment I ever had in the game. Pardon the pun, but you can imagine the shit I took over that episode.

Keenan always tried to stay one step ahead of his players, particularly with regard to controlling our lives through curfews and practices and so forth. It's said that Keenan learned all of his tricks to control players from the great Scotty Bowman when Keenan was an American Hockey League coach in Rochester. At the time, Bowman was in charge of Rochester's parent club in Buffalo.

When we were on the road, Keenan would give the bellman a hat and tell him to ask every player who came in after curfew to sign it. Keenan could then inspect the hat the next day and know who had violated curfew. Other times, he would sit in the lobby reading a book and catch his drunken players stumbling in at three in the morning.

Some of us had our ways to beat the curfew setup, most of which involved making sure we didn't return to our rooms through the lobby. At the Los Angeles Airport Marriott, for example, we would use rocks to make sure that the side doors remained ajar so we could sneak back into the hotel.

Early in my career, we had back-to-back games in Calgary and Vancouver. We flew from Calgary to Vancouver after the game, and with the time change, it was still after midnight when we got to the Westin Bayshore hotel. With a game against the Canucks the next night, we were supposed to go directly to our rooms. But players always liked going out in Vancouver because the Roxy was a favourite player hangout. We were only going to Vancouver twice a season, so you couldn't waste a trip. Several of the guys, me included, took the elevator to our rooms and then took the stairs back down to the ground floor and fled out the side door.

Several beers later, it was past three in the morning, and I returned to the team hotel by myself. I was standing in front, wondering whether I was walking into a well-executed Keenan trap. Had he paid the night manager to keep a list of players coming in late? Would there be an autograph seeker waiting for me by the elevator to essentially ask me to sign my own death warrant? Would Keenan himself be standing watch? Anything was possible with Iron Mike.

Wanting to avoid any possibility of a Keenan ambush, I went around the side of the building to find the loading dock. That was locked down tight, as was the entrance to the hotel kitchen, which was on the same side of the building. But as I inspected the area, I noticed a ventilation grate; and peering through it, I could see into the hotel's kitchen. Back then, hotels were still issuing metal keys, not key cards, and I used my key to unscrew the grate. Within a couple of minutes, I had the grate removed and was scooting through the air duct, attired in a suit. I ended up breathing in plenty of soot and dust, but it was a small price to pay to pull one over on Keenan.

Once in the kitchen, I grabbed a ham sandwich and a Bud Light and took the service elevator up to my floor. I remember sitting in my room at four in the morning, munching on my sandwich and sipping my beer, feeling like I had just pulled off the crime of the century.

Truthfully, NHL coaches had to play babysitter and night watchman in that era because I believe my generation had more of a frat-house attitude than today's players. Modern players are far more concerned about rest, eating properly and following a training regimen that doesn't include consuming mass quantities of Molson Canadian. When I played, it was expected that you would go out on the road and drink with your teammates until it was nearly dawn. Today, players seem to live in the weight room. We lived primarily in taverns and bars. I didn't start spotting abs on players until I was about 26 years old.

Keenan tried to keep track of us on the road mostly because he was trying to discourage us from finding trouble. When I was a young player, it did often seem as though I was only two or three steps ahead of finding myself in hot water.

One night, during a trip to Calgary, a bunch of the Blackhawks met people at the bar who invited us to a party at a house outside of town. The invitation came at about 1:30 in the morning, but stupidly I decided to go. One other Blackhawk decided to go, but we ended up in separate cars. We were driving well outside of town when the situation turned bad. In wintry conditions, we ended up in an accident. The car completely flipped over. Even though I was a passenger and not the driver, I could see the headlines in the morning paper: Drunken young Blackhawks star Roenick detained after late-night traffic accident.

Panicked by the thought of what Keenan would say, I embraced the only strategy that offered me any hope of getting out of this mess: I ran. I got the fuck out of there. I ran through the snow into a neighbourhood. The problem was that I was on foot, more than 30 miles from my hotel. I was in a residential area. No stores or pay phones were anywhere. Plus, it was now after two in the morning. My only option was to knock on someone's door and ask to use a phone to call a taxi.

That's what I did, and when the man came to the door in his pajamas, he opened his storm door and his eyes bugged out.

"Holy shit," he said. "You're Jeremy Roenick."

"I am," I admitted, "and I need to use your phone."

Only in Canada or Chicago would I have been recognized. Even bleary-eyed, in the middle of the night, this man recognized an NHL player when one showed up on his doorstep.

The funny part of the story is that the guy invited me into his kitchen and offered me a Molson Canadian. In the 45 minutes it took for the cab to find the house, the Good Samaritan and I talked hockey and finished off his case of Canadian. I imagine he had quite a story to tell his buddies at work the next day. Meanwhile, it was almost four o'clock when I returned to my hotel. But I was up in time for the morning skate, hoping I had dodged a bullet. Clearly, the people in the car that night and my friend with the beer didn't rat me out, because no one from the Chicago organization ever brought it up to me.

The closest I ever came to being arrested involved an incident that occurred when Keenan took the team to the resort area of Banff, Alberta. The team was scheduled to play Calgary and Edmonton in the same week.

At about two in the morning, after spending most of the night in a bar, five or six players and four or five local women, decided to visit a nearby hot springs that was closed to the public. Since it was located halfway up a mountain, we hired cabs to transport us and then paid the drivers handsomely to come back in 45 minutes to retrieve us. Snow was falling, and we had to scale a fence to get inside. We had brought beer along, and in short order we were drinking and jumping into the springs just to keep warm. Even with the steam rising, it didn't take long for us to start feeling the cold.

When the cabs didn't come back on time, we decided to start walking down the zig-zaggy road. I remember I had a brown suede coat that I wrapped some of my clothes in. That meant I had no coat on, and it was freezing. I remember joking that we should just cut through the woods, because it was a shorter trip back to the hotel. Everyone laughed, because there was probably six feet of snow covering the ground. There was no way we were going to do that.

We kept hoping the cabs were on the way, and when we heard cars coming up the mountain, we were initially relieved. But when we looked over the side, we could see it was a police car and what looked like a paddy wagon. Immediately, we figured the police had heard the taxi drivers talking on their radios about coming to get us and they planned to arrest us for trespassing before we were rescued. Quickly, we decided our only option was to leave the road and start trudging through the snow. One by one, we climbed over the ledge to start the snowy descent. Holding my clothes under my arm like a football, I must have looked like Herschel Walker high-stepping my way through the snow.

Not knowing we had gone down the side of the mountain, the cops drove to the springs. When they arrived, they could see us scrambling down the mountain. They came after us. Some of the snow was up to my chest, but we all reached the hotel's parking lot right before the cops arrived. They thought we had already made it into the hotel, but we hadn't gotten that far. There was so much snow, they couldn't see we were on the other side of the parking lot.

When the cops left, we strolled into the hotel lobby and came across an employee cleaning the floors. We were covered in snow, our hair turned to icicles by freezing sweat as we hustled down the mountain.

"Why did you guys have a snowball fight at three o'clock in the morning?" he asked.

Keenan didn't catch us that night, either.

Another time in Banff, Michel Goulet left the ice early at practice. He went into the coach's office and lifted one of Keenan's credit cards out of his wallet. That night, all of the players went out together, and Goulet ordered five full trays of Jägermeister shots. The trays of liquor kept coming all night, and Goulet paid the $4,000 bill with Keenan's credit card. Of course, this was going on without his permission.

By luck of the draw, Goulet had taken Keenan's Blackhawks team credit card. When Keenan got the credit card statement, he didn't want to get the team's bean counters mad by submitting the large bill. Instead, he paid it out of his own fucking pocket. Many guys didn't like Keenan, but they did like him on the night that he unknowingly took his team out for dinner and drinks. I recall that he was toasted with Jägermeister many times that night.

As I tell all of these Keenan stories, I hope my readers don't get the impression that I didn't like Keenan. I love the man for moulding me into the player I became. He was Dr. Frankenstein, and I was his creation. He was a father figure for me, and he nurtured my game through a tough-love approach. We fought regularly in my years in Chicago. More than once, I screamed, "Go fuck yourself, Mike."

Even though my emotions would boil over, I understood that Keenan was always simply trying to find a way to help me become the best player I could be. But when I needed guidance early in my career, it was Keenan who often provided it. I remember Tracy and I were going through a rough patch in our relationship. We were young people entering adulthood differently from our peers. I was a teenage professional athlete who had money and growing fame. In retrospect, it was one of the most difficult periods in our lives, and it was Mike Keenan who sat us down and helped us work through the issue. Neither of us has forgotten that kindness.

Keenan never complimented me about my performance on the ice, because that was not his style. But after games, he would tell Tracy that no matter what he said to me, she should know that he felt that "Jeremy was going to be a great player someday."

It wasn't as if Keenan was the only tough coach in his era, nor was he the only coach to attempt to unify his team by making them all mad at him. That was a tactic that famous coach Herb Brooks used to bring together the Americans before they took down the Soviets at the 1980 Olympics. But many of those who played for Keenan would probably argue that he took coaching meanness to a new level. Keenan's toughness never bothered me, because I was accustomed to that approach. My father often yelled at me to get his point across, and Thayer coach Arthur Valicenti wasn't peaches and cream in his approach to prep school hockey. Alain Vigneault also had a hard edge to his coaching style. I wouldn't say I liked being criticized or yelled at, but I got used to it.

Maybe the Blackhawks' dressing room would have been better off with less friction. But you always knew where you stood with Keenan. I don't believe there was any aspect of his coaching style that players truly enjoyed, other than the fact that we were improving as a team. He wasn't there to make friends. He was there to win hockey games. And the way he viewed it was that his players' flaws were in the way of his attempts to win games. He did whatever he felt was necessary to correct your imperfections, and he didn't care what you thought about his methods. Either you did what he wanted you to do, or you were in his doghouse and every day at the rink was going to be a day in hell. Yelling was part of the culture in a Keenan dressing room. Either you could live with that or you couldn't. There was no middle ground.

In my rookie season in the NHL, it felt as if I was a character in the soap opera *Days of our Lives*. Every day there was anger, passion, bad behaviour, subplots and drama in the Chicago dressing room.

It was during my second season in Chicago, when I was just 19, that I grew comfortable enough to hold my ground with Keenan. He would yell at me, and I yelled back. That was the way it worked in Chicago. Mike had the power but allowed us to vent our frustration through anger at him. If you didn't respond to him with anger, he viewed it as a sign of weakness. In Keenan's dressing room, it was acceptable, maybe even encouraged, for players to confront each other about how we were playing. Mike wanted the fires always burning in his dressing room. He wanted everyone always mad at him, and he liked it when players held each other accountable. There were some fistfights in the dressing room as players fought, not like sworn enemies but like brothers who would still love each other when the scrap was over.

Today's NHL dressing rooms are tame by comparison to what Chicago's dressing room was like back then. Today's players don't confront each other the way we did. In my opinion, today's players are too touchy about criticism. When you came into our dressing room under Mike Keenan, it was like joining a house of gladiators. There would be pain and suffering. But in that environment, I matured into a very good player, and the Blackhawks became a quality team.

# CHAPTER 4

# Finding My Bluster in the Windy City

The late Chicago Blackhawks owner Bill Wirtz once promised me that I would never be traded. In Chicago Stadium, he told me not to worry about my upcoming contract negotiations because a deal would be reached.

"You will be a Blackhawk forever," he said emphatically.

I believed him. Maybe I should have been skeptical of the commitment, because a year or two before that meeting, Mr. Wirtz didn't recognize me when I bumped into him at a grocery store on the north side of Chicago. It was an awkward moment for both of us. I approached him and said, "Hello, Mr. Wirtz." He nodded, and I could tell immediately that he thought I was a fan, or some stranger, who had recognized him.

"I'm Jeremy Roenick, sir," I said.

He was clearly embarrassed, but we ended up having a pleasant conversation. Although Mr. Wirtz didn't recognize me without a helmet, I think he liked me, or at least he liked how I played on the ice. He probably meant it when he said that I would spend my entire career with the Blackhawks.

Unquestionably, that was my plan. In 1991, I signed a five-year contract with the Blackhawks for just over $5 million. The deal started with a yearly salary of $750,000 in the first season and ended with a salary of $1.4 million in the fifth year. My decision to accept a long-term deal was questioned around the league because I was viewed as a rising star that might be best served by taking a short-term deal and then waiting to see how the market would escalate. When Bob Goodenow became executive director of the NHL Players' Association the year before, he had introduced salary disclosure as a tool to raise salaries. By making sure that agents knew what every player was earning, league salaries could be used as a basis for comparison during negotiations. When no one knew what everyone else was making, agents relied on guesswork to determine their players' salary demands.

My agent, Neil Abbott, and I discussed the pros and cons of a short deal versus a longer deal until we were weary of the debate. You have to remember that hockey salaries hadn't yet spiked when I signed that contract. By averaging just over a million dollars a season, I was being paid more than Boston standout Cam Neely or Edmonton sniper Jari Kurri. Both of those players were earning less than a million dollars per season in 1991–92. Detroit's Steve Yzerman was only making $1.4 million that season, and he was coming off four consecutive seasons of scoring 50 or more goals.

The important issue, according to Neil, was that $5 million would set me up for life, and when the contract expired I would still only be 26 years old. His concern was that my aggressive playing style left me vulnerable to a catastrophic injury. This deal would protect me from that risk, and when the contract was up, I would still be young enough to land a "home run" deal.

At the time, the Blackhawks even fought the idea of making me a millionaire player. Fortunately for me, negotiations were ongoing during the 1991 Canada Cup, and I was having a strong tournament. Blackhawks general manager Bob Pulford was co-general manager of Team USA, and his fellow team executives were razzing him about how my price tag was rising with every shift I took.

*Sports Illustrated* published an article on October 7, 1991, in which writer E.M. Swift offered that, after I had scored a pretty goal, Pulford, in response to the needling he was taking, jokingly yelled, "Will you get that kid off the ice?"

A day or two later, Pulford agreed to the contract that would make me a million-dollar player.

I trusted Neil's instincts because it was clear from the beginning that he only had my best interests in mind when he ventured an opinion. What I can say about Neil without fear of contradiction is that he treats his clients like they are family. Besides, by the 1991–92 season, I felt like there was no better National Hockey League city than Chicago. Keenan had scared me into becoming a 50-goal scorer, and he had bullied the Blackhawks into becoming a quality hockey team. Defenceman Chris Chelios and I were the centrepieces of the team. I had replaced the great Denis Savard as the team's offensive catalyst, and Chelios was the defensive star. The Blackhawks were an Original Six team led by two American stars. Who would have thought that possible even 15 years before?

That was starting to become a theme around the NHL in the early 1990s. Brian Leetch, whom I had battled with in high school, was the New York Rangers' best weapon. My archrival Mike Modano was becoming a star with the Minnesota North Stars. There were certainly indications around the NHL that the American program was beginning to produce premium NHL talent.

Chelios was born and raised in the Chicago area, and Blackhawks fans loved him for that and because he played hockey as if it were mortal combat. Even though I was from Boston, Chicago fans also embraced me as if I were one of their own. Everyone in Chicago knew us, and everyone seemed to want to know us better. Chelios and I were treated like royalty everywhere we went. As a general rule, the Blackhawks always had a good time away from the rink. Chelios and I had a better time than most. Both of us liked to prowl in the celebrity world. We met many of them, none nicer than the late Canadian actor John Candy. He grew up in Toronto and seemed to like spending time with the NHL community. He was also friends with then-Kings owner Bruce McNall and Wayne Gretzky. The three of them became partners in the purchase of the Canadian Football League's Toronto Argonauts.

When Candy's 1991 movie *Only the Lonely* was filmed in Chicago, scenes were shot at Comiskey Park, as well as the famous Emmitt's Pub and the Ambassador East Hotel. Candy invited Chelios, my wife, Tracy, and me to visit him on the set. After we knocked on the door of his trailer, he appeared at the door and said: "Sorry folks, park's closed. Moose out front should've told you." Then he shut the door.

It was his famous line, delivered in character, from his role as the Walley World security guard in the 1983 movie *National Lampoon's Vacation.* It was a hysterical greeting. Seconds later, Candy reopened the door and we were in his trailer, where we helped him drink the tub of beer he had on ice. While he sat and talked to us, he had ice packs all over his knees and back from the stress he put on his body from a day of shooting. It was like watching an athlete ice down after competition. Candy was a big man, and 14-hour shooting days were clearly stressful on his body. We always wanted to talk about the movie business, but Candy preferred to discuss the Toronto Maple Leafs, the Blackhawks and Wayne Gretzky. He always wanted to talk about hockey. "What is it like," he would ask, "to play against Mario Lemieux?" Of course, we were more interested to hear tales about Chevy Chase or Hollywood movie sets.

At the time, there were celebrities who wanted to hang with us as much as we wanted to be with them. That was such a strange feeling for me, because I didn't view myself as a celebrity. I saw myself as the interloper, someone who had been invited into the celebrity world, not someone who belonged there. One time, Charles Barkley was in town to play against the Bulls and decided to take in a Blackhawks game. I don't remember what happened in the game, but I do remember Barkley bursting into our dressing room, bellowing: "Where's that Roenick kid? I want to meet that Roenick kid."

After we were introduced, he said: "Man, you remind me of myself when I was a younger player. You play hockey the way I played basketball as a young man, aggressive!" It was one of the nicest compliments I ever received. A major NBA star had given up his free time to come down to tell me that he liked the passion I showed when I competed. To this day, I don't think I've ever met an athlete who is more respectful than Barkley. I mean that sincerely. Some people listen to you only to find an opening to allow themselves to talk again. Barkley is always interested in what you have to say. He treats people with respect. We chatted for 15 or 20 minutes in the dressing room, and I told him some of the Blackhawks were getting together at the nightspot Excalibur to shoot pool after the game. I invited him to join us. I hoped he would show up, but I didn't expect to see him there. But around one o'clock in the morning, in strolled Barkley. He shot pool and drank with the Blackhawks until the bartender booted us out at closing time.

In 1996, I took my wife to the Olympics in Atlanta and was walking down the street when this giant of a man picked me up from behind and whipped me around. It was Barkley, who was just as friendly and cordial as the night we met. Every time I see him, we pick up our conversation right where we left off; I have man love for Barkley to this day.

I always had time for the NBA players in Chicago. I played some golf with Michael Jordan, and I was friends with Dennis Rodman and Ron Harper after they came to play with the Bulls. Rodman, Harper, Chelios and I used to drink together at the Martini Bar in Chicago. We had our own little area in the bar, and employees would keep us segregated from the other patrons. You had to be on "the list" to come back to our area to see us. Of course, Rodman had told the employees that any attractive blonde was automatically on his list, and Harper ordered employees to send back every good-looking brunette. Chelios and I would laugh at the parade of women coming back to see these two guys.

It was always a wild night when we hung out with the sake-drinking Rodman. He could do some crazy shit. You never knew which Rodman was going to show up. He dressed differently and he acted differently every time we saw him. One night, he invited us to his party and he was dressed like Cleopatra.

One of my all-time favourite nights came when the Blackhawks were playing in Toronto and comedic actor Dan Aykroyd invited us to come to his local bar there. Aykroyd had live music at his bar, and he went up on stage and jammed away for our entertainment. When it was time to close for the night, he kept the bar open, and then we all went up on stage and jammed with him. Chelios was leading the pack, and I believe Joe Murphy, Tony Amonte and Bernie Nicholls were there. I remember playing the drums very badly.

On the ice, we were having just as much fun. In 1990–91, with Keenan screaming at us all the way, the Blackhawks led the NHL with 106 points. We then self-destructed in the playoffs, losing in the first round to a Minnesota team that was 12 games below .500. Showing no discipline, we accumulated 46.4 penalty minutes per game, and Minnesota netted 15 power-play goals in the six games. Although Minnesota ended up reaching the Stanley Cup final, we were still embarrassed by the loss to the North Stars.

Going into the 1991–92 season, I thought we had figured out what we needed to do to win. The Minnesota series had taught us some lessons about the fine line between aggressiveness and taking dumb penalties. Personally, I believed I had a better understanding of the sacrifice I needed to make to be successful. I believed I learned that more from opponents than teammates. When I played against Edmonton's Mark Messier in 1989–90, during the Edmonton Oilers' march to their fifth Stanley Cup championship, I probably learned everything I needed to know about winning. Messier looked scary. He resembled what a gladiator from centuries ago must have looked like, just before he cut off your fucking head in the arena. I probably could not have looked that scary, but I believed I could replicate Messier's commitment to winning.

Meanwhile, Keenan had pieced together the kind of team he wanted to coach. We had a roster full of guys who were ready to play the game as if they were medieval warriors. The Blackhawks had traded Dave Manson to Edmonton to land heady defenceman Steve Smith. Hard-nosed Brent Sutter was brought over from the New York Islanders for Steve Thomas and Adam Creighton. Heavy hitter Bryan Marchment was acquired from Winnipeg in a deal that sent Troy Murray to the Jets.

To me, the Smith acquisition seemed the most important, because he had helped the Oilers win Stanley Cup titles in 1987 and 1988 and 1990. He understood how a team needs to become disciplined as the playoffs progressed.

We weren't the most skilled team in the NHL in 1991–92, but we were certainly one of the most difficult to play against. Three of our defencemen—Smith, Marchment and Chelios—combined for 717 penalty minutes. Mike Peluso had 404 penalty minutes. I had 98, and I wasn't even in the top five on our team. By then, Ed Belfour had established himself as a fiery, battling goalkeeper. It took work to score against us. The Montreal Canadiens were the only team to give up fewer goals than we surrendered that season.

On March 7, 1992, I became only the third Blackhawk to score 50 goals in a season when I bounced a shot off Boston Bruins defenceman Raymond Bourque's knee and into the net for the game-winner in a 2–1 win against the Bruins.

The goal was my league-leading 12th game-winner of the season, breaking Bobby Hull's team record. As happy as my teammates were for me, Chicago captain Dirk Graham said that he was more impressed that night by a skating dash I made for a puck in the closing minutes of the game than he was my 50th goal. As we were trying to hang on to our one-goal lead, I outraced Boston defenceman Gord Murphy to negate an icing call that would have put the faceoff deep in our zone.

After netting my 50th, I still had 13 games remaining to make a run at Hull's team record of 57 goals. But a suggestion in the newspaper that I would be trying to pursue that record earned me the wrath of Keenan.

On the night I scored my 48th and 49th, in a 4–4 tie against the New York Rangers, I made what Keenan considered a risky play in an effort to score my 50th in that game. My status as the team's leading scorer offered me no immunity from Keenan's persecution. He yelled at me as often as, if not more than, he did in my rookie season. He chewed me out aggressively for trying to make a play that he didn't believe was in the team's best interest.

"I don't want to get in trouble again," I told the *Chicago Tribune*. "So [the record] will be in the back of my mind. The team is always first."

Not daring to take any risks in the final few weeks of the season, I finished with 53 goals.

The Blackhawks were only the NHL's seventh-best team that season with a record of 36–29–15, but everyone in the hockey world understood that we would be a bigger force in the playoffs because of our grittiness.

Although Chicago fans were initially miffed at the decision to trade away Savard, it took only a few games for everyone to realize that Chelios's presence completely changed the culture of our team. He was the most ruthless competitor I've ever known. He was skilled, and he was mean. Nobody liked playing against Chelios, and that's why Keenan wanted him.

When Chelios got tangled up with opponents, he would put

them into headlocks. He would squeeze them so tightly they would start kicking the ice and screaming that they couldn't breathe. I don't remember who the opponent was, but I can vividly recall him yelling, "I'm going to die, I'm going to die! You're squeezing too hard."

Back then, the Blackhawks tested the strength of our grip with a device that measured it on a scale of one to a hundred. You would squeeze a lever, and the needle would rise like a tachometer. Most of the players could push the needle to the mid-70s. The strong players pushed it to 78 or 79. Chelios grabbed it and gave a quick squeeze, and the needle rocketed to 100. Chelios has vice-grip hands. In the 1990s, Chelios went through what I called his "arm-wrestling phase." He was always challenging the biggest guy in the bar to an arm-wrestling contest. Sometimes, he would entice opponents by offering to put up a hundred dollars against anyone who would be willing to bet twenty that he could beat Chelios. The five-to-one odds usually drew some takers. My guess is that Chelios won over a hundred of those arm-wrestling matches.

Pity the fool who didn't know all of Cheli's tricks; if you tried to hit Chelios, you often found yourself chewing on his stick. The closer you got to Chelios, the higher his stick would come up. And Chelios was also the king of chop. If an opponent violated his personal space, Chelios would fucking chop him across the ankles.

Although Chelios and I often partied together, we had a business relationship when it came to what happened on the ice. Chelios was among the few teammates I had who was comfortable critiquing my performance or my conduct. Even though Chelios and I were close, he had no problem pulling rank on me if he believed it was necessary. If he felt I was out of line, he told me.

One year, I was injured in the postseason when we were playing against Toronto at Maple Leaf Gardens. While the guys were preparing for the game, I felt like I was getting in their way. The visitors' dressing room was cramped in that vintage arena, and they didn't need an extra body in there. I decided to leave the rink to have dinner. The food was not a problem; the cocktails *were* a problem. By game time, I was amped up. I decided to watch the game from ice level. I stationed myself at the Zamboni entrance along the glass. I was banging on the glass and yelling to Eddie Belfour and Chelios all night long.

After the game, Chelios said he needed to talk to me. He brought me into one of the small rooms at the Gardens and started to yell.

"You were acting like an idiot out there," Chelios said. "It was embarrassing."

He told me never to behave like that again. If anyone else would have said that to me like that, I might have been livid. As soon as Chelios was finished with his tongue-lashing, I apologized and thanked him for setting me straight. I never acted that way again.

The Blackhawks had every type of player we needed to be successful. Marchment was a madman when he played. He would slash guys, make game-changing hits and fight anyone. Smith certainly didn't accumulate all of those penalty minutes for delay of game. He was a very confident player and an intimidating presence. He had an aura that rubbed off on all of us.

It's not a coincidence that my best goal-scoring numbers came when I was playing alongside Hall of Famer Michel Goulet and Steve Larmer, should-be Hall of Famer. Those two players taught me more about playing offensively than anyone else. They also drove me fucking crazy with their teaching methods. But the lessons stuck with me. Keenan always says I was a "sponge" back then because I soaked up information. But I can say that it wasn't easy processing all of the "tips" they were providing me when I was a 20-year-old playing between two established stars. We would be sitting on the bench after a shift, and Goulet would be chirping in my right ear about what he needed me to do while Larmer would be yelling into my left ear about what *he* thought I should be doing. Fucking "J.R., do this." Fucking "J.R., do that." Fucking "J.R., be here." Fucking "J.R., be there." Essentially, I learned to be a top offensive player by doing everything in my power to serve two masters. I knew if I didn't give them the puck when they wanted it, they would bitch-slap me.

One time, I remember we came back to the bench and Larmer climbed all over my ass for not serving the puck to him at the optimum moment.

"You should have given me the puck as soon as I started to cut in," he said.

"I tried, but—" I said, before he cut me off.

"Don't try," he said curtly. "Just do it."

Their constant harassment helped transform me into a star, but don't believe for a minute I didn't grow weary of constant bitching about how I was playing. We are like family in an NHL dressing room, but sometimes family members get mad at one another. Once, Larmer was yelling at me on the bench while I was trying to get a drink of water. I became so pissed off at him that I spit water all over him. That was truly spitting on the hand that fed me, because Larmer taught me much about positioning and seeing passing options before they are visible to others.

Keenan always loved Larmer. When Keenan coached Team

Canada, he always told us it wasn't easy to find guys who could play with Wayne Gretzky because Gretzky just saw the game differently. It was like we were all playing chess, and Gretzky was playing three-dimensional chess. Keenan said Mario Lemieux was the best at playing with Gretzky, but the other winger who could do it was Larmer.

Larmer passed along one trick that I used for most of my career.

"If you don't see me," Larmer would say, "I'm going to the spot that you just vacated."

When two linemates think like that, they will score on plenty of give-and-go plays. And our line scored often on that play.

All of our changes had been made with the idea that we needed to be tough to play against in a seven-game series. We proved that in 1992, when we lost two of the first three against St. Louis and then rattled off 11 consecutive wins to put Chicago in the Stanley Cup final for the first time since 1972. We were trying to win Chicago's first Stanley Cup since 1961.

Going into the final, the media asked me how the Chicago Blackhawks were going to beat the Pittsburgh Penguins; I thought they should have been asking the Penguins how they were going to beat us. Even though the Penguins were the defending Stanley Cup champions and boasted a roster that included Mario Lemieux, Jaromir Jagr, Ron Francis, Bryan Trottier, Kevin Stevens and Rick Tocchet, the players in our dressing room believed we were the favourites.

It seemed like we were correct in that assessment when we claimed a 4–1 lead halfway through game one. Even when Tocchet and Lemieux scored late in the second period to pull the Penguins within a goal, we still believed we could hold the lead. We thought we were mentally tougher. We thought we could outwork the Penguins. We thought wrong.

The Penguins were relentless, and Lemieux and a 20-year-old Jaromir Jagr took over the game. With just under five minutes left, Jagr claimed a loose puck and wove through five Blackhawks, including Brent Sutter and Dirk Graham, skated through the slot and beat Belfour with a low backhander. My recollection is that Jagr turned Sutter inside out twice. In the newspapers the next day, Lemieux called Jagr's goal "the greatest goal I ever saw."

Lemieux had his own heroics, scoring the game-winner, on the power play, with 13 seconds remaining in regulation. Five seconds before, referee Andy Van Hellemond had whistled Smith for hooking Lemieux. Smith had to do it to prevent Lemieux from breaking in on Belfour.

The Penguins were the first team since 1944 to come back from a three-goal deficit to win a game in the Stanley Cup final. We actually led twice by three goals because we had scored the first three goals of the game.

One news account of the game prophesized that Lemieux and Jagr "may some day be remembered as hockey's equivalent of Babe Ruth and Lou Gehrig."

Keenan was livid over our performance in general, and he was particularly incensed over Jagr's goal. "Both defenders played the puck, not the man," he said, referring to Sutter and Graham. "And our goaltender never made a save, and it wasn't a very hard shot. He beat three players on a solo effort."

The sentiment around the hockey world seemed to be that Keenan gave up on us after the first game. I didn't feel that way. I thought his quotes after the game were typical Keenan mind games, designed to spur us to a higher performance level in the second game. But in hindsight, anyone can see that we never recovered from game one. In game two, we started slowly, and I found myself at the end of the bench with my linemates, Steve Larmer and Michel Goulet. Keenan wouldn't even look at us. Stu Grimson and Mike Peluso, two of our tough guys, received increased ice time while we sat. Grimson was six foot five and weighed 220, and Peluso was six foot four. Keenan said he was trying to "wear down" the Penguins with some size. We lost the game 3–1.

The buzz after the game was about Keenan benching his top line.

"I can't decipher what his reasons are," I told the *Tribune*. "It was very frustrating. I knew the position we were in. I feel I was working hard. I was getting good hits. And he sat me on the bench. It was tough to take. He sat me out three or four shifts, the last eight minutes of the game. But I can't worry about what he's going to do. I have to worry about what I'm going to do."

The media questioned Keenan's in-game tactics for benching his three best offensive players. The theme of the criticism was that the Stanley Cup final is not the time to make statements to your players. It wasn't the time to take the switch to your players. It wasn't the time to teach lessons.

Keenan wasn't done with his theatrics. Before I was benched in game two, Stevens slashed me. Fortunately, it resulted in a bruise and not a break. But that didn't stop Keenan from telling the doctors to put a cast on my injury. He told me I was going to the press conference that morning, and he told me that I shouldn't say a word. When we got there, Keenan held up my cast as Exhibit A of his case that the officials had missed the Penguins taking liberties with his players. My cast was Keenan's prop. My "injury" was also his explanation for why his 50-goal scorer had been on the bench for such a long time.

There were far more reporters snickering than believing in Keenan's theatrics between games two and three. When I was able to play game three, famed *Chicago Tribune* columnist Bob Verdi, who knew by now the way it works for the Blackhawks, wrote: "Let the healing begin! Jeremy Roenick lives! At 7:44 Saturday evening, in a miracle of modern science, the Blackhawks' 22-year-old superstar left his death bed and skated onto the Stadium ice to take his first shift."

Near the end of his column, Verdi even suggested that Bill Wirtz should sell copies of my X-rays for $19.99. Late in his column, he added this: "Bite your tongue if you even dare think Keenan choreographed this entire scenario. To deflect criticism of his coaching in game two? To work the officials? To get some strokes for Roenick, who plays golf with Stevens all summer back in Boston? Shame on you. Then again, if Roenick was too hurt to play Thursday night, what about Steve Larmer and Michel Goulet? Where were their one-day casts, or were they being benched in sympathy for Roenick? Just asking."

No one should have been shocked by Keenan's move, because he's not the kind of man who is going to change his approach because the stakes are higher. He's going to do it his way, because at that point his way had worked out well for him.

Down 2–0 heading back to Chicago, we knew our belief that hard work would trump skill was misguided, at least for this particular series. We were swept in four games. I was crying as I left the ice. Veteran players always tell you to savour every moment in

This is me at 18 months old, living in Connecticut and already gearing up to launch my athletic career.

This is me with my younger brother, Trevor (*below*), and my dog, Sparky.

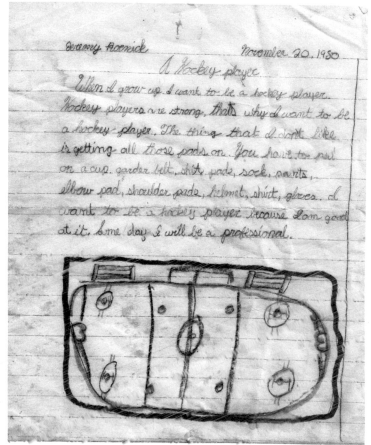

You can it see from this homework assignment: I always knew I wanted to play in the NHL.

When I was 10 and living in Northern Virginia, it seemed just as likely that I would end up a top soccer player as a top hockey player. I was as dominant on the soccer field as I was on the ice. I'm in the centre row, second from the right.

Here's my Thayer Academy high school team the season before I was drafted. I was a junior at the time. Can you pick out Tony Amonte and me?

American players hone their skills the same way that Canadian players do: by shooting in their driveways. I'm 16 in this photo.

Tracy and I are 16 years old here. Are you kidding me with that pizza face and 1980s fashion?

Here are Tony Amonte (*left*) and I horsing around in 1987, when we were in high school. Do we look like two guys who would combine for 929 NHL goals?

This is me with some of my best high school buddies. That's Matt Mallgrave in the back, then (*left to right*) Dan Greene, Matt Collins and Joe Caswell. Greene played on a line with Tony Amonte and me at Thayer Academy. Collins and Caswell also played at Thayer. Mallgrave played at St. Paul.

Shortly after the Blackhawks selected me as the eighth pick in the 1988 NHL draft, I had my photo taken with team executives. Of the seven players chosen before me, only Mike Modano, picked first overall by Minnesota, scored more goals than I did.

At the 1988 NHL draft, the Boston area was well represented, with me going eighth to Chicago, Tony Amonte (*centre*) chosen 68th by the New York Rangers and Ted Crowley (*right*) going 69th to the Toronto Maple Leafs.

Can you believe how young Mike Keenan (*left*) looked at the 1988 NHL draft? He was my first coach, so it's funny that we sometimes appear together now as hockey analysts on NBC telecasts. I was scared of Keenan when I first played for him, but today we're friends.

Neil Abbott (*left*), shown here with me at an NHL awards dinner, was my agent for my entire playing career. But he seemed more like a family member than an agent because he always took care of me.

Look what a handsome kid I was when the Blackhawks drafted me in the first round at the Montreal Forum on June 11, 1988. Within 11 months, St. Louis Blues forward Glen Featherstone would knock out a few of my teeth with a high stick.

Although I was upset and angry when Chicago coach Mike Keenan assigned me to Hull in the Quebec Major Junior Hockey League, it turned out to be a great experience on and off the ice. The Hull roster included Stéphane Matteau, Karl Dykhuis, Martin Gélinas, Cam Russell and Joe Suk, among others. Alain Vigneault coached.

This larger-than-life Michigan Avenue storefront display in Chicago seemed unreal to me when I was in the early days of my NHL career. It was pretty great, especially for an NHL player who didn't weigh more than 160 pounds soaking wet.

In 1991, just before my 21st birthday, I was in the midst of my first 40-goal season for the Chicago Blackhawks. This was my third year with the NHL, and I was already starting to think I might be a Blackhawk my entire career. Chicago fans loved the way I played, and after that season, general manager Bob Pulford gave me a five-year deal worth about $5 million overall.

I was very close to Tracy's parents, Richard and Dorothy Vazza, shown here at our wedding on June 20, 1992. Tracy's mom died while I was playing with Philadelphia, and her dad died suddenly in 2007. The news of his death ran me over. I was devastated because he was one of my sounding boards. Still miss him.

The Roenick family gets up close and personal with a trio of dolphins on our trip to Hawaii.

No matter where we go on vacation, I somehow end up on a horse. Here I am riding slowly in Santorini, Greece.

This is me with my daughter, Brandi, and my son, Brett. If you can't figure out where we are by the statue in the background, then you don't know American history.

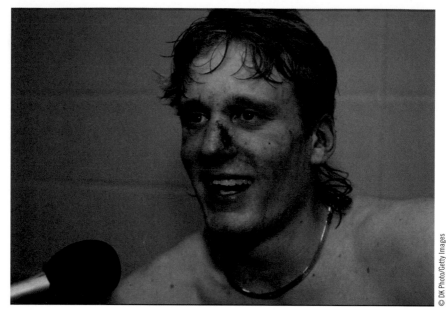

Here I am after the 1989 playoff game that became my "coming out party." First, St. Louis's Steve Larmer gave me a skate blade to the nose. Then, in the second period, Glen Featherstone smashed in my teeth with his stick. My face looked like a train wreck, but I came back to score and we won our series that night. That game changed how people saw me and gave me a reputation for toughness.

ROENICK
27
CHICAGO—
THANK YOU
FOR
THE BEST
SEVEN YEARS
OF MY LIFE

When I was traded from the Blackhawks to the Phoenix Coyotes in 1996, I authorized a Chicago Staples store to hang this banner to thank the city's fans for all their support. We tried to do something nice, but the Blackhawks made the store manager take it down immediately.

a Stanley Cup final because you never know whether you will ever return. Those words went right over my head, because I felt as if the Blackhawks had arrived and we would have more chances to win a Stanley Cup. I could not have been more wrong.

While the Penguins were celebrating their victory in our building, the Blackhawks were in our dressing room, talking about what had gone wrong. Keenan recalls that Dirk Graham told him immediately after the series that it had been over before we realized what the requirements were for winning the Stanley Cup. The Penguins had a superstar in Lemieux, and they had won the Cup just 12 months before. They knew what they needed to do, because they had done it recently.

What I remember most about that night was sitting with Keenan in the dressing room, drinking beer until three or four o'clock in the morning. Mike told me that we had to learn from our experience, and we talked about how this loss would make us stronger. We had a tough, skilful team. I was 22. Ed Belfour was 27. Chelios, Steve Smith and Steve Larmer were still in their prime. Michel Goulet was 32. At 42, Keenan was still a young coach. In my mind, I believed Keenan would push us back to the Stanley Cup final. In my mind, I was going to be a better player in my next Stanley Cup final. I didn't get a point in my first three games of the series, and then I scored twice in game four. My second goal pulled us within one with 8:42 remaining, but we just couldn't get the tying goal. I believed I would get another chance to redeem myself.

But, six days after the Penguins finished us off, Mr. Wirtz informed Mike that he had to choose between being general manager and being coach. Keenan was told that Darryl Sutter had become a hot coaching candidate, and the Blackhawks didn't want to lose him to another team.

At that time, Keenan was mentally drained. He had coached Team Canada to a gold medal at the 1991 Canada Cup before guiding us to the Stanley Cup final. That meant he had been coaching 11 consecutive months. Anyone who knew Mike knew he still wanted to coach, but he chose to be general manager.

Then, on November 6, 1992, less than five months after taking us to the final, Keenan was summoned to what he thought was a meeting to negotiate a new contract. Instead, he walked into a room to find the team's lawyer, Gene Gozdecki, and Mr. Wirtz's son Peter, then a team vice-president. They informed him he was being fired. No reason was given. To this day, Mike tells me he still doesn't know for sure why that decision was reached. The presumption is that Mr. Wirtz didn't enjoy having a strong-willed executive pushing him to make moves he didn't want to make. My guess is that Mr. Wirtz preferred a "yes man" in that position, or at least someone who wasn't as strong-willed as Keenan.

Keenan had pushed Mr. Wirtz about trading Denis Savard, and I don't believe Mr. Wirtz truly wanted to trade Savvy. Keenan had brokered the deal for Chelios with Montreal's Serge Savard. Mr. Wirtz went along with the trade, but maybe Mr. Wirtz resented Keenan for pushing him to trade a popular player. My hunch is that Mr. Wirtz didn't appreciate how much power Keenan expected to have.

The mistake the Blackhawks made in dismissing Keenan was clearly evident 19 months later. By then, the New York Rangers had hired Keenan, and he had taken them to the Stanley Cup championship in 1993–94. It was the Rangers' first title in 54 years.

Some players were happy to have Keenan out of their lives, but I was devastated. I was angry. As I mentioned, he was a father figure to me. He always gave it to me straight. The decision to fire Keenan was probably my first true exposure to the ugly politics of sports. When you negotiate contracts with teams, you certainly understand that the NHL is a business. But when Keenan was fired, I realized for the first time that decisions weren't always made on the basis of how successful a team was on the ice. If Keenan had been judged solely on how his team performed, he would have never been fired. I learned that day that talented people can be cast aside simply because someone doesn't like them. Remember, I had stepped from a high school classroom into the NHL. These life lessons were all new to me.

My wife, Tracy, believes that losing Keenan at that time changed my life's course. I was a young man with a lot of money and time, and I was just starting to be the party guy that I hadn't been in high school. I started to hang out more with people who wanted to be with me because I was a star player. They didn't even know Jeremy. They only knew J.R. Tracy tried to warn me what was happening, but I wasn't listening. Perhaps if Keenan had been there, it might have made a difference. I was afraid of Keenan. He was the most intimidating coach I ever had. Strangely, I liked the power he had over me. But honestly, I don't think even Keenan could have stopped me from exploring my celebrity status. It was intoxicating to be a star in Chicago in the 1990s. When you are on the top in the sports world with thousands of fans, it's very easy to feel like you are the king of the world. You feel invincible. I'm sure Tiger Woods felt he was invincible. My situation was far different from Tiger Woods's situation, but I do understand the feeling that nothing bad is going to happen to you. When you are a top young athlete, you are coddled and sheltered. Then you end up with money and popularity; it's easy to get caught up in that superstar-hero mentality. When that happens, then you are fucked.

# CHAPTER 5

# Showing Me the Door

During my time in Chicago, there was an impression around the NHL that I didn't like Darryl Sutter as a coach, but that wasn't true. I thought he was a smart hockey guy and a quality coach.

I have said for years that I've felt fortunate to have played with some of the Sutter brothers. I respected the Sutters individually and as a family. I admired the way the Sutter family honoured the game. They played the game with grit and fire. They played the game the way it was supposed to be played. Frankly, I hope fans believe that I played the game with Sutter-like passion. I certainly tried to play the game like that.

Brent and Duane also had a good sense of humour. In my early years with the Blackhawks, Brent and Duane always nailed me with practical jokes. Baby powder in the hair dryer. Pants tied in knots. Socks cut in half. Bengay on the toothbrush. Bengay on the jock strap. Shaving cream where it didn't belong. Furniture moved out of your room. I always knew when I had been punked by a Sutter.

One time, our captain, Dirk Graham, had a trainer tell me that Bob Pulford wanted to see me. Not knowing that Pulford had made no such request, I hustled into his office and sat down in front of him.

"What the fuck do you want?" he grumbled.

"I was told you wanted to see me," I said.

"Why the fuck would I want to see you?" Pulford said. "Get the fuck out of here."

Graham received extra credit for using Pulford as an unwitting participant in a prank, because Pulford never seemed like he was having a good day. He was always mumbling and complaining under his breath. Pully was a stubborn cuss, but he was mostly good to me. I viewed him as a loveable curmudgeon. But it could be painful to talk to him.

Today, players sleep on team planes. But I never slept on a team plane because it was guaranteed that if you did, you would have your tie cut in half, or worse.

One night, I went to bed, and as soon as my head hit the pillow I was overwhelmed by a smell that seemed like someone had taken a dump in my pillowcase. When I got up and turned on the lights, I realized that was exactly what had happened. Later that season, I climbed into bed one night and stretched out my legs until my feet hit something cold and squishy. Upon further investigation, I realized someone had dropped a deuce under my covers. Never did uncover the culprit of those smelly pranks.

When it came to practical jokes, I was both a giver and a receiver. One night, Brent Sutter decided not to go out with the boys. He decided to stay in the room and have room service. With many of my teammates listening on a speakerphone, I called Brent in his room and pretended I was a reporter doing an interview. Each question got a little nuttier. It was a hoot. In retaliation, Sutter emptied my room and moved all of my furniture into the hallway by the elevator. He even plugged in the clock and set it for the right time.

Shaving-cream pies in the face. Stealing teammates' clothes. Fake messages. I saw it all in my career, and I enjoyed every fucking minute of it. Although it may seem like it is all sophomoric nonsense, there is some value to it. Teams often bond through practical jokes. Younger players feel like they belong when they are victimized by veterans.

I liked all of the Sutters, but Brent was my favourite. I thought he was the most talented of the Sutter brothers. He had a different personality; he was a bit more laid-back, more polished than his brothers.

What I liked about Darryl Sutter as a coach is that he was similar in style to Keenan. He was tough, demanding and unwavering. It is true that our personalities sometimes clashed. About 18 months into Sutter's tenure as coach, my relationship with Sutter was the primary topic of conversation at the 1994 All-Star Game in New York.

The local newspaper headline read, "Sutter-Roenick row has league talking." But it wasn't a feud as much as it was a disagreement. And Keenan and I had disagreements every day. My big mouth was guilty of contributory negligence in making our squabble seem more hostile. With all of the media gathered in one spot, I aired all of my grievances. Sutter wanted to exclusively play dump-and-chase, and I thought it was limiting us offensively.

"It's hard when I try to be creative on the ice and get chastised for it," I told the media. "When he browbeat me and Joe Murphy after we won a game in Boston for not playing good enough defence, that's when I had to sit down and think about things the most."

The ridiculous aspect of my gab session with the media was that one of my complaints about Sutter was that he was only communicating with me through the newspapers and not directly.

"Roenick probably says things he shouldn't, but no one is perfect," Pulford told the media. "He basically only says them when he's frustrated. There's nothing wrong with the kid. He's a good person."

Sutter is also a good person, and there was nothing wrong with us disagreeing on how we should play. The mistake we made was fighting through the media. We should have just yelled at each other, like Keenan and I did. I fed off the passion of the fights I had with Keenan, and he knew that. Keenan believed we all played better when we were on edge. His style wasn't conducive to a happy dressing room, but we were all spitting fire when we got on the ice.

Newspapers speculated about Sutter possibly getting fired because he and I were having some issues. But that certainly wasn't what I was hoping would happen. I liked his coaching style, and I proved that years later, when I came very close to signing with him when he was with the Calgary Flames.

Despite what Pulford said, I wonder today whether the Blackhawks were growing weary of my personality. Certainly, I was no troublemaker, but I'm guessing they wished that I would keep my mouth shut more often. That wasn't going to happen. They knew that. Maybe that played a role in why I ended up getting traded.

When it was time to negotiate my third contract with the Blackhawks, the NHL salary landscape had changed dramatically.

When Eric Lindros forced the Quebec Nordiques to trade him to Philadelphia and then received a salary of three-and-a-half million dollars per year in his first NHL season in 1992–93, salaries in the NHL were redefined. Two years into my deal, I was underpaid by the standards of the marketplace. But renegotiation wasn't in my makeup. I figure if you shake hands on a deal, you live with it regardless of how it works out. I took the long-term deal because I wanted security, and I got that. But as my contract was in its final months, Neil told the Blackhawks we would be looking for a new deal in the vicinity of $5 million per season.

On May 5, 1996, Mr. Wirtz told *Chicago Tribune* columnist Bob Verdi that he planned to make sure I remained a Blackhawk.

"Jeremy is an integral part of this franchise," Mr. Wirtz said. "We intend to keep it like that for a long time. It's going to take a lot, but that's all I do anymore, anyway. Sign checks."

When Verdi approached me to tell me what Mr. Wirtz had said, I was overjoyed. "All I've wanted from the beginning," I told Verdi, "is to stay a Blackhawk."

As soon as we began negotiating with general manager Bob Pulford, Neil and I quickly discovered that Wirtz was far less willing to sign that cheque than he was willing to admit publicly

At that point in my career, I had already scored 50 or more goals twice in a season, and I had also netted 41 goals and 46 goals in two other seasons. I had registered at least 100 points three times. Beaten up by injuries in 1995–96, I had still netted 32 goals and produced 67 points in 66 games, and added 7 goals and 5 assists in the playoffs. Just as important, in my opinion, was the fact that they could count on me to produce 100 penalty minutes. I took pride in the truth that I was a pest on the ice.

But when my agent, Neil Abbott, told Pulford we were looking for a deal in the $4 million to $5 million range depending upon the length of the deal, Pulford acted as if we had asked for ownership of the team.

"You will never get $4 million to play in this league," Pulford scoffed.

Mr. Wirtz told me I "wasn't worth" the kind of money I was seeking. His words stung me because I always felt Mr. Wirtz liked the way I played. I felt like I had served the Blackhawks well. To this day, I'm one of only three 50-goal scorers in Chicago history.

The Blackhawks thought my value was closer to $3 million per season. Neil told them I would be looking to leave if they didn't pay me what we believed to be my market value. At the time, Gretzky was making more than $6 million. Mark Messier was right at $6 million. Steve Yzerman was at $3.7 million. Mike Modano was at $2.9 million. Salaries were rising daily, and the Blackhawks didn't seem to want to admit that.

As a rising star in my prime, I was highly desirable in the marketplace. My problem was that I was a restricted free agent, meaning that a team that paid me the kind of money I wanted would have to give the Blackhawks five first-round draft picks. At the time, general managers viewed acquiring a player this way as the hockey equivalent of buying a baby on the black market. The St. Louis Blues were the only team ever to give up five first-round picks to sign a restricted free agent, when they signed Scott Stevens in 1990.

But Neil was convinced that a team would give up the draft picks to sign me. When my contract expired on July 1, we heard from 15 teams. None of them were initially willing to give me an offer sheet, but all were willing to talk contract in hopes of working out a deal with Chicago. New York Islanders general manager Mike Milbury seemed closest to handing out an offer sheet, but his people were concerned about giving up five first-rounders while the team was rebuilding. He has said that he carried around an offer sheet in his briefcase for weeks but never sent it. He told us he thought I could do for the Islanders what Bobby Clarke had done for the Philadelphia Flyers in the early 1970s. The Washington Capitals, St. Louis Blues and New Jersey Devils were also interested.

Meanwhile, every day seemed to bring a new rumour about where I might be traded. One day, I was going to Winnipeg for Teemu Selanne; the next, I was going to St. Louis for Brett Hull. Mike Keenan was the Blues' general manager and coach at the time, but the Blues had traded away one of their first-round picks, meaning they weren't in a position to put forward an offer sheet. Keenan would have to swing a trade to get me. We were essentially close to agreeing to terms on a contract, but Keenan couldn't work out the deal with the Blackhawks, despite four hours of negotiations.

While all this was happening, I kept hoping that the Blackhawks would up their offer and begin serious negotiations. But the Blackhawks never budged. Assistant general manager Bob Murray kept telling the media it wasn't about the money, and perhaps that statement was partially true. If you look at the Chicago Blackhawks organization in that era, it was a totalitarian regime led by Mr. Wirtz. It was as if most of the NHL teams were in the free world, and the Blackhawks were behind the Iron Curtain. Mr. Wirtz wanted to be in complete control. Remember, this was a man who didn't believe in televising home games. I'm sure Mr. Wirtz and Pulford viewed me as a radical. While they didn't always say so directly, I sensed that they wanted to muzzle me. When Mike Keenan had wanted too much power, they fired him. Maybe my spirit of independence didn't fit with their idea of what an athlete should be. I don't know that for sure.

On August 16, 1996, the Blackhawks announced that I had been traded to the Phoenix Coyotes for Alexei Zhamnov and Craig Mills. Neil's first thought was that Chicago had turned down better offers than they received from Phoenix.

Even though I knew a trade was likely coming, it was still shocking to the system. I had been in Chicago for eight seasons. I was in Chicago longer than I was in Boston. As unhappy as I was about leaving Chicago, I tried not to say anything bad about Mr. Wirtz. To him, this was a business decision, and I believe that a person who owns a business has the right to run it the way he or she wants to run it. Although I didn't always understand or appreciate some of Mr. Wirtz's decisions, I always respected him. Today, I believe that Mr. Wirtz's son Rocky has done a fantastic job of transforming that franchise into one of the league's best.

After my trade to Phoenix, I was still technically without a team, still a restricted free agent. The Coyotes owned my rights, but I had no contract and was still eligible to receive an offer sheet. And the Islanders, among other teams, called the Coyotes with the hope of working out a deal, but Phoenix said they wanted to keep me. The team had just moved from Winnipeg, and they were hoping I could be a fan draw. The negotiations didn't immediately go smoothly. But Massachusetts native Sean Coady was a scout with the Coyotes then, and we were friends. Coyotes executive vice-president Bobby Smith asked him to call me directly and see if there was a way to bridge the gap.

Frankly, there were teams willing to pay me more than $4 million per season. The Islanders and Blues were chief among them. But now they would have to complete a trade with the Coyotes, and we had no idea whether that was possible.

I didn't want to be in limbo into October. Coady and I talked about what I wanted, and I explained to him that there was a principle at stake in my mind because Pulford had told me no team would pay me $4 million to play hockey.

"What's it going to take to get you to Phoenix?" Coady asked me.

"Tell Bobby Smith if he will give me five years, $20 million, I will sign today," I replied.

Smith agreed to my asking price, and I climbed on a jet to Phoenix.

I never wanted to leave Chicago. But once I agreed to be a Coyote, I committed myself fully to the idea of being both a player and ambassador in Phoenix. The idea of trying to sell hockey in the desert excited me. I've always liked to challenge myself. This would be a major challenge.

# CHAPTER 6

# Selling Ice in the Desert

On my first day with the Phoenix Coyotes, team captain Keith Tkachuk sat me down to explain how our relationship would work.

"I have two rules for you," Tkachuk said. "The first rule is that you have to get me the puck. The second rule is don't forget the first rule."

The speech was Tkachuk's version of an icebreaker, a way to bond with his new teammate. It must have worked with me, because Tkachuk and I became instant friends. What I discovered later is that Tkachuk had the same introductory conversation with every new player who joined the Coyotes.

It always sounds odd when I hear someone refer to Tkachuk as Keith, because no one on our team ever called him by his given name. To us, he was Walt or Big Walt. He received that nickname early in his career because there had been a Walt Tkaczuk who played for the New York Rangers from 1967 until 1981. There is no relation between Keith Tkachuk and Walt Tkaczuk. Their last names are not even spelled the same. But that didn't matter to Tkachuk's teammates in Winnipeg, who started calling him Big Walt. They liked the nickname. So it stuck. Today, Tkachuk seems to prefer being called Big Walt over Keith.

There was frequently an impression in the hockey world that Tkachuk and I didn't get along, even though the truth was that we were the best of friends. We were a couple of Boston guys. We ate together on the road. We partied together. We drank together. We played golf together. We gambled together. We enjoyed each other's company, and we still do today.

The first time I ever talked to Tkachuk was in 1990, after I had already played two NHL seasons. Tkachuk was two years younger than me, and the Hull Olympiques were trying to recruit him to come up and play in the Quebec Major Junior Hockey League. Hull general manager Charlie Henry asked me to call Tkachuk and tell him how much I enjoyed playing in the QMJHL. Henry figured a sales pitch coming from another Boston-area player would mean more to Tkachuk than Henry calling him again.

Although I didn't know Tkachuk at the time, I felt comfortable calling him. I was an NHL player, and I figured if an NHL player had called me when I was deciding what to do, I would have appreciated it. When Tkachuk answered the phone, I quickly told him who I was and that I wanted to talk to him about playing in Hull.

"No thanks, bro," he said. "Going to BU." Then he hung up the phone on me.

It always makes me laugh today when I tell that story. But that was Tkachuk. He has always been headstrong and confident in his own decisions.

In my first couple of seasons in Phoenix, we had our own Boston gang. We were called the "Massachusetts Mafia." Tkachuk had played at Malden Catholic High School and then attended Boston University. He looks and talks like a Boston longshoreman; he's big, beefy and gruff at times, and he has a thick Boston accent.

His father was a U.S. Marine and a Boston firefighter. If Tkachuk hadn't been a talented hockey player, I could have seen him being a firefighter; Bob Corkum was from Salisbury, Massachusetts, and played at Triton Regional High School before playing college hockey at Maine. Craig Janney played at Deerfield Academy in Massachusetts and then went to Boston College. Janney was three years older than me, and he was already in the NHL when I spent my 15 minutes as a Boston College student.

Corkum was an old-school player, a 220-pound forward who could hit, fight, kill penalties, block shots, win a key faceoff and score an occasional big goal. He's the style of player that coaches always love because he's versatile. What I also remember about him is that he could drain a bottle of beer faster than anyone I have ever seen. The contents of a Budweiser longneck could disappear down Corkum's gullet in under two seconds flat. It was a breathtaking feat.

I would see Corkum and Janney pedalling like madmen, side by side, on the stationary bikes, and then 45 minutes later I would see them at the corner of the bar, side by side, drinking just as aggressively.

Janney never received enough credit for his talent. He might have been one of the most skilful setup men the league has ever seen; it's certainly not a coincidence that he ended up centring Brett Hull, Cam Neely and Tkachuk. You don't centre those players unless you can thread a pass through a mail slot.

The four of us were inseparable. We ate together, and we liked to spend time at the bar together.

One story I will always remember, during a road trip to Florida, was the Massachusetts Mafia's late-night escapade to Miami's

South Beach. When we were finished howling at the moon at the Highlander, we had obliterated Jim Schoenfeld's 11:30 curfew by a few hours. I believe we crawled back to the hotel about four o'clock in the morning. All of us could have had the swine flu and been in better condition to play than we were the next day.

I've always believed that if you are going to dance, you have to pay the band. If I wasn't right, I always prided myself on digging deeper to find my competitive best. To be honest, I always thought I played better if I was feeling a bit guilty for drinking the night before. But in the game against the Panthers, I just couldn't seem to escape the slow lane. It seemed like I was skating in mud or sand, and Corkum and Janney seemed stuck in that lane with me. Meanwhile, fellow reveller Tkachuk was skating around the ice like he was Superman. He was unstoppable, scoring three goals in our win against the Panthers.

Burned into my memory bank is the image of Big Walt strolling into the team bus after the game, singing the Semisonic tune "Closing Time" as he shuffled past Schoenfeld's seat. When Tkachuk arrived at the back of the bus with the rest of us, he said loudly, "Okay, boys, I did my part. The rest of the road trip is up to you."

As captain, he had also delivered a message: having fun at night doesn't excuse you from being at your best at work the next day.

Although general managers and coaches loved Tkachuk as a general rule, it doesn't mean that he didn't find himself in trouble now and then. One time, the team was in the midst of a losing streak, and we had a game on Long Island, followed by two off-days and then a game in Manhattan against the New York Rangers. We were all looking forward to going into New York City after the game against the Islanders. One of the social highlights of the season was the opportunity to party in New York City.

The problem was that we played poorly again and lost to the Islanders. Our general manager, Bobby Smith, was boiling with anger, and he burst into the dressing room and scalded us with criticism. Schoenfeld quickly piled on, blaming us for defensive lapses, lack of effort and probably unrest in the Middle East.

Then Schoenfeld handed down the player equivalent of the death penalty.

"Curfew tonight," Schoenfeld announced loudly. "I want you in the hotel, in your room, by 11:30."

That got our attention. Now everyone in the dressing room was seething with anger, particularly our captain.

Smith then announced that there would be a meeting at 10 o'clock the next morning in his room. He wrote his room number, 241, on the chalkboard and told everyone there would be consequences if anyone was late. That made us madder, because we knew we were going to be screamed at again in the morning.

We looked to Tkachuk to make the call about what we were going to do, and he said we would all go out to eat and then gather in trainer Stan Wilson's room to drink. When we got back to the hotel, it was one o'clock in the morning, and Tkachuk said he would pick up some beer and meet us in Stan's room. As only Tkachuk can do, he cut a deal with someone at the hotel, and he now possessed two cases of beer he was bringing up to Stan's room. The problem was that Tkachuk's memory was fuzzy about Wilson's room number. The number that popped up in his head was 241. He was convinced it had to be the right number. Why else would that number be in his head? He rapped on the door, heard a commotion inside, and when the door swung open, Tkachuk found himself staring at his bleary-eyed general manager, standing there in his bathrobe.

If you are a GM of a struggling NHL team, the last person you want to see at your door, at 1:30 in the morning, is your captain, particularly if he's holding two cases of beer.

Truthfully, your body will tell you if you are overdoing the night-life before a coach or GM ever will. Most athletes have competitive personalities, and if you feel your effort is shortchanged because you are out too late, you will correct that yourself. But sometimes athletes—maybe less today than in my era—need a jolt from management. In this season, Smith eventually decided we needed to be reminded that we were NHL players, not frat boys. He decided to call us out with a meeting in his office. It was like getting called into the principal's office.

The members of the Massachusetts Mafia were hauled in together, and Smith, in a 45-minute meeting, told us we should have been ashamed of ourselves. He said we were spending too much time at the bar and we were staying out too late.

Smith said I was acting like an overpaid, spoiled brat. As I recall, he said Janney was out of shape. He might have even called him "fat." I think he told Tkachuk he should be embarrassed to call himself a captain. He sprayed all of us with .50-calibre criticism.

In some respects, it was comical because we were almost always the best players on the ice whether we won or we lost. Even if we stayed out late, we were still scoring goals. It wasn't as if we were playing poorly, or that we were getting drunk every night.

We didn't hate Smith for yelling at us, because we all understood he was just trying to fire us up. It's a general manager's duty to inspire his players to play at their highest level. The team was sputtering at the time, and Smith was looking for someone to pick up the team. It wasn't fun being verbally flogged. But all he was really doing was asking his top players to give more. I respected Smith for trying to see if we had more to give. The four of us didn't quit drinking, and we still continued to have some fun. But we started to be more mindful of our schedule when we were out on the town. We wanted to win as much as Smith did, and if he thought cutting back on alcohol intake might help, we were willing to give it a try.

That meeting didn't change our relationship with Smith. Actually, I think general managers don't challenge their players enough in the modern game. When Smith hammered on us, the real message was that he cared greatly about his team. As a player, you want to know that your general manager is passionate about what's happening on the ice.

We had a fun group in Phoenix. Dallas Drake was a dependable, hard-working player and one of the funniest. He was one of the best trash-talkers I ever heard. Once, when we were playing the Detroit Red Wings, Darren McCarty skated by our bench and Drake yelled, "Hey Darren, get off the ice because your face is scaring the kids in the front row."

Rick Tocchet and Jim McKenzie are both Canadians, but they probably could be called honorary members of the Massachusetts Mafia. Still today, Tocchet remains a close friend. The Coyotes had plenty of guys who would have your back when the situation turned ugly on the ice, but Tocchet, McKenzie and Tkachuk would always be at the front of the line.

When I talk about Tkachuk, most people figure we played on the same line in Phoenix. But it didn't happen as much as I would have liked. In five-on-five situations, Keith played with Janney more often than he played with me. Maybe that's why the media believed we didn't get along. It bothered me when I would see that written, because it wasn't close to being the truth. Certainly, we had our spats, but it was mostly about how we were playing or what was best for the team. You argue with your wife, but that doesn't mean you don't love her. We both had to adjust our thinking to coexist because we are both similar and dissimilar at the same time. In our own ways, we liked being the centre of attention. But Tkachuk wanted to be the centre of attention on the team, and my desire was to be the centre of attention everywhere.

"Would you just stay out of the newspapers?" Big Walt would ask me. It never bothered me when he said that, because I knew he was always trying to look after the team's best interests. He was always telling me to focus more on what was happening in the dressing room, although over time I believe he figured out that I put my heart into everything I did. I never had any issue accepting that Tkachuk was the Coyotes' captain. To me, he was always the boss.

I have never played with a captain who took care of people like Tkachuk did. He looked after his teammates, trainers, equipment guys, clubhouse attendants and anyone else who made his life better. He always carried a wad of cash, and he dispensed tips more freely than any man I've met. For example, he would ask the visiting clubhouse attendant to place a cold case of beer on the back of the bus. Once the attendant accomplished that task, Tkachuk would hand him a hundred-dollar bill.

Tkachuk was always buying dinners for our trainers and support staff. He demanded that rookies tip well. Woe upon any younger player who didn't take care of Keith's guys.

"Our lives would be so much more difficult without these guys," Keith would say.

There is no question that Tkachuk was the most caring team-mate that I've ever known. When we were on the road, Tkachuk would meet people down on their luck, and he would check on their well-being when he came to town. In Alberta, Keith knew an old-time hockey guy named Red. When Tkachuk was in town, Red knew he had a job as our dressing-room attendant.

Current Toronto Maple Leafs coach Randy Carlyle introduced Big Walt to Red when Carlyle and Tkachuk played together in Winnipeg. Carlyle took care of Red back then, and Carlyle made Tkachuk promise he would take care of Red after Carlyle retired. Frankly, Red was a mess, but one time Tkachuk took him on the team charter from Edmonton to Calgary. Tkachuk would park Red in front of our dressing room door and would tell everyone he would look after our stuff. After the game, he would ask every player for twenty dollars, and then he would kick in a couple of hundred dollars and give Red the entire wad of cash.

He had another guy in Vancouver that I called "Crazy, Wacko Joe," and Big Walt followed the same plan with him. When Tkachuk was in town, he made sure they had a good meal and a high-paying job for one night. They always had money in their pockets when Tkachuk came to town.

"My parents always taught me to take care of people," Tkachuk would say. "You should show respect for everyone in your life."

No matter which city we were in, Tkachuk knew the guys who worked in the visitors' dressing room.

While Tkachuk was busy tending his flock, I tried to do my best to take care of Tkachuk when he needed it. It bothered Big Walt to use his celebrity status to his benefit. He didn't like to say, "I'm Keith Tkachuk, an NHL player, can you give me special consideration?" I had no such problem. When he needed a special hotel, airline or restaurant reservation at a trendy place, he would call me and I would make sure the red carpet was rolled out for him. The funny aspect of this story is that I would sometimes merely present myself as "Keith Tkachuk's personal assistant" to accomplish what Tkachuk needed done. I've never told Big Walt that story because it would drive him bonkers to be perceived as having a personal assistant.

Tkachuk and I had many memorable times together, like the time that he and I and Tocchet planned to go to Las Vegas over the All-Star break. Our flight was scheduled for midnight, giving us time to make it unless our scheduled game that night went into overtime. Naturally, the game did go to the extra period, threatening our travel plans. Plus, the game had too many stoppages. We were pressed for time. Big Walt was livid on the bench. Within the first minute of overtime, he scored the game-winner on an exceptional individual effort. Thanks to a police escort that I arranged, we arrived at the airport in time to make the flight.

It was Tkachuk who stuck me with the nickname of Styles because of my interest in expensive clothes, fine cars and trendy restaurants or nightspots. He gave me the name, and I embraced it. Then he had the audacity to harass me daily when I purchased Arizona vanity licence plates with the word STYLES on them.

One issue that Keith and I did disagree on was coach Jim Schoenfeld. Keith considers him one of his favourite NHL coaches, but Schoenfeld and I didn't see eye to eye. I liked Schoeny as a person, but we clashed in our coach–player relationship.

My experiences with coaches in my five years in Phoenix ranged from terrible to exceptional. My first Phoenix coach was Don Hay, and he is the only coach I ever played for that I didn't respect. He had gone from junior hockey to assistant coach in Calgary to head coach in Phoenix, and as far as I could tell, he didn't have the tools or the confidence for that leap. As I've stated, I prefer tough, straight-shooting coaches, and Hay was neither. He avoided making decisions. While he was telling us what to do, he would look to the team leaders to see how his words were playing with them.

Members of the Phoenix organization told me that Hay wanted to trade me for a couple of "hard-working Canadians." However, he never had the courage to tell me that to my face. He talked behind my back, which is always a coward's route. Considering how much my mouth has gotten me in trouble, I think people around the hockey world know that I will tell you to your face how I really feel.

My third coach in Phoenix was Bob Francis, and I loved playing for him. He was a fiery guy whose style reminds me of the New York Rangers' John Tortorella. He was an energetic person, and his energy trickled down to the team.

During my NHL career, several coaches probably wanted to take a swing at me, but Schoenfeld was the only one who came close.

Schoenfeld was my second coach in Phoenix, and he is a big, likeable man whose greatest claim to fame as an NHL coach is hurling the now-famous insult "Have another doughnut" at referee Don Koharski during the 1988 Wales Conference final. Schoenfeld, who was then coaching New Jersey, confronted Koharski after the Devils had lost 6–1 to the Boston Bruins. Schoeny, as he was known to everyone, didn't like a penalty call Koharski made late in the third period that left the Devils a man short for four minutes. In the runway, Schoenfeld began yelling at Koharski, and he seemed to stumble. Koharski immediately accused Schoenfeld of pushing him. Koharski yelled, "You'll never coach another game in this league."

"You're crazy, you fell, you fat pig, have another doughnut," Schoenfeld screamed.

The whole scene is available for viewing on YouTube.

I tell you this story to explain that Schoeny could get worked up. He was a passionate coach, full of energy. We didn't always see the game the same way. I couldn't say whether he did or didn't like me, but I would probably guess I wasn't one of his favourites. He liked to dig at me, and he seemed to find fault with me too often for my taste. But I didn't see it going the way it did.

That season, I was playing with Dallas Drake and Greg Adams. We played pretty well as a line, particularly defensively. One night, we were matched up against Eric Lindros's line in Philadelphia and we shut them down. Then we had a string of seven or eight strong defensive games. And the big thing was, the team was winning. Then a story appeared in the newspaper suggesting I might win the Selke Trophy for best defensive forward. And then other writers saw that story and wrote their own versions.

A local newspaper also did a story on my candidacy, and Schoenfeld was even quoted as confirming that I would probably be a candidate if I continued to play well.

The guys started needling me in the dressing room by calling me "Frank Selke." It was good fun to a point, as long as everyone realized that I viewed myself as more of a goal scorer than a defensive zealot. My attitude was that I didn't want, or need, to be a Selke

Trophy candidate. No hockey player sits around saying, "I want to win the Selke or Lady Byng Trophy." You want to score the goals that win the hockey games.

Then my luck changed and I had a couple of bad games. In one of the losses, I made a brain-dead play and allowed my guy to score. The next day, we were watching the game film in the dressing room, and my poor decision-making was on display for all to see. Schoeny rewound the play and showed it again. I was shaking my head in an affirmative manner—*Yep. I get it. I screwed that up, and I can't let that happen again.* Every athlete goes through the indignity of being called out for a poor play.

But my acknowledgement of guilt wasn't enough for Schoeny. He rewound it again and replayed the moment. And then again. Now it was becoming embarrassing for me and every player in the room. Watching myself make the same mistake over and over, my patience reached its limit. Schoeny played it one last time and said, "And J.R., if I hear any more of this Selke Trophy bullshit, I'm going to sit you on the bench. Do you understand me?"

That sent me over the edge. "Schoeny, you can go shove a fist up your ass," I screamed. "You are the one who started the Selke bullshit."

"Excuse me?" he says.

"You heard me. Go shove a fist up your ass," I said

Schoeny got up and told everyone to leave the room.

"What's with you?" he asked.

I looked at him and said: "I'm not one of your young kids that you can embarrass in front of my team. If you're going to embarrass me, then I'm going to embarrass you."

As everyone filed out of the room, he was kicking off his flip-flops, removing his jacket and rolling up his sleeves as if we were going to brawl right in the Coyotes' dressing room.

I sat there, trying to act cool. But inside, I was nervous because Schoeny is strong as an ox. He would destroy me in a fight. My mind was racing at full speed, trying to come up with a scenario that didn't finish with me lying bloodied on the floor.

And I swear that the only tactic that occurred to me was to bite him in the balls. I swear it's true. That was my battle plan. And I intended to keep biting him. I always laugh at that memory. But I was quite serious when I developed that plan.

Later, the players told me they were all listening on the other side of the door because they believed they would have to come in and break up the fight before Schoeny killed me. Tkachuk told me later that he asked Phoenix assistant coach John Tortorella to stand by the door in case my life needed saving. "I would like Jim Schoenfeld's chances in that fight," he said.

About the time we were reaching the point of no return, I embraced the idea of trying to talk my way out of trouble. It wasn't the first time I had embraced that strategy.

"If you don't want me on your team, just say the word, and I will go tell Bobby Smith or [owner] Richard Burke that I don't want to play for you anymore," I said. "They can decide whether it's you or me who goes."

I could sense Schoenfeld starting to realize that kicking my rear end wasn't going to be in his best interest. Whether I deserved the beating or not, it wasn't going to look good for him in the newspapers. I wanted to drive home that point.

"We don't have to have a peaceful coexistence," I said. "I can ask for a trade today."

Whether Schoeny didn't like the scenarios I laid out or whether he simply decided it wasn't worth the aggravation, he started to stand down.

"Let's sit down and work this out," he said.

The tension began to evaporate. I couldn't tell you what was said because I was too busy pulling myself together after being on the verge of annihilation. We talked about our issues, and he said what he needed to say and I said what I needed to say.

The meltdown we had didn't make our relationship any better or worse. I wasn't his favourite player and he wasn't my favourite coach.

One reason why I was so bothered by Schoenfeld's attack on me is that I always cared greatly about my team. I always gave what I had to my team. For him to think that I was focused on the Selke Trophy was insulting to me. I cared about my team to the point that I once pummelled one of my Phoenix teammates, Oleg Tverdovsky, in practice because I didn't believe he cared enough.

Tverdovsky and I played three seasons together, and he ranks among my least favourite teammates of all time. Few players have had more talent and done less with it than Tverdovsky. He was a highly skilled defenceman from the Ukraine who rarely wanted to work on his game. He seemed to believe that he could get by in the NHL on his talent alone. He never put forth a consistent effort in practice, and it always infuriated me. He never listened to the coaches, never cared about what we were doing. No matter what drill we were doing, he would foul it up.

One day in practice, he screwed up another drill and I skated over and dropped my gloves. Tverdovsky had never had a fight in his NHL career when I beat him up. Just to further make my point, I thumped him again later on when it seemed like he still wasn't putting forth the effort that I thought he should.

# CHAPTER 7

# Guts

The Phoenix Coyotes probably hold the unofficial National Hockey League record for the highest-stakes poker game ever played on a team charter. One night, our card game in the back of the plane ended up with $110,000 in the pot for a single hand.

That's a league mark you won't see listed in any NHL publication.

Some of my favourite off-ice moments with the Coyotes involved playing poker with my teammates at 35,000 feet. As soon as the landing gear on the plane went up, the dealing began. Rick Tocchet, Keith Tkachuk, Craig Janney, Jim McKenzie and Bob Corkum were regulars in the game, but occasionally others would play. Most of the guys were afraid of our game because the stakes were high. My practice was to have five to ten thousand dollars in cash, or close to it, when I boarded our charter. I know Tkachuk would have that much or more. But the cash wasn't a requirement because we always accepted IOUs when pots began to escalate. The $110,000 was a one-time event, but we had other pots in the range of $80,000, and we routinely had games with pots in the range of twenty to thirty thousand.

The danger of teammates playing against each other in a big-money poker game is the hard feelings or ill will that can result from a bad beating. The NHL celebrates, and depends upon, team chemistry more than any other sport. If linemates, for example, were at odds over the outcome of a poker hand, it could have a negative impact on the team. But we truly never had issues with our game, probably because every player was a veteran, and most of us had lucrative contracts. It also helped that we were good friends.

We played dealer's choice, meaning that when it was your turn to deal, you could choose any game you wanted to play. When we played games such as five-card stud or draw poker, the action and pot sizes were tame by our standards. However, whenever we played a game like acey-deucy or Guts, where there is a risk of a player having to match the pot, then the pots would begin to spiral and the adrenaline would begin to flow like beer from a tap. As a general rule, athletes have competitive personalities. We believe in our own abilities. We believe we are going to win, and we enjoy the rush that washes over us when we have success. That kind of thinking builds poker pots quickly.

Tocchet was the most skilled player in our group. He had the perfect poker face; it was impossible to know whether he had the nuts or rags in his hand. He was street smart, a guy who had played enough cards to understand when to be aggressive and when to sit back. Much like on the ice, the best poker players are those who can read the game and anticipate what is about to happen. As is often the case in neighbourhood poker, the money would move from one player to another in our game. You would be up, and then you would be down. But occasionally we would have some big winners. I remember on one trip McKenzie used his fucking winnings to purchase a new SUV with cash.

Obviously, everyone on the team knew we were playing poker in the back of the plane, but not everyone knew how much money was at risk. I don't believe the coaches knew what the stakes were. Our game was "protected" by the fact that our captain, Big Walt, was a primary participant.

Playing poker was a routine pastime for players when I first came to the NHL in 1988. When I arrived at my first NHL training camp in Chicago, I played in my first big-league poker game before I played in my first NHL game. In August, I was bumming ten dollars off my parents to go to the movies, and in September I was betting four hundred on two pair in a poker game.

When Denis Savard, Doug Wilson, Steve Thomas and Keith Brown and the boys invited me to play in their poker game, I felt honoured. I really did. I was proud to be invited. I thought they were mentoring me, making me feel as if I belonged. However, it didn't take me long to figure out that the boys might have been more interested in acquiring my money than my friendship. I was a naive teenager with plenty of money in my pocket. I'm a believer in the old poker adage that if you can't identity the patsy at the table, then it's probably you. The attitude of the veteran Blackhawks when I showed up in their game was, "Welcome to the team, kid. Now put your money in."

When I started playing cards with the Blackhawks, you might lose a few hundred dollars, maybe a thousand or fifteen hundred if you had an unlucky night. If a pot was more than a thousand bucks, it would have been huge in those days. Chicago players educated me about poker in those early days. I have vivid memories of losing $500 one day and a thousand the next, and a veteran pulling me aside and telling me, "Don't worry. Tomorrow will be another day, and it could be *your* day." Then tomorrow would come and I would lose another $500. That seemed like a big loss to me, considering that two months before I would feel rich if I had $40 in my pocket. But even though the boys might have taken advantage of me in those early days, I would not have traded that experience. Whether their motives were pure or not, the older Chicago players did mentor me by inviting me to those games. I learned to be my own man in those games. When you are a teenager, it's just cool to be hanging out with people you look up to and admire. I loved hanging out with those guys. They got to know me as a person, and they all began to look after me on the ice. I think I entertained them, or at the very least, they were amused by me. I didn't win at cards very often in Chicago, and when I did win, I didn't keep quiet about it.

The bigger poker pots in my Phoenix days simply reflected how much more money players were earning after Bob Goodenow took over as the executive director of the NHL Players' Association in 1992. We played for larger pots because we could. In 1990–91, Wayne Gretzky was the league's highest paid player at $3 million per season, Mario Lemieux was making just over $2 million, and there were only a few players making a million. By 1995–96, Gretzky was making six and a half million, and a year after that, Lemieux was being paid more than $10 million to play for one season. In the days I was playing poker on the Coyotes' charter, I was making $4 million per year. Tkachuk was playing on a five-year deal worth more than $17 million. The season before I joined him in Phoenix, he made $6 million. When I left Phoenix, Tkachuk was earning $8.3 million, while Craig Janney was making $1.6 million per season. Tocchet was making more than $2 million per season. Corkum and McKenzie were probably the two in the game with the greatest risk, because their salaries were in the range of $500,000.

Although we were in the back of the plane playing poker for what most fans would consider big money, the truth is that on a percentage basis, I was probably taking a bigger financial risk back in Chicago when I was in a $500 pot while earning $100,000 than I was participating in a $20,000 pot when I was earning $4 million.

Still, I'm sure every Coyotes player at our table realized our poker game was out of control when there was more than $100,000 in the pot. What made the situation scarier was the fact that we were playing Guts, a poker game that has a provision that losers of each hand must match the pot.

Here is how Guts is usually played: each player is dealt three cards, and then the player must decide whether to stay in the hand or fold. Since there is an advantage in knowing how many players are in, every player must reveal their intention to play or fold at the same time. You do that by placing a coin, or not placing a coin, in your hand under the table. When your hand returns from under the table, your fist is closed. The dealer says "play or drop" and the players open their clinched fists. Those holding a coin have chosen to play and risk matching the pot. The players with no coin in their hands have dropped out of that hand. They cannot win, nor are they at risk to match the pot. At that point, players still in the game reveal their hands. The player with the winning hand claims the pot, and the losers must match the pot.

But this night, we were playing a variation of Guts that I call Squares. You still receive three cards, but then cards are placed in front of you, *Hollywood Squares* style, that you use to complete a traditional five-card poker hand.

Honestly, I don't recall the sequence of events that led to $110,000 being in the pot. But I remember that most of the money in the pot previously belonged to Tkachuk and me.

In some games of Guts, there is a "maximum burn," meaning no matter how much money is in the pot, a loser won't pay more than a predetermined limit. At that point, we didn't have a "maximum burn" in our game. Because of that, I expected most of the players to "drop" rather than risk putting $110,000 in the pot. Even if you are earning millions, it's hard not to blink in the face of a risk of losing more than a hundred grand. Nervous laughter filled the back of the plane as the pile of cash and IOUs sat on the table. With that amount of money in play, the game suddenly seemed far crazier than it had seemed 15 minutes before.

Given my personality, you know I had to go in. When the call was made to declare our intentions, there was only one other player holding a coin. It was Big Walt. That created a buzz in the back of the plane, because everyone realized instantly that one of us was going to have to put $110,000 in the pot. Remember, loser has to match the pot. Big Walt and I looked at each other with forced grins that said neither of us was happy to be in this position. Neither one of us wanted to show our hand. I'm not sure either of us was breathing at that point. The insanity of this confrontation was clear to both of us. Our "friendly" poker game had become dangerous; it was a threat to team harmony, to friendships and probably to marriages.

"Do you want to just split the pot?" Tkachuk offered.

"Yes," I said.

I think both of us exhaled at that point. Guys were complaining as Big Walt divided up the money. They protested that the game should be continuing with another $110,000 in the pot. But the grousing didn't last long because in their hearts they knew Big Walt had made the proper decision for a variety of reasons. First, Tkachuk and I had fuelled that pot by losing previous hands. It wasn't as if we were going home with $55,000 profit. Second, Tkachuk and I were the only likely participants for pots this size. It wasn't in the team's best interest for their two prominent players to be facing off for that much money. Third, everyone understood that we had no business playing for that much money in this setting. It was daring to play for $25,000; it was irresponsible to be playing for $110,000.

Finally, the unrest died quickly because Big Walt was a highly respected leader. Once he decided that splitting the pot was the right course of action, no one was going to argue with him. Everyone always looked to Big Walt to make the right decision.

After that hand, we decided to dial back the stakes of the games. We instituted a maximum burn limit. My observation is that that $110,000 pot shocked us all back to reality. We decided to move to safer ground. The poker game continued, but we were all more keenly aware of the line that shouldn't be crossed. We never again ended up with that much money in a pot.

What you probably really want to know is who would have won that hand. Yes, after we agreed to split the pot, Big Walt and I did compare hands. Big Walt would have won with four of a kind. I had a full house. I would have been on the hook for $110,000.

In the spirit of full fucking disclosure, let me say that the poker game in the back of the Phoenix Coyotes' charter wasn't my only experience with high-stakes gambling. I won $120,000 playing blackjack one night in Las Vegas. Another time, I started with

$85,000 in chips and was down to my final $500 chip before I began to rally. Before I left the table, I had turned the $500 chip into $100,000. What looked like an $85,000 loss ended up being a $15,000 profit.

I enjoy most forms of gambling. I like playing cards, and I've cashed at some. I played in three World Series of Poker satellite tournaments; cashed in one and came within 10 people of cashing in another. I like going to casinos. I've had some good nights and some bad nights. I think some athletes get drawn to betting because they like living in an arena where there are wins and losses. Gambling is a competitive venture where there is both success and failure. Athletes are comfortable in that arena.

Based on what I'm hearing, there is far less poker being played among NHL players today than there was when I was playing. Today's NHL players are all into video gaming. That seems to satisfy their competitive cravings when they are away from the rink.

My presumption is that guys still like to bet a few bucks when they golf. When I was a player, I didn't play too many rounds of golf without some money changing hands. When I played for the Coyotes, I always played for money against Tkachuk and Janney. It wasn't for big money. If you had a bad day, you might lose a thousand dollars. Since I regularly flirt with par, I was usually giving five or six strikes.

When Tkachuk heard that I was working on a book, he jokingly said to make sure that I include a sentence that I'm not to be trusted on the golf course. He and Janney never trusted my ability to find my golf ball, no matter what level of shit I found myself in on the course. When we first started playing, they would become incredulous when I would yell "found it" when I was three feet into the thick brush on a woodsy course. After a while, they would just start mockingly yelling "found it" before I even entered the problem area.

Frankly, it angered me that the boys thought I was cheating. The truth is that I have a GPS-like sense about where my golf ball is going. I do have an uncanny ability to locate my golf ball. Of course, that doesn't mean that Big Walt's accusatory "found it" didn't piss me off to the point that I felt justified in using the "foot wedge" to give myself a better lie.

# CHAPTER 8

# Payback Was a Bitch

No one during my NHL career inflicted more pain on me than Dallas Stars defenceman Derian Hatcher. On April 2, 1995, when I was still playing for Chicago, Hatcher hit me knee on knee and caused a slight fracture and severe hyperextension. I missed 23 games. Almost exactly four years later, when I was playing with the Coyotes, Hatcher brought his elbow up on a high check and blew apart my jaw as if it had been constructed out of Lego bricks.

The story behind the latter incident starts with a hit I laid on Mike Modano of Dallas with twelve games left in the 1998–99 regular season. Given that I had a rivalry with Modano that dated back to our youth hockey days, I always took advantage of any opportunity to sting him with a heavy hit. I measured myself against him on a daily basis, and I always wanted to make it clear that I was the more physical player.

Modano was coming around the net, and I smoked him. Knocked him out. The general consensus was that it was a clean check, but the Dallas Stars believed it was a late hit. A jury would probably call it a borderline hit. But there is no disputing that I crushed him.

The problem was that we were playing Dallas three weeks later, and there had not been nearly enough time to heal Modano's wounds or any ill feelings that the Stars had for me. Just by reading the newspapers, I suspected there would be retribution. I didn't know when it would occur, or who would deliver the message, but I knew punishment was coming.

The Stars didn't waste time. In the first period, as I came around the back of the net, Stars defenceman Craig Ludwig broke my thumb with a slash. Seconds later, six-foot, six-inch, 240-pound defenceman Derian Hatcher leaped elbow-first into my face. It was the most vicious hit I ever took in my NHL career. My jaw was broken in three places. Eight of my teeth were either cracked or broken.

I knew right away that I needed surgery. It felt like pieces of my jaw were flapping around under my skin. If it weren't for the skin, it felt like I could have pulled pieces of jaw out of my mouth. There is a video on the Internet that shows me moving my jaw for the trainer in front of the Plexiglas, and it is so gruesome that a lady in the front row passes out.

At the time of the hit, we were already on the power play. Now we had a five-on-three advantage, and all I could think of was beating these guys. I started heading back onto the ice to play, and Phoenix trainer Gordon Hart said, "Where are you going? Your jaw is broken."

I said I knew it was, but it wasn't going to get worse than it already was. "Let's see what we can do on the power play," I said.

As I was skating around, I could hear my jawbones smacking against each other. We did score on the power play, but it wasn't my goal. I came close but couldn't put it in. My focus might not have been what it should have been. Near the end of my shift, I got hit again, and the pain in my jaw was indescribable. As soon as I got to the bench, I told the trainer I needed to go to the hospital. "This is bad," I said.

When you are playing at home and you are injured, your team physician shepherds you through the hospital process. You receive immediate care. In Dallas, I waited, by myself, in the emergency room. A half-hour passed, then an hour, and I still wasn't seeing a doctor. Having grown impatient, I stood in the doorway, spitting blood into a cup just to remind everyone I was still waiting for the doctor. As I stood there, believing I wasn't receiving enough attention, an ambulance came roaring in and paramedics brought in a teenager who had lost his leg in an automobile accident. The severed limb was on the gurney with him. As doctors and nurses scurried to treat him, I remember thinking, "This broken jaw isn't that bad." I returned to my seat.

Eventually, the doctor came in and recommended immediate surgery, after which I would need to spend two days in a Dallas hospital before I returned to Phoenix.

"Fuck that," I said. "I'm getting my ass out of Dallas. I don't want to be anywhere near Dorian Hatcher. I don't want to be near the Dallas Stars."

The doctor seemed surprised that I didn't want to have it taken care of immediately. But 10 minutes later, I was in a cab, X-rays in hand, heading back to the arena to rejoin my team. While I was taking a shower, the Coyotes trainers were making arrangements for me to have immediate surgery performed by noted Phoenix oral surgeon Reed Day. Since I was scheduled for surgery as soon as I could get to the hospital, I couldn't take pain medication, nor could I have anything to eat or drink.

My memory of the charter trip back to Phoenix involves playing cards in the back of the plane. Throughout the game, I spit blood into a plastic cup. I filled up two cups. I was a mess.

When I walked off the team jet in Phoenix, I climbed into a limousine and headed directly to the hospital. I remember the doctor explaining to me around six in the morning that my mouth would be rubber-banded shut. The idea of not being able to open my mouth terrified me. I asked the doctor to take out a couple of bottom teeth so I could drink through a straw.

As hard as this may be to believe, I have never harboured a grudge toward Hatcher for fucking me up that night. Going into that game, I felt as if I had a bounty on my head. I was jacked up because I knew I was going to be targeted. I love that kind of shit. I loved entering games when there was a secondary storyline, a subplot, to raise the game's drama. I loved the challenge of being able to determine how that storyline would play out. I knew the Stars were coming after me. I didn't know who would attack me, or when it was going to happen, but I knew someone was going to try to hurt me. Obviously, I didn't expect Hatcher to redesign the bone structure of my fucking face. But in hindsight, I view what happened as just another epic chapter of my NHL journey.

I certainly would have loved to break Hatcher's fucking ankles that night. I would have loved to knock his fucking jaw into the back of his fucking throat. But I didn't hate him for what he did to me. I respected Hatcher as an extremely competitive person and a winner. I had always admired the way he played. His intensity level was two levels higher than most players. In a weird, maybe perverse, way, I respected Hatcher for doing what he did to me, for avenging Modano.

The hit did change me. It added another layer of toughness that I didn't know I had. It proved to me that I could walk through fire and play the next day.

Hatcher was suspended the final two regular-season games, plus five playoff games, for his hit. Given the extent of my injuries, the sentence seemed light. Hell, I'm sure people have received jail time for hurting someone less severely in an assault. But at that time, the five-playoff-game suspension represented the longest postseason suspension since Maurice "Rocket" Richard was suspended the final three regular-season games, plus the entire playoffs, for punching a linesman in 1955.

When the suspension was announced, I told the media: "I hate to say what's fair or unfair. My opinion is I can't play in the playoffs, so I don't see why he should get to play in the playoffs. That's why I hope they get knocked out in the first round." Even without their captain, Hatcher, for five games, the Stars weren't knocked out in the first round. They ended up winning the Stanley Cup. Hatcher sipped champagne out of Lord Stanley's bowl that summer after I was sipping my meals through a straw that spring.

My wife, Tracy, tried to make it as normal as possible for me, even blending up filet mignon and pasta. One of my favourite dining dishes is osso bucco, which is veal shanks braised with vegetables, white wine and broth. Tracy even put that in a blender in an effort to help keep me from losing too much weight. I still dropped 17 pounds. But I didn't lose my desire to be back in the lineup as soon as possible. We had a 3–1 series lead against the St. Louis Blues in the first round, and then we allowed the Blues to come back to tie the series and force game seven. Nineteen days after my surgery, I told the Coyotes I was going to play in that game seven. I was outfitted with a special helmet that looked like a cross between a goalie mask and football helmet. I looked like an imperial storm-trooper from the Star Wars movies.

Dr. Day addressed the media, saying: "Jeremy understands the risks. If he was a regular patient, six to eight weeks would have been required. Certainly, he could break his jaw again. . . . He has accepted the risk that if he breaks his jaw again, we will repair it."

I felt like I could make a difference, and I took a regular shift, including playing on the power play and killing penalties. We lost a 1–0 game in overtime on Pierre Turgeon's goal. I played more than 26 minutes in that game. It was one of the most disheartening losses of my career.

Schoenfeld was fired after that season and replaced with Bob Francis. It certainly wasn't Schoenfeld's fault that we were knocked out in the first round. I believe that if Hatcher hadn't broken my jaw, we would have won that first-round series.

My one regret about my five years in Phoenix was that we couldn't advance beyond the first round. My honest assessment of why that never happened is that we had bad luck. In 1997, we had a 3–2 lead against Anaheim in the first round, and I blew out my knee and we lost that series. In 1998, we took a 2–1 series lead against the defending Stanley Cup champions, the Detroit Red Wings, and then Keith Tkachuk and Nikolai Khabibulin got hurt. In my fourth year, we were steamrolled in five games by a Colorado team that lost to Dallas in seven games in the Western Conference final. I tried to stir up our passions in that series, calling the Denver media "morons" because they said before the series that we had no chance to win.

Raymond Bourque had been acquired to be Colorado's spiritual leader, and after game two, I mocked him by saying: "Ray Bourque is the messiah. You can't touch him."

Hey, you do what you can to get your team involved in the series. Remember what Keenan said: negative energy is still energy. And if Colorado is chasing after me for a game, maybe they forget what their mission is. That turned out not to be the case, but it was worth a try.

CHAPTER 9

# Not All Rainbows and Butterflies

While this book was being written, my daughter, Brandi, was 17. At the time, her boyfriend was 18.

"Do you know her boyfriend is the same age you were when you played your first season in the NHL?" Tracy said to me one day.

It takes the wisdom of age to appreciate how immature we truly were when we were teenagers.

When Tracy told her parents we had something to tell them when I was 18, I remember her mom's reaction was, "Oh my God, you aren't pregnant?"

No, but I was leaving Boston College to play pro hockey, and that might have seemed just as irresponsible to Tracy's parents. Given the career I had in the NHL, it was the correct decision. I loved every minute I had wearing an NHL jersey. But that doesn't mean there were no negative consequences to my decision to turn pro when I was 18.

I was a teenager with a six-figure income in 1988. I was a popular Chicago celebrity by age 20, a 40-goal scorer by 21, a 50-goal superstar at 22, and a million-dollar athlete by the time I was 23.

By the time I was traded to the Coyotes, I was 26, but I was still trying to find the proper balance between my job, my family and my fame.

If you don't believe that that level of popularity, or money, can fuck up your thinking a bit, then you either haven't been around many young adults, or you don't pay attention to celebrity news. The sports and entertainment landscape is littered with pop icons who have made unwise decisions when they were young and rich.

When I received my second Blackhawks deal, paying me more than a million dollars a season, I remember showing the contract to Tracy's father and saying, "Do I earn enough now to take care of your daughter?"

Of course, by then, her late father had revised history by saying he knew all along that I was going to be a star player.

As I was gaining money and fame, it never occurred to me that I was losing who I really was. No one wants to hear a professional athlete bitch about his, or her, life, because many people would gladly trade places with them. But the truth is most people can't comprehend the difficulty and pressure that come with being a pro athlete. In addition to the aches and pains that come from training and competition, there is the pressure of living up to expectations. You are trying to win for your city and your team, and your effort is constantly being scrutinized by the media and fans. Always, there is someone coming up that wants to knock you off your high horse. People believe the life of an athlete is all glamour, but it is far from it.

I have so much respect for players like Mike Modano, Joe Sakic, Steve Yzerman, Wayne Gretzky, Mario Lemieux and others who reached the top, handled the pressure and were able to stay on top. My issue wasn't about dealing with the pressure. My issue was letting the stardom change who I was. For a period of time when I was in my 20s, I lost my way. My priorities became fucked up.

You don't realize what's happening to you, because you just start to accept your abnormal life as being a normal existence. You miss family weddings, birthdays, holidays, etc., because you have a game, practice or road trip. I believe I missed my first seven Thanksgivings after I joined the Blackhawks because of the team's schedule. It's always about putting the team first. Imagine how a normal bride-to-be would feel if the groom came home and said, "We have to change the wedding day because I'm going to have to work later into the summer." That's what happened to us when the Blackhawks made their long playoff run in 1992. But that was my fourth year in the NHL, and by then Tracy knew how this all worked.

To be the wife of an NHL player is a thankless role, because the player hears the applause and the wife inherits the problems that accompany stardom. When a player is traded, he heads off to his new city immediately, while his wife stays behind to sort through the ruins of their life. It's like a player has two families: one at home, and one in the dressing room. And sometimes, it's the family at home that ends up taking the back seat. Nothing sums up that reality better than when you see a professional athlete stopping to sign an autograph at a restaurant, while his wife is standing a few feet away, waiting for him to finish.

Once, when I was playing for the Blackhawks, I took Tracy to Chicago's renowned Pump Room restaurant for Valentine's Day. We were sitting there in the famous number one booth, maybe the best table in the city. It had a rose and candlelight. We were settling in for a romantic dinner when a Blackhawks fan stopped by our table and began to chat with me. Within minutes, he had sat down at our table. One night, we had to leave Maggiano's restaurant in Chicago because fans were lining up at my table, making it difficult for the waitstaff to navigate around the dining room.

Believe it or not, when I joined the Blackhawks, they had a rule that players couldn't live in the city, probably because they feared that we could get caught up in the nightlife.

When I played, I believed it was important for me to give back to fans, and I still believe that today. But when I look back at my years in Chicago, I realize I was naive about what was happening to me. I was probably too trusting of too many people. Tracy tried to warn me. In my dealings with people, she often ended up playing the heavy. By the time we were married, Tracy had her college degree and she had other life experiences as a dressage competitor. She kept trying to tell me that I needed to understand the difference between my true friends and those who wanted to be with me because I was an NHL star. I wasn't listening to her back then.

At that young age, I had a hard time saying "no" to anyone. I always blamed Tracy for everything. She saw my personality changing and my family life unravelling long before I realized it was true. Now that I'm older, I realize I was unfair to her in those early years. I had no life experiences when I signed my NHL contract, and then suddenly I was a star in the Chicago social scene. I didn't handle that situation particularly well.

No one understands better than me that fame can fuck up your home life. As an NHL athlete, I had a schedule that couldn't be changed. Tracy accepted that that was our life. The tension was caused by decisions I was making about how to spend my free time. At that point in my life, Tracy says, there were only four people around me who were willing to be brutally honest with me about what was happening: Tracy; her dad, Richard Vazza; my agent, Neil Abbott; and Mike Keenan. The other people in my life were telling me every day how great I was.

Keenan was hard on me, and he would piss me off. But Tracy always loved Keenan because she felt that he was hard on me because he was trying to help me become a better player. When people shit on Keenan because he was a hard-ass, Tracy always defends him: "When you peel back the layers of that onion, you find a big heart." She wishes that Keenan would have been my coach longer, because she believes he would have spotted the warning signs that my real life was spiralling away from me.

For several years, Tracy believed I was gambling too much and picking the wrong friends. I placed too much emphasis on the next big party and not enough on what was happening in my family life. When I was playing for the Coyotes, she often confronted me.

"You are 28 and living like a rock star," she told me. "What are you going to do for money when you are 60?" To her, it was clear that I was so busy trying to be "J.R. the superstar" that I forgot who Jeremy was.

Tracy's frustration finally boiled over on October 9, 1999. My Phoenix Coyotes were in Chicago to play the Blackhawks. Tracy came to Chicago. Fed up with my unwillingness to confront the problem, she confronted me at the Coyotes' dressing room, between the second and third periods of a game at the United Center. I am sure Tracy established a new league standard that night by becoming the first NHL player's wife to scream through an open dressing-room door that her husband was an asshole. The pressure had been building for a long time, and Tracy couldn't keep it bottled up any longer. She went nuclear on my ass in the dressing-room doorway as my teammates looked on.

When I tried to calm her down, it got worse, not better. Our heated argument extended beyond the start of the third period. Whatever words I used in that situation were not the right words.

"I'm out of here," she screamed, before stalking off.

I was enraged. By the time I arrived on the bench, I was an angry bull, and someone was going to pay a price for my anger. It turned out to be my best friend for many years. Although no one believes me, I would swear on the bible that I just slashed the first person who came near me, and it was Tony Amonte.

I don't know where my mind was, but it wasn't on the game, or Tony, when that event happened. The one regret I have about my career is going on the ice that night with that level of fury in my heart. But I will go to the grave swearing that I didn't know it was Tony when I slashed him in the face, opening up a gaping wound. Whether Tony and his family believe that, I am not sure. All I can say is that I was in a blind rage when I stepped on the ice.

Although I apologized for my actions, Tony and I didn't speak for a year and a half after what I did. We didn't truly reunite until we were roommates at the 2002 U.S. Olympic orientation camp. He eventually forgave me. He later said: "I consider us friends. He's like a brother. People ask me, 'How can you not hold a grudge?' I ask, 'How can I? Life is too short.'"

I still consider him one of my best friends. We get along, and we have a blast when we are together. But to be honest, we really haven't been quite the same since that day when I went crazy on the ice. I received a match penalty for that slash, and the NHL suspended me five games, and I lost over $100,000 in pay. But the biggest price I paid is knowing that a good friend believed I tried to hurt him.

Even though this was the pre-Twitter NHL, there were plenty of hurtful rumours that circulated around the hockey world about what had caused the blow-up that night. The truth about what happened that evening was that Tracy was trying to convince me to bring back the man she had married. The one who had been lost in my climb to stardom and replaced by someone she didn't recognize.

"You need to get your shit together," she said to me that night.

When the emotions gave way to honest dialogue about what was happening in our life, I knew Tracy was right. She said I had lost my gratitude. She was right. By nature, I'm sentimental. I don't want to be the guy who takes his family for granted. I had lost my focus, not only about my life, but also my career. Tracy told me that she believed I had never recovered from the hurt I felt when the Blackhawks said I wasn't worth the money I was demanding in my final negotiation with them. I started working with sports psychologist Gary Mack, and both of us went to see him to work through the issue of how to regain my focus on my career and family.

"I want to go to find out how this sweet kid I fell in love with became a devil," she said.

The psychologist helped me find my way back home. Maybe I became more Jeremy and less J.R.

Mack's counselling helped me reprioritize my life, with a greater emphasis on Tracy and my family. Although I had a gambling problem, what I really had was an ego problem. I didn't believe anyone could tell me what I was doing wrong. I didn't believe I needed to be fixed. If there was an issue, I didn't want to deal with it. I didn't want to talk about it. I felt that if you didn't acknowledge a problem, it would go away.

I liked to pull down the black shade. Tracy hated that about me. I refused to communicate. Gary forced me to deal with that issue. The funny thing about counselling is that you have to do most of the talking. Gary wouldn't say much; he just had a way of getting me to say things I didn't want to say. He got me to work through my problems. He forced me to be accountable in all areas of my life, including my career. He stressed daily preparation of your day in terms of what you want your life to be like and what kind of person you want to be. He made you decide how you want others to perceive you. He wanted you to get out of yourself and look back to see who you really were. He wanted you to have pride in yourself. Mack didn't "fix" me, but he helped me know that I wanted to be a better person. That's really what Tracy wanted. She wanted me not to hide from my problems. She wanted me to be able to discuss problems when I have them. And today I'm able to do that.

My friend Matt Mallgrave came out to talk to me as well. We were friends before I came into fame and money, and our talk helped guide me back on the right path.

It's not as if I completely quit gambling or stopped going to parties. When we stay with friends at a hotel in Las Vegas, Tracy jokes that "Jeremy helped pay for this floor." But the confrontation at the United Center in 1999 caused me to consider for the first time that I had a gambling problem. Plus, it made me think about who my friends were.

More importantly, it made me fully cognizant of the importance of Tracy to my career. She says now that people who knew her back in Chicago probably think she is a "cold, hateful person" because she always had to play the bad cop while I played the good cop in our dealings with the people in our lives. Tracy had to be the responsible one in our marriage, while I was busy playing the role of NHL star. It's fair to wonder if I would have the money I do today if Tracy had not been with me on this journey. She was a strong person the first day I met her, and she remains strong to this day.

When Brandi was born, I do remember partying like a rock star, dancing on the top of a big speaker at a nightclub. That was one of the happiest days of my life.

When Tracy and I were first married, we talked about having five children. But her pregnancy with Brandi was problem-filled. She was bedridden at times, and she had to be fed intravenously. We had to get her a nurse. I remember staying at a hotel during the playoffs, because Tracy didn't want me distracted during the playoffs.

Honestly, I was scared for her to have another baby. Proving again how tough she is, Tracy decided to have a second child. By then, Zofran was available to pregnant women for nausea, which was helpful.

We were on Cape Cod in Massachusetts when Tracy went into labour with Brett. She got up one morning and announced calmly that her water had broken.

"What do you mean, your water broke?" I said, jumping out of my chair as if someone had just yelled "fire."

Tracy was starting to make breakfast.

"What the fuck are you doing?" I said. "We have to go to the hospital."

"Relax," she said.

"Relax? What the fuck are you talking about?" I said. "Your fucking water just broke."

"We are fine," she said.

She finished making breakfast. We ate it. Then we left for the hospital.

Tracy knew what she was talking about, because her labour lasted long enough for me to make seven trips to Blockbuster Video to rent movies. The baby was in breech position and he wouldn't turn. I remember telling the doctor after 24 hours that Tracy had gone through enough pain and I thought we needed a Caesarean. Fortunately, the doctor agreed.

As the anaesthesiologist was preparing the epidural, Tracy put her head on my chest. When I saw the five-inch needle that was inserted into her back, my knees buckled and I saw stars. I was going down to the ground. It was Tracy who held me up. People say I was a warrior in my NHL career, but Tracy is the true warrior.

After Brett was born, we then had both a boy and a girl, and both were healthy. We were thankful enough for what we had; we decided not to risk any more pregnancies.

# CHAPTER 10

# Exit Strategy

During my fifth season in Phoenix, it became clear that I was going to be wearing another team's sweater in the 2001–02 season. Effective July 1, 2001, I was going to become an unrestricted free agent for the first time in my career. The Coyotes couldn't afford me. They had been having money issues, and general manager Bobby Smith had made it clear they wouldn't be able to re-sign me, especially since I was definitely going to get offers much higher than the $4 million I was being paid.

Even after Steve Ellman and Wayne Gretzky completed negotiations to buy the Coyotes in February 2001, nothing changed from the perspective of keeping me. Gretzky became the team's managing partner, and he fired Smith. Cliff Fletcher was brought in as general manager, and it was immediately clear that his mandate was to shed payroll in the name of getting younger.

On March 5, the Coyotes traded goaltender Nikolai Khabibulin to the Tampa Bay Lightning for defenceman Paul Mara, forwards Mike Johnson and Ruslan Zainullin and a second-round draft choice.

Nine days later, Keith and his $8.3 million contract were traded to the St. Louis Blues for Martin Handzus, Ladislav Nagy, Jeff Taffe and a first-round pick. At the time, Tkachuk had been the franchise's captain for seven years.

The Coyotes finished the 2000–01 schedule tied with the Vancouver Canucks for eighth place in the Western Conference. Each team had 90 points, but Vancouver got the final playoff berth by racking up 36 wins to our 35. Undoubtedly, Tkachuk and Khabibulin would have made a difference in that final month. It was the only season of my five in Phoenix that we didn't make the playoffs.

With all of the controversy surrounding the team's future, it has been forgotten that we drew reasonably well when the team played in the America West Arena in downtown Phoenix. We averaged over 15,000 fans per game in an arena, built primarily for basketball, that had 4,500 obstructed-view seats when it was set up for hockey.

Unquestionably, the location of the new arena—near the NFL's Arizona Cardinals' stadium in Glendale, northwest of Phoenix proper—has hurt the team. If the arena had been built in Scottsdale—to the east of Phoenix, where most of the Coyotes' fan base lives and where the Ellman group originally hoped to build— there is no question attendance would be better.

When I came to Phoenix, I had made it my mission to help our sport grow in the desert. After the gates had opened in the America West Arena, I would put on my sweater and step out into the runway between the dressing room and the ice to do my stretching. From there, I could converse with the fans. I tried to connect with people. If you ask Arizona fans from those days, they will tell you that Roenick always signed autographs.

On the ice, I never had fewer than 24 goals or 102 penalty minutes in any of my five seasons, and our record was .500 or better in all five seasons I was there.

I have fond memories of my days with the Coyotes. I still call Arizona home today. I've been there longer than I've lived anywhere else. My two children were raised there. When the Coyotes announced in 2011–12 that they were going to add me to the team's Ring of Honor, I felt humbled and gratified. I think people in Arizona understood that I was as proud to wear the Coyotes sweater as I was to wear the Blackhawks logo. Keith Tkachuk also joined the ring that same season, making the honour even greater. I would always want to be a member of any club Tkachuk is in.

My hope is that the Blackhawks will someday follow the Coyotes' lead by retiring my number, 27. I played only six seasons in Phoenix, and I played eight in Chicago. I'm still one of only three 50-goal scorers in Chicago history. My relationship with the Blackhawks is good enough that I still hope it is possible. It's hard to explain why I want so badly to see my jersey hanging from the rafters in Chicago. But to put it simply, that city means so much to me.

# CHAPTER 11

# Hitch in My Giddy-Up

On July 2, 2001, the Philadelphia Flyers signed me for $37.5 million over five years to add energy and goals to their lineup. The deal was completed on just the second day of the NHL's free-agent season because the Phoenix Coyotes, knowing they couldn't re-sign me, had allowed teams to talk to me before the July 1 deadline.

After reviewing my options, my choice came down to two teams: Detroit and Philadelphia. If you ask my wife, Tracy, she thought for sure we were moving to Detroit. Even though my decision to join the Flyers was well thought out, that's how close I came to signing with the Red Wings.

When the Flyers were wooing me, Rick Tocchet and Mark Recchi took me to an NBA Finals game between the Los Angeles Lakers and Philadelphia 76ers. Similarly, the Red Wings brought me into Detroit, and general manager Ken Holland wined and dined us. He drove Tracy and me around the area. His sales pitch was an aggressive one: he told us that if I came to Detroit, I was giving myself the best opportunity I'd had to win the Stanley Cup since Chicago reached the championship series in 1992.

At the time, Detroit was only four years removed from winning back-to-back titles, and they still had a talented roster. They played an offensive style that was very appealing. They were also offering a five-year contract with similar money to what the Flyers were offering.

The only negative about Detroit was that the area didn't have enough places where Tracy and my daughter, Brandi, could stable their horses and train.

While we were still in Detroit being wooed by Holland, the Flyers called and said that they had to have an answer from me that night, because if I wasn't signing with them they wanted to make an offer to another player before he ended up somewhere else. They sweetened their offer by agreeing to front-load a bit of the money. When you receive a front-loaded contract, it's like getting an advance on your salary. For example, a team might agree to pay you $40 million over five seasons, with an $8 million salary every season. But in a front-loaded deal, the player might earn $12 million in each of the first two seasons and only $4 million in the last two. As a rule, players prefer front-loaded deals because they like their money now. By getting another $4 million up front, a player can earn interest on that money for an additional two or three years. Even in a salary cap league, big-market teams that can afford to front-load deals have an advantage when bidding for free agents.

However, the money wasn't the deciding factor. Rick Tocchet, then playing for Philadelphia, convinced me to sign with the Flyers. He lobbied aggressively on the phone, convincing me that the Flyers had an excellent chance to win the Stanley Cup if I came aboard. He believed I could be the missing piece.

"If you sign, we would have the most talent I've seen in a dressing room since I was in Pittsburgh," Tocchet said, referring to the Penguins team that had defeated my Blackhawks in the 1992 Stanley Cup final. Trusting Tocchet, I called my agent and told him to take the Flyers' offer.

Meanwhile, my hometown Boston Bruins offered more money than both the Flyers and Red Wings. But I didn't believe the Bruins were close to being ready to compete for a Stanley Cup. Plus, I didn't believe it would have been good for my career to play in my hometown, where I would be on the friends and family plan. Throughout my career, I've created distractions without trying very hard; I didn't need distractions built in.

What the Flyers may not have understood is that when you buy the Roenick deluxe package, it also comes with a disco ball at no extra cost. On game days, at about 5:40 in the afternoon, I was the warmup act for our team meetings. I would haul my disco ball into the dressing room, turn down the lights, turn on music from the 1970s or early 1980s and dance the night away. The Gap Band's 1983 hit "Party Train" was usually the featured song. Fourth-liner Todd Fedoruk often accompanied me with his hockey-stick guitar. Don't know why I started this 15-minute pre-game ritual, because I had never done it at my previous NHL stops. But once I started, I couldn't stop.

Coach Ken Hitchcock could never make peace with it.

"Can't you just be serious for once?" he would say.

"I *am* being serious," I would reply. "This is what I do to keep everyone loose and ready to go."

It was made clear to me that Hitchcock would prefer that I be more like Flyers legend Bobby Clarke and less like Hollywood legend John Travolta. Maybe he would have been happier with me if

I'd sat at my stall and scowled at my teammates. The old-school Hitchcock just never could relate to my flamboyant tendencies.

"J.R., you are never on the same page with us," Hitchcock would whine.

"But the page I'm on is more fun," I would say. "Why don't you come on *my* page for a while?"

Hitchcock and I had some special moments, such as the time, during a game, when he was trying to yell instructions to me as I was carrying the puck into the offensive zone. After I dumped the puck, I hit the brakes, turned to the bench, and screamed: "Will you shut the fuck up, Hitch? I'm trying to play a game out here."

Everyone on the bench doubled over in laughter.

Although Hitchcock and I would battle over issues, I always felt like there was mutual respect between us. Hitchcock primarily liked the way I played, although he was always trying to convince me that I needed to be more defensive-minded. Probably, he was right. I've always said that Hitchcock was the smartest coach I ever had.

On the days when he would irritate the shit out of me, I would think, "What does he know? He never played in the NHL." Other times, I would be honest with myself and realize that his coaching tactics and defensive structure gave us a chance to win the Stanley Cup. When I'm objective about Hitchcock, I see that the issue we really had was that he wanted his dressing room to have a 1950s mentality, while I wanted to let some fresh air into a sport that can sometimes be too stuffy. Hitchcock always wanted to be in control. He wanted things done the way he wanted them done. I never wanted to be controlled, and I like to do things differently.

Once I arrived in Philadelphia, it seemed as if I was born to play there. As soon as I ran over someone for the first time, the crowd adopted me as one of their own. After I retired, my Twitter account blew up when I was quoted as saying Philadelphia fans were "crazy sons of bitches." Philadelphia folks were upset because they felt I was turning my back on the fans who had supported me. Never. In terms of what Philadelphia fans mean to the Flyers' success at home, I view "crazy sons of bitches" as a term of endearment. The minute you run someone over while wearing a Flyers sweater, the fans in Philadelphia are with you for life. The players from the Broad Street Bullies era are viewed as gods in Philadelphia. Anyone who knows me well knows I liked the music loud and the fans amped up when I played. When the crowd is revved up, the Flyers feed off the energy. I saw it happen often.

The Flyers were signing me to be a replacement for Eric Lindros, who hadn't played for an entire season because of a falling-out with general manager Bob Clarke. My relationship with Hitchcock was a lovefest compared to what occurred between Clarke and Lindros before I got there. Lindros had refused to play for the Flyers and sat out the season.

At the press conference to introduce me to Philly media, I tried to signal a new era in my own way: I made owner Ed Snider hug it out with me on stage at the practice facility in Voorhees, New Jersey.

"Come here and give me a hug," I said to Snider before wrapping him in my arms. He had no idea what I was trying to do, which made it even more amusing.

"You'd hug him too if he gave you that kind of money," I told the assembled reporters.

The way I saw it, the Flyers were a team in need of feel-good moments, and it was my mission to provide the franchise with the most upbeat press conference in team history. I would have held hands with Clarke and sung "Kumbaya" if I thought it would have helped.

When reporters asked me what Tocchet had said to convince me to sign with Philadelphia, I told them, "He said, 'Come here, or I'll kick your ass.'"

I told the media that it used to scare me to play in Philadelphia because the Flyers always had a big team that was willing to hit. I said I wanted to be part of their assault team.

"I just want to take someone's head off and score goals," I said.

I said I believed my best chance to win a Stanley Cup would be in a Flyers jersey, and I meant every word of that. The Flyers had an impressive roster that included Tocchet, Mark Recchi, Keith Primeau, Éric Desjardins and Simon Gagné. We had seven former All-Stars, three former 50-goal scorers. At the press conference, I kept telling everyone how good I thought I looked in the Flyers' sweater.

My first captain in Philadelphia was Desjardins, and he was a solid, dependable, hard-working man. When we were opponents, we didn't like playing against each other. Since I had knocked out some of his teeth on a hit earlier in my career, we probably had an awkward beginning as teammates. I respected Desjardins, but he was never a guy I would go out with on a Saturday night. He was too blah for me. I preferred captains who could take over a room verbally or physically. I prefer a captain who could snap, like Keith Tkachuk would in Phoenix or Chris Chelios did in Chicago. Desjardins wasn't that guy. Given his personality, I knew I wouldn't be stepping on his authority by doing what I do.

Although my time in Philadelphia is usually associated with playing for Hitchcock, Billy Barber was actually my first coach in Philadelphia. At our first meeting, I knew I would like him. He was old school, and he was a good man. I didn't always agree with his tactics, but I always liked him. He was tolerant of my personality, as long as I was doing the job on the ice. Probably, his days playing for the wild-ass Broad Street Bullies had taught him you can have a good time and still win a championship. Based on what I hear, the Broad Street Bullies weren't choirboys.

Although other leagues have started to loosen up, the NHL remains conservative in terms of how it expects athletes to conduct their business. We still want our athletes to be careful on how we celebrate goals, and we still don't appreciate athletes whose personality doesn't fit into the sport's definition of what is considered normal. Throughout my career, my antics always played to mixed reviews. Some of my teammates considered me a sideshow, while others understood that I believed we would play better if we had an entertaining, fun-filled work environment. Between the whistles, I always played with the intensity of a gladiator. But before the game, or after, I didn't need to walk around with a scowl on my face to prove that I cared about winning.

The truth is that only one team wins the Stanley Cup, and the other 29 are left to come up with an answer for why they didn't win. No one wants to say we weren't deep enough, or we had bad luck, or our goaltending sucked, so the conclusion that is usually reached is that the team wasn't on the same page, or they weren't fully committed to winning.

That's all bullshit. When my teams were winning, I was always considered entertaining, fun-loving and good for the game. When we were losing, I was considered a distraction or self-absorbed. When we were winning, I was selling the game by doing 10 or 12 radio interviews per week. When we were losing, I was self-promoting when I did those same interviews.

The truth is that I cared as much about winning as everyone else. I just didn't believe that having a winning attitude meant you couldn't have some non-hockey-related fun two hours before game time. If Wayne Gretzky had boogied to the Bee Gees' "Stayin' Alive" two hours before every game in 1983–84, I'm reasonably fucking confident he still would have registered 205 points and helped the Edmonton Oilers win their first Stanley Cup. Maybe if he had purchased himself a disco ball, he might have put up 230 points that season.

But when I arrived in Philadelphia, the Flyers seemed like a team in need of levity. The Clarke–Lindros feud had stained the organization, and I saw it as my mission to be the stain remover on and off the ice. Lindros's rights were traded the summer I arrived. My arrival seemed to signal a new beginning for the organization.

"Exactly the breath of fresh air we needed," goalie Brian Boucher told *Sports Illustrated* during my first season in Philadelphia. "For years it seemed like everybody on this team was the same type of quiet, serious guy. Almost like we were robots, clones. Now J.R. comes in, the room's loose, happy. We're feeding off it."

This was a quality group of teammates. John LeClair certainly makes my list of all-time favourite teammates, and Boucher is certainly among the funniest players I've known. He does a vocal impression of Dominik Hasek that is spot-on and priceless.

The Flyers started the 2001–02 NHL season with great promise, but it didn't go the way any of us expected. From mid-December until the 2002 Olympic break, we went on an 18–5–2–1 run to claim first place in the Eastern Conference, but then we won only nine of our last 26 games and were ousted by the Ottawa Senators in the first round of the playoffs. We only scored two goals in those five games.

During the season, Barber's wife, Jenny, passed away after battling lung cancer. He kept working through the illness, never missing a game. None of that mattered when the season was over and we were cast as an underachieving team. Our late-season collapse cost Barber his job.

Barber had played for legendary Flyers coach Fred Shero, who apparently didn't believe in regularly practising five-on-four play. Billy took that approach with us, and our power play struggled all season.

"We had the worst power play in the league—why are we not practising it?" our captain Keith Primeau said about Barber. "All season long, we said if someone makes a mistake, they're getting yelled at. We say when we come to the bench, make that adjustment. He wants the player to make the adjustment. Our job is to play."

Personally, I felt bad that Billy was fired because we didn't play well. I was disappointed, even though most of the players were happy he was gone. Barber was the kind of coach I was used to dealing with. His style didn't bother me.

Hitchcock was hired on May 15, 2002. He was the only person the Flyers interviewed for the job, because they were worried he would end up with the New York Rangers. My two seasons with Hitchcock were what you would expect if you were to place a rigid conformist in charge of a rebel with a cause—the cause being to have a good time while trying to win a Stanley Cup.

My time with Hitchcock wasn't nearly as contentious as the media made it out to be, but we had our challenging moments. In October of 2003, we met for over an hour to hammer out the difference of opinion we had about how I should be playing. The headline in the next day's *Philadelphia Inquirer* was "Roenick and Hitchcock giving peace a chance."

Afterward, I told the media that Hitchcock and I "were at each other's throats," but I actually came away feeling like it was a positive meeting. Hitchcock always seemed to like the energy I brought to the ice, but he just wanted more out of me in terms of being a leader and setting an example by being the best at playing his system. He was always preaching that I could become a "great player" if I would simply follow his program. Whenever Hitchcock needed to criticize a player to get a point across to the team, I was his favourite target.

His methods were not always to my liking, but I always believed he knew what he was doing. He just wanted me to be all that I could be. All that I wanted from him was to loosen up a bit. I was always poking at him verbally in the hope that he might lose it one day in a fit of uncontrollable laughter. Never happened. The best I could get out of him was a shake of his head or a roll of his eyes. Pulled jokes on him regularly, too, like filling up his shoes with shaving cream, and other such nonsense. None of it worked.

It was as if Hitchcock was addicted to winning, and when he wasn't winning he was cranky, grumpy. He could be unbearable. In January 2004, we were playing poorly, and then we lost a 3–0 game to the Edmonton Oilers and Hitchcock called us out in the media. We were a good team, and when we didn't play well, I didn't mind Hitchcock slapping us around. Mike Keenan would have done the same thing if he was coaching a team that played as poorly as we'd played against Edmonton.

When I was asked about it, I said about Hitchcock: "He's a son of a bitch right now. He's no fun right now. He's a pain in the ass. But anybody in their right mind who is coaching a team that is sputtering like we are right now would be a pain in the ass."

I said Hitchcock was treating us like dogs because we were playing like dogs.

# CHAPTER 12

# The Gambler

It's fair to say that coaches didn't like it very much when I was gambling in the offensive zone, and general managers didn't like it very much when I was gambling in casinos.

Although I never found myself in any legal trouble through gambling, my life was put under a microscope twice because I liked to bet on NFL and NBA games.

My gambling problem probably was most out of control when I was playing in Philadelphia. When I got a new deal worth an average of $7.5 million per year, I purchased a new $150,000 Porsche. But what the deal really meant to me was that I could bet more money. My $500 bets became $2,000 wagers, and I was betting on more games.

The most distressing gambling situation I had involved my relationship with Rick Tocchet, who was then an assistant coach in Phoenix. In 2005–06, when I was playing for the Los Angeles Kings, the story broke that he was being investigated by the New Jersey state police for financing a sports gambling operation. That was a difficult time, because I've said for many years that Tocchet was among the best teammates I've ever had. He epitomized what a good NHL player should be about. He had leadership, grit, tenacity and skill. He knew when to open his mouth and when to keep it shut. Tocchet always stood up for his teammates, and he was very proud to be an NHL player.

The investigation involved some betting I had done when I was playing with the Flyers. Initially, I assumed the investigation was misguided; my impression was that Tocchet was simply placing bets, just like I was. Knowing I like to bet on sporting events, Tocchet had hooked me up with a way to lay bets over the phone. I liked to bet on football games, and I would regularly bet a thousand dollars or so on three or four games a week. Occasionally, I would bet on some college and NBA basketball, but I preferred to bet on the NFL. Tocchet introduced me to New Jersey state trooper James Harney. He was the betting connection, as far as I knew. There was another man involved, named James Ulmer, whom I didn't know. But the state police painted a different picture. The media reported that Tocchet had to answer charges of promoting gambling, money laundering and conspiracy. They called it a New Jersey–based betting ring and said their investigation showed that at least a thousand people had placed bets, worth a total of more than $1.7 million, on professional and college sports. State police colonel Rick Fuentes called it a "highly organized sport betting system."

The press reported there were six active NHL players who had placed bets with the New Jersey ring, but none had bet on hockey. I was certainly happy to see that fact reported.

Never was I worried that I would be in any trouble, because I knew that placing a bet was not a criminal act. I had checked that out before I ever started betting. As long as you report your earnings to the U.S. Internal Revenue Service, you are not committing an illegal act. I have always been very aware of the legalities of gambling, and very confident of the fact that I was staying legal and following all of the NHL rules.

The other fact I want to make clear is that I never bet on hockey games. I loved the sport too much. To make it clearer, I would have cut off one of my testicles before I would bet on an NHL game.

When I was being deposed in the investigation of Tocchet, they asked me how I felt when I learned that Tocchet was the money man behind the gambling operation. I told my interviewer that I didn't believe that he was. Then the interviewer informed me that law enforcement officials had tapped Tocchet's phone and had me listen to several tapes that made it clear that Tocchet was more involved than I knew. I was surprised, to say the least, but it wasn't as if that revelation made me believe that Tocchet was evil.

"Now, how do you feel now that you know Tocchet was involved?" the interviewer asked me

"To tell you the truth, I don't give a shit," I said. "Tocchet is my buddy, my friend."

I tried to stand by Tocchet the best I could, given the circumstances. I was that blunt about it. I told the interviewer that I would rather give my money to a friend than someone I didn't know. I'm not condoning what Tocchet did. I'm not advocating that what Tocchet did is acceptable behaviour. All I was saying was that if I was going to lose a bet, I would rather the fucking money end up with Tocchet. And I tried to make it clear that Tocchet was a good man who had apparently made a bad mistake.

Tocchet essentially served a two-year suspension from the NHL and did not return to the Phoenix bench until 2008. He eventually ended up as Tampa's head coach, although today he is out of the coaching ranks. I still consider him a close friend. I know I'm sorry those events ever happened, and Tocchet is, too.

After the New Jersey investigation, the NHL completed its own investigation and was satisfied that no one involved in the hockey world ever bet on NHL games.

Before all of this happened, I had quit betting for a period of time because Flyers general manager Bob Clarke had asked me to stop. In January 2004, Clarke had confronted me and a couple of other players after hearing gossip around the dressing room that some of us liked to place bets. Clarke asked me to quit because he felt it could be a distraction. At the time, the Flyers weren't playing very well. And when a pro sports team isn't playing well, all outside activities are scrutinized. If the team loses a big game, and someone overhears you talking about some extracurricular activity, then you're called in because you aren't focused solely on the team. It didn't have to be my betting. It could have been someone's golf or girlfriend or hanging out with the wrong people. If the team isn't playing well, you can certainly count on everyone's leisure activities being called into question.

I was confident that I didn't have a problem, but I stopped for a short period of time because I respected Clarke and the Flyers organization. Even when I started up again, I scaled back, deciding not to lay any bets on days when I had a game.

As it turned out, my gambling history was revealed that summer, after law enforcement officers raided Florida-based National Sports Consultants, a gambling ring that also sold betting tips. My name was listed among the company's clients, and officials said I had spent more than $100,000 for tips on how to bet.

Truthfully, I only spent a fraction of that amount. Basically, the way it worked was I would pay about $2,000 for the company's "experts" to give me tips on games I was betting. What I quickly discovered was that I was an idiot for believing what these assholes told me, because they would recommend that half of their clients bet on one team and their remaining clients bet on the opposing team. The idea was that at least half of their clients would be happy and come back for more tips. Depending upon how lucky the handicappers were, it could take a while before some bettors figured out that the "touts" didn't know any more than they did. The touts were scam artists.

When the story came out in the newspapers, I admitted that I had bet between $50,000 and $100,000. Even though my name was mentioned, law enforcement officials admitted that I had done nothing illegal and that I had never bet on hockey.

When my name came out, I called and apologized to Clarke, assuring him that my association with the company had come before I quit betting at his request. Some of the touts said I was using their service right up until they were raided that spring, but that was not true.

Clarke asked me if I thought it would be better if he traded me. I told him that I wanted to stay with the team.

It's hard to understand how I fucking let myself dive so deep in the gambling culture. My sports psychologist, Gary Mack, had died of a heart problem in 2002. At the time, I thought I had my life back on course. But clearly, I was mistaken.

The tougher conversation was with my wife. We had worked through our issues with Mack, and we had started to communicate more. We were doing better as a family, but I had slipped back into old habits. When I told her that a newspaper story was coming out that was going to say I had paid for handicappers' advice on betting, she called me a "fucking idiot."

"You are an asshole for dragging us into this story," she said.

I didn't disagree.

Although I admit to having had a serious gambling problem during my days in Philadelphia, I never sought professional help other than the time spent with the late Gary Mack. Today, I still gamble, but not at the same levels I did years ago. Since I don't make the big money anymore, I don't bet big money.

# CHAPTER 13

# Born in the USA

In the 1980s, when most boys in Canada wanted to be Wayne Gretzky when they grew up, I wanted to be Mike Eruzione.

When Eruzione beat Soviet goalkeeper Vladimir Myshkin with his wrist shot on February 22, 1980, he changed his life and mine. As I watched the television broadcast of the Americans celebrating their amazing Olympic triumph on Lake Placid ice, I knew at that moment I wanted to be a hockey player. I wanted to experience the exhilaration and overwhelming joy that the Americans knew as they hugged each other on the ice after recording what has been called the greatest upset in sports history.

As I watched the mob scene on the ice, I was wearing my Richfield (Connecticut) Bruins jersey. I was standing in teammate Matt Heisen's living room. We had a game scheduled that night, and our equipment went on in front of the television. Our eyes were glued to the screen until we realized that we were in danger of missing our opening faceoff.

The funny aspect of this story is that when we arrived at the arena, it looked like a vacant warehouse. No cars. No people. But right after our car squealed into the parking lot, there was a parade of vehicles pulling in behind us. Everyone had stayed home to watch the American win. The start of our game was delayed, mostly because everyone was talking about what the Americans had done.

Today, watching Stanley Cup celebrations is probably one of the primary motivators for American children becoming involved in hockey. But if you ask any American player in my generation, the inspiration of their career was that American win over the Soviets. Mike Modano. Keith Tkachuk. Brian Leetch. Bill Guerin. Tony Amonte. All of America's great players in the 1990s were descendents of that one victory over the Soviets. The American triumph over Canada in the 1996 World Cup came from the seeds of inspiration that were planted on Lake Placid ice. When my American generation started thinking about a career in hockey, it started with the desire to wear a USA jersey, not to win the Stanley Cup.

One of the accomplishments that I'm proudest of is being a member of the generation that made the USA a world power in hockey. When I was growing up, the Americans went to international tournaments hoping to be competitive. When my generation arrived in power, we didn't hope to win; we *expected* to win. In the 1990s, the Americans had Pat LaFontaine, Doug Weight, Modano and me at centre ice. That's plenty of fucking firepower down the middle. Then, on the wing, we had toughness in Tkachuk and Guerin, plus Amonte, who could fucking fly up ice like an F-15 fighter jet. On defence, we had Brian Leetch, who had matured into a dominant puck mover, and Chris Chelios, who played every game like he was engaged in mortal combat.

One of the major changes in American hockey post–Lake Placid was that the sport started to attract better athletes, and we started to seek better competition, and that was usually found in Canada.

By the time my generation arrived in the NHL, we were not in awe of our Canadian rivals. We respected the Canadians, but we did not fear them. We did not view them as invincible.

My first tastes of high-level international competition came at the World Junior Championship in 1988 in Moscow, and then in 1989 in Alaska. In that second tournament, Modano, Amonte and I were matched up against Alexander Mogilny, Sergei Fedorov and Pavel Bure. We didn't have team success in those tournaments, but I can tell you that when we lined up against that Soviet trio, we were anything but intimidated. We could skate with them, and they knew that. In my two WJC tournaments, I registered 13 goals and 12 assists in 14 games. Modano had 10 goals and 10 assists in those 14 games.

The U.S. program was the beneficiary of the Modano–Roenick rivalry. Because we had been competitors since we were 10 years old, we pushed each other to be better players. Both of us wanted to be known as America's best young player. I believe Modano helped me become the player I became.

As proud as I've been to wear the Team USA sweater, the truth is that I've had a sometimes-rocky relationship with USA Hockey. My early years with the American program were all good. I have fond memories of the 1991 Canada Cup. I played well in that tournament. That was the tournament where the younger American players began to believe that we were going to eventually be a world fucking power in hockey. My buddy Gary Suter made a statement to that effect when he drove Wayne Gretzky into the boards from behind in the game against Canada. I remember going into the dressing room between periods and telling Suter, "You just hit Wayne fucking Gretzky. Nobody hits Gretzky."

He just shrugged. That was Sutes. He didn't give a shit what people thought about the way he played. He had that Mark Messier attitude—"I'm going to do whatever I need to do to win the fucking game."

Gretzky was hurt on the play and missed the start of the NHL season. I know Suter wasn't deliberately trying to hurt Gretzky. But I also know that Suter never wanted you to feel comfortable playing against him. He wanted you to worry about what he might do to you. He was among the league's best-conditioned athletes. He wasn't a big man, but he could inflict pain when he hit you.

Suter and Chelios were great friends, even though they had contrasting personalities. Chelios always liked to be the centre of attention, while Suter always liked sitting at the end of the bar by himself. More than once, I would walk into a tavern and find Suter in his favourite spot, like a less-talkative and fitter version of Norm on the television show *Cheers*.

"Hey, Sutes," I would say.

"Hey, J.R., you sexy sonofabitch," Suter would say in a very low, monotone voice.

My issues with USA Hockey started in 1996. By then, players from America's greatest hockey generation were well established. There was an expectation that the Americans were going to give the Canadians and Russians a battle in the 1996 World Cup. Some analysts said the Americans were among the favourites. I said the Americans were going to win the fucking tournament. I just flat out made that prediction in a press conference. Team USA general manager Lou Lamoriello was not pleased with my public prediction. Lou was happy I felt that way; he just didn't understand why I needed to say it. I needed to say it because I wanted the Canadians to know we were a confident bunch. He didn't want any bulletin board material. I didn't give a shit. That's how I felt. I believed the team had too much talent to lose. Ron Wilson was going to be our coach. He can be a prick and a snide bastard, but he is considered a good coach for a short tournament.

My relationship with USA Hockey started to deteriorate more when I decided not to play in the World Cup because I didn't have an NHL contract. I wanted to fucking play—no doubt about that. But my agent, Neil Abbott, pointed out the financial risk of playing without a contract. If I suffered a long-term injury, the loss of income would be enormous. Abbott thought playing for the USA would be irresponsible, given my circumstances. But don't blame Neil for that decision. It was my call in the end. He was doing his job by pointing out what was at stake. I made the final call not to play. Remember, this was the summer when the Blackhawks traded me to the Coyotes, and we couldn't agree on a deal. I hadn't yet received a "home run" contract.

I remember Keith Tkachuk called me when the U.S. team was coming together and said, "Get a fucking deal done and get your ass in here and let's go win the fucking tournament."

I didn't budge. I think USA Hockey people were pissed off at me, and I think my refusal to play hurt me at various times in my career. But I can tell you this: I loved watching my American boys beat Canada in Montreal. No one was rooting for them more than I was.

The truth is, we measured ourselves against the Canadians, and we didn't start having success until we adopted the Canadian mentality. We'd been getting pushed around by the Canadians for years and years. Finally, we realized that if we were going to beat them, we'd have to play like them, have to act like them. We realized that we had to enter tournaments as if we were preparing for a brawl in the alley. We had to prepare as if we would do anything to win.

Given my disappointment, I was hoping that the 1998 Olympics would help me forget my absence from that 1996 World Cup team. Instead, the 1998 Olympic experience in Nagano ended in a shitstorm. This was the first time the NHL sent its players to the Olympics, and based on the World Cup results, the Americans were considered one of the favourites. Basically, it was the same roster that won the World Cup, except I was now playing. Maybe I am a fucking jinx, because we played terribly as a team and lost three of four games, including the quarterfinals to Dominik Hasek's Czech team. The Czechs ended up winning the gold medal over the Russians.

To make matters worse, the American team became fucking embroiled in the controversy involving broken chairs and a fire extinguisher being unleashed in an athletes' village room. What I can tell you about that is that it has to be among the most over-blown and exaggerated controversies in Olympic fucking history.

Although I was out with my wife and friends when the events unfolded, I can tell you all that really happened was that some of the guys filled goalie Mike Richter's room with fire-retardant foam as a practical joke. Honestly, I have no idea who pulled the trig-ger. Sure, it shouldn't have happened, and the timing was ridic-ulously awful because we had played poorly. But the amount of damage inflicted in the room was grossly overstated. A thousand dollars in damages, my ass. The shop vacuum in your garage could have cleaned up the mess in under an hour.

And the most ludicrous charge was that players purposely broke chairs. Yes, we broke several of them, by putting our asses in them. The good people of Japan make quality electronics and cars, but they did a piss-poor job of constructing Olympic village furniture. These chairs were made of flimsy material, similar to balsa wood. They seemed to be designed for smaller Asian people, not hockey players who weighed more than 200 pounds. Every day, one of us would sit in a chair and go crashing to the floor because it would disintegrate beneath us. Every room had a pile of sticks in the corner made from the remains of our chairs. A week before the so-called room-trashing, I was quoted in a media story about how the Olympic village experience was great except for the fact that our furniture kept breaking.

The 2002 Olympic experience made up for my previous disappointments in playing or not playing for the USA. Certainly, I was disappointed that we didn't win the gold-medal game against Canada. But I'm fucking proud of the silver medal. That was some of the finest hockey I've ever seen played. The 3–2 win against Russia was the most exciting, nerve-fraying, pressure-filled game I've ever been in. In the third period of that game, we were desperately trying to hold on to our lead, and the tension was unbearable. I remember taking a puck in the stomach to block a shot on a penalty kill. I would have never fucking forgiven myself if I hadn't blocked that shot.

It was a satisfying win over Russia, but it took too much out of us. Meanwhile, the Canadians had an easier game against fucking Belarus. We couldn't get up to speed again against Canada in the gold-medal game. I hated to lose to Canada, but it's not like we lost to a bunch of scrubs. We lost to the best players in the world. You could tell the Canadians needed it. It was their first Olympic gold medal in hockey in a half-century. Al MacInnis said that competing in that tournament was like carrying an anvil around on your back for 10 days. The Canadians were facing overwhelming pressure.

In 2005, my past issues with USA Hockey began to hurt me again. I believe that strongly. USA Hockey officials decided to start phasing out members of American hockey's greatest generation, and I was one of the first to be pushed to the sidelines.

Don Waddell, then-general manager of the Atlanta Thrashers, was the GM of the U.S. Olympic team, and in the late summer of 2005 he left me a voice message saying that I wasn't being invited to Team USA's Olympic orientation camp, but I was still in the mix to make the team.

Bullshit. They had already decided I wasn't in their plans. I knew it as soon as I heard the message. I've never forgiven Waddell for the decision to write me off before the season. I felt like I deserved more consideration than he gave me.

In retrospect, I'm very proud of my days in a USA sweater. I believe my generation put American hockey on the map in terms of being a world power. Even though the 1980 team won the Olympics and the gold medal, we weren't considered a world power then. When the Americans won in 1980, I think the reaction was, "Holy shit, we just pulled off the greatest miracle of all time." Today, we don't need a fucking miracle to beat Russia, Canada or anyone else.

In my generation, we were at least a threat to win a gold medal every time we took to the ice. Obviously, we didn't win any gold medals after 1996, but we didn't back down from anyone, particularly the Canadians.

My relationship with USA Hockey has been strong for a few

years. But you know I can't leave well enough alone. When Brian Burke picked his U.S. Olympic team in 2010, I said that Chris Drury had no place on the team.

I have to say what I feel. That's just who I am. But Burke was pissed at me, and USA Hockey officials were displeased. As it turned out, I was wrong about Drury, who played well for the Americans in Vancouver.

But a few months later, my big mouth was overlooked, and I was elected to the U.S. Hockey Hall of Fame. One of the great ironies was that Derian Hatcher, my Dallas nemesis, was elected at the same time. During my induction speech, in Buffalo, I said: "Everywhere I go, everybody asks me about Derian, and I'll put this one to rest right now: Derian, I respect you, and I'm envious of you because of your Stanley Cup. But never, ever, did I feel any animosity for what happened on the ice between us."

At the induction ceremony, Hatcher said he always felt awkward around me after breaking my jaw, and he was thankful that I always went out of my way to make him feel at ease.

Another person I thanked at the induction ceremony was NHL commissioner Gary Bettman. "Thank you for letting me speak my mind," I told Bettman, who was sitting in the audience. "Thank you for letting me have a personality."

# CHAPTER 14

# Death in the Family

My decision to sign with the Philadelphia Flyers in 2001 turned out to be important to my wife, Tracy, but not for the reason I intended.

When I was sorting out my free-agent options, Tracy said she understood that I needed to do what was best for my career. Hockey came first. She kept that same attitude throughout my career. Certainly, I had to consider the NHL implications first. But I also wanted to factor in Tracy and my daughter Brandi's horse-riding interests. In choosing Philadelphia over Detroit, I believed I was putting my wife and daughter in a better situation to pursue their careers. It made me happy to factor my family into the decision. It truly did.

Today, Tracy believes that decision to go to Philadelphia was divinely inspired, because in February of 2002 her mother, Dorothy Vazza, was diagnosed with cancer in Florida. Tracy drove down to Florida and brought her back to Massachusetts.

"I was there for you all of those years, and now it has to be about my family," she told me. "I'm going to take care of my mother, and you are going to take care of our kids. You are going to have to do that, regardless of what is happening with your team. Do you understand?"

I told Tracy that I understood, and I was ready to do that. I needed to do that. I owed Tracy that much. For a few months, I was both a mom and dad to my children.

The cancer was aggressive, and in late August, it was clear that Dottie was dying. At that time, a very eerie event started to unfold.

On August 21, Tracy's mother began to tell us all that she wanted to stay alive until her son Rick's birthday on August 23. The oddity of that was that Rick's birthday was August 17. We just dismissed it as medicine or confusion having an impact on Dottie's thinking. Then, the next night, her condition deteriorated and everyone came to say goodbye. Rick wasn't able to get there on time, and she died shortly after midnight on August 23. Rick was devastated that he had not made it in time.

We all stayed up that night, drinking wine and telling stories about Dottie and her life. At around 3:30 in the morning, Rick's cell phone went off, and Rick looked shocked as he stared down at his screen. The message read, "Happy Birthday."

There was no telephone number attached to the message.

We all almost shit ourselves.

"Are you fucking kidding me?" I asked.

That was the most unexplainable moment I've ever had in my life. I don't know what I believe about the afterlife, but that was a moment I will never forget.

CHAPTER 15

# The Bomb

The scariest moment of my career came on February 8, 2004, when a slapshot from New York Rangers defenceman Boris Mironov caught me square in the jaw. It was as if my face exploded. Picture a hammer striking a glass bottle. That's what the impact felt like.

The Rangers' team physician, Andrew Feldman, was quoted the next day in the newspaper saying that I was unconscious for three to four minutes. All I remembered was seeing Mironov's screaming rocket shot coming right at my mouth, and I turned away and it caught me in the side of the face. When I woke up, the ice looked like a crime scene. Blood was everywhere

When I was able to rise and skate off the ice with assistance, I was witness to an event I never thought I would see: an opposing player, particularly a Flyers player, receiving a standing ovation in Madison Square Garden.

The injury did seem like a case of fate piling on, because four weeks earlier teammate Mark Recchi had struck me in the jaw with one of his shots in practice. The wound took 27 stitches to close, and my face was a mess.

My face was still recovering from that injury when I produced one of the famous rants of my career. It came January 14, 2004, after referee Blaine Angus watched me get cut with a high stick right in front of him and didn't make a call.

We were playing Buffalo, and I had already been cut twice in the first 40 minutes of the game. During the third period, I was sliced again, by Rory Fitzpatrick, as I skated into the Sabres' zone. When I realized no penalty was being called on the play, I exploded at Angus, who was looking at me when it happened. My mouth was a fountain of blood. Droplets were spitting out of me as I screamed at him.

"What do you mean you didn't see it, you fucking cocksucker?" I shouted. "It was right in front of your fucking face. Are you fucking blind? You are a terrible fucking referee."

Somewhere in the midst of those four sentences, Angus threw me out of the game. I received a minor for unsportsmanlike conduct and a gross misconduct penalty.

That just escalated my rage. I was still screaming at him from the bench as he went to the penalty box to report my crimes. Recchi was over there, pleading my case, explaining to Angus that I didn't mean what I was saying. That I was pissed off that I had been cut.

Just as Recchi was wrapping up his plea for mercy, I threw a water bottle that hit Angus in the leg on one bounce.

"Did Roenick just throw a water bottle at me?" Angus said.

Recchi told me that he realized at that point that there was nothing more that could be said on my behalf. He told me he just turned to Angus and said: "Best we just get this game over with as quickly as we can. No whistles."

After the game, I was over-the-top pissed off. "NHL, wake up," I shouted into the television camera. "Blaine Angus is standing right in front of me and he says he doesn't see it. What's he looking at? The National Hockey League has to step in and tell these guys to open their eyes." Not done quite yet, I continued my rant by saying, "Blaine Angus did an absolutely terrible job."

Not surprisingly, the NHL suspended me for one game, which cost me $91,463 in salary. Frankly, I'm surprised the league didn't tack on more after I criticized their decision to suspend me.

"I'm the one who gets punished and has money taken out of his pocket," I said. "Not Blaine Angus, but me, because they refused to do their job correctly. Certain referees, and they know who they are, are held unaccountable for their poor, poor decision-making in how they do their job."

I added that there were three or four referees who "stuck it up the Flyers' ass any time they had the opportunity."

"The league is too Neanderthal to change it," I said. "That's why the game is sputtering the way it is."

It was worth every cent of that ninety grand just to get that off my chest.

By the way, Blaine Angus was fired by the NHL in 2006.

With all that had already happened to me that season, I certainly had the right to feel like I was the unluckiest player in the league when Mironov's explosive shot detonated on my face. The Recchi shot and Fitzpatrick slice were flesh wounds compared to the damage that the Mironov bomb had inflicted. X-rays at St. Vincent's Hospital painted a gruesome picture of the wreckage that was once my jaw. Twenty-one official breaks—18 smaller spider breaks and three major fractures. Surgery was required immediately to stabilize my jaw and wire it shut. Doctors said that I was going to be out of the lineup for a lengthy period.

But my initial thought about the Mironov shot was that I was fortunate it wasn't even worse. After I lost the faceoff, the puck went immediately to Mironov at the point. He pounded it. If I had not been able to turn away, it would have destroyed all of my teeth and my facial structure. Essentially, one twist of my head probably spared me from major reconstructive surgery. We can assume that the puck was travelling faster than 90 miles per hour when it found my face.

Initially, I was feeling optimistic about my recovery. I called my wife from the Garden to assure her I would be fine. Through a wired jaw, I talked to teammates and told them I was being treated well in the New York hospital. I even did a newspaper interview and joked that I would take the reporter "out for soup" when I was discharged from the hospital.

The surgery went fine, but then I started to experience nausea and severe headaches. Suddenly, I had lightheadedness and dizziness. It was clear to me that I had suffered a concussion. Within days, I was wondering whether my career was over. Was this a depression brought on by the concussion? Maybe I just didn't like the frighteningly ugly man I saw when I looked in the mirror and saw the aftermath of Mironov's bomb in the face. I had a four-inch scar on my jawline. My cheeks were sunken.

I didn't know why I was feeling this way, because no injury had ever made me feel this worried before. I just felt like this was a bad injury, and I didn't know why. My agent, Neil Abbott, immediately secured an appointment for me with Montreal's noted neurologist Karen Johnston.

Ken Hitchcock was quoted in the newspapers as saying he believed I was "riding an emotional wave" and simply needed time to rest and come to grips with my injury. He said he expected me to return, and he was right. The symptoms never went away, but I was able to come back. With five games left in the regular season, I returned to the lineup wearing a shield. By the playoffs, I had removed the shield because I'm not the kind of player who wears one.

In the first period of the first playoff game, the New Jersey Devils decided to find out if I was still the same player. Sean Brown challenged me, and instantly we were throwing punches to the head.

I probably should have sent a fucking thank-you note to the Devils, because that scrap helped me realize I could still be the same player, even if I still didn't feel perfect. It freed my mind.

Although I was never 100 percent healthy in the 2004 playoffs, I will always remember that time as one of the most memorable playoff runs of my career. The postseason began with me playing right wing on a line with my buddy Tony Amonte and centre Alexei Zhamnov, whom we had acquired to help us win in the playoffs. How ironic that I should end up playing with a guy who was supposed to replace me in Chicago. That line had good chemistry, and I had points in six of the first seven games of the postseason.

In 2003–04, Hitchcock had given me great responsibility, putting me against the other teams' top stars. I was killing penalties as well.

"He's always been a good friend to everyone," said Hitchcock. "Now he is being a good teammate."

In the second-round series against Toronto, I probably scored the most meaningful goal of my career. It was an overtime game-winner to beat the Leafs 3–2 in game six. It was meaningful primarily because it pushed us into the Eastern Conference final to face the Tampa Bay Lightning. But it was also memorable because Amonte had set me up with a perfect two-on-one pass.

Believe it or not, I had visualized how that goal was going to happen.

Shortly before the winning goal was scored, the Flyers' Sami Kapanen had been levelled on a vicious check by Darcy Tucker. It was one of the hardest hits I ever saw delivered. The Air Canada Centre crowd just erupted with delight.

This hit should have destroyed Kapanen, who is about five foot eight, 170 pounds. But he pulled himself up and made his way off the ice. The fortitude and guts Kapanen showed by staggering to the bench is one of the more impressive athletic feats I've ever seen. Keith Primeau stuck his stick out to pull Kapanen the final few feet. After Kapanen fell into the bench, I jumped on the ice, picked up a loose puck and found myself on a two-on-one break with Amonte. Bryan McCabe was the only Toronto defender between us and the net.

What made the situation so eerie was that between periods I had a vision of myself being in that position and burying the puck top shelf against Ed Belfour. Now, just over seven minutes into overtime, my premonition was about to become reality. Belfour knew I liked to shoot over the right pad on the far side. That's my go-to shot. I knew Eddie knew that. So, in my mind, between periods, I had made the decision to shoot high over Belfour's glove. When I was picturing this situation between periods, I kept repeating the two-on-one sequence many times. Each time, I shot the puck high over the glove and Belfour couldn't stop it.

When I had that opportunity in overtime, I shot the puck exactly as I had pictured it. Belfour was both surprised and beaten. My 15-footer zipped under the crossbar, popping Belfour's water bottle into the air. The building that had been a joyous madhouse after Tucker's wallop of Kapanen was now as quiet as a tomb.

Visualization works.

The Lightning was the number-one team in the Eastern Conference in the regular season, and they were 4–0 against us in the regular season. They had rolled over Montreal in the previous round, but we had learned much about ourselves, and about winning, in the first two rounds.

In game four, Fredrik Modin checked me against the boards, and my head slammed against the Plexiglas. The next day, I felt nauseous and I had a splitting headache. It was clear that I had had another concussion.

Under today's NHL concussion protocol, I would have been out of the lineup. But in 2004, I never considered not playing. The series was tied 2–2. I wasn't going to miss game five. We lost the fifth game by a score of 4–2, but in game six my linemate Simon Gagné scored in overtime to force a seventh game. After Gagné scored, my legs surrendered. I collapsed to the ice. I felt as if I couldn't move. It was as if my body was overrun by exhaustion. Concussion-related? I have no idea. But I can tell you that I had some scary moments as Primeau and Gagné helped me off the ice. Only after I had a shower and a massage did I feel well enough to exit the dressing room. Those playoffs took more out of me than any other period of my career.

As we prepared for game seven, it seemed like we were readying for a Stanley Cup final game. No one would have said it, but all of us probably believed that if we won our next game in the St. Petersburg Times Forum, we were going to win the Stanley Cup. The Calgary Flames had been an upset winner in the Western Conference, and we felt we could handle them. We were definitely a better offensive team than the Flames.

For the older players, this game almost seemed like a last chance. I was 34, and so was Amonte. John LeClair and Mark Recchi were older than us. Primeau was 32. We were all closer to the end of our careers than the beginning. Plus, the collective bargaining agreement was expiring the following September, and Bob Goodenow, the executive director of the NHL Players' Association, was warning us that the 2004–05 season might be lost because of a lockout. Would I be able to come back after a year off?

Those concerns added to the view that game seven was a last chance for us to make a run at the Stanley Cup. My experience in Chicago had taught me that this is the only sensible way to approach these kinds of big games.

We believed we were ready to win that game seven. We thought we wanted it more than the Lightning. It felt like we were a team of destiny. But in hindsight, we were too beat up to be successful against a healthier, quicker Tampa Bay team. Plus, our power play had not been sharp in that series.

The Lightning claimed a 2–0 lead in the game, and we could only get one back. The 2–1 loss left me crying at my stall for 20 minutes after the game.

When you think of athletic competition, you visualize winning. You think of celebrations. Jubilant players. Equipment fired into the air like bottle rockets. Tears of joy. Grown men hugging each other. But for every one of those celebrations, there is a losing dressing room where every player is suffering from an ache that pain medicine can't relieve.

This loss hit me harder than any I ever suffered. It was even worse than losing game one of the Stanley Cup final in 1992.

The season had been a roller-coaster ride, and it had drained me emotionally and physically. My body was wrecked. My head throbbed. My stomach churned. I felt like throwing up. As I sat at my stall, I felt incapacitated, paralyzed by my emotions.

You feel betrayed. As an athlete, you learn to believe that if you sacrifice and commit fully to your quest, you will be rewarded. All of us had given all that we had, only to discover it wasn't enough. It felt as if this playoff run had been conducted with our troops at half-strength. Most of the guys were beat up, and yet every day a new hero would rise from our ranks. Concussed Primeau had carried us on many nights, scoring some big goals. He had 9 goals and 7 assists. Kapanen played his heart out. Gagné was great. Alexei Zhamnov, once traded for me, had come over from the Chicago Blackhawks and played terrifically for us in the playoffs. He had 14 points in 18 playoff games. Playing at about half-strength, I had 13 points in those 18 games.

After we came up short in game seven, Hitchcock went from a grizzly bear to Mr. Complimentary. "I don't think anything less of them," he said about us after the game. "They've already gone to the well far too many times than they should have had to." He knew we were out of gas. We had desire but no fuel to carry us the rest of the way to our destination.

"We emptied the tank in game six," Hitchcock was quoted in the *Philadelphia Inquirer* as saying. "The board battles we won in game six and at the tail end of game five, we weren't able to win in game seven. They won them in their zone, and they came at us."

After the game, I sat at my stall, half-dressed, for a very long time. I was overwhelmed by sadness and despair. Maybe it was my concussion. Maybe it was my feeling that my career might be over. Maybe it was the realization that my last chance to win a Stanley Cup had fallen one goal short. But I couldn't stop crying that night.

# CHAPTER 16

# All in My Head

Anyone who wants to know what life as an NHL player is like should simply review my medical records. I've received 600 stitches in my face, broken all of my fingers, had my shoulder rebuilt, suffered two knee injuries, broken my jaw once in four places and another time in 21 places. Then there is the matter of 13 documented concussions and probably 10 to 20 others that were not diagnosed.

The concussion I suffered when Boris Mironov hit me with his shot in 2004 was probably the scariest, because the symptoms seemed to alter my personality and they persisted for many months. That summer, it was as if someone else was inhabiting my mind. I never felt right. It was the worst summer of my life.

When Pittsburgh Penguins captain Sidney Crosby was still having symptoms in the summer of 2011, seven months after suffering a concussion, I could relate to what he was going through. There was a day during the summer of 2004 when I slept roughly 23 hours.

As a general rule, I'm an upbeat person. That summer, I was a hater. I was irritable, moody and grumpy. I slept a lot more than usual because I was tired all the time. It was a struggle to get out of bed. I treated my wife, Tracy, poorly. I treated my kids poorly. I sat

Tony Amonte and I have been friends since we were teenagers, and Tracy and Laurie Amonte, Tony's wife (*far left*), have been friends since they were toddlers. Here, we're hanging out at the 1998 Olympic Games in Nagano, Japan.

Tony Amonte and I played on the same team at the Olympic Games in Nagano. It's really wild to think that Tony and I were prep school linemates who ended up playing together on two NHL teams and then the U.S. Olympic team.

At the 1998 Olympics, I hit Wayne Gretzky with a check for one of the few times in my career. I have great respect for the way Wayne Gretzky played the game and carried himself as the league's ambassador. But when I played for Gretzky in 2006–07, we did not get along. We were not on the same page — not even in the same book.

Brett Hull and I chummed it up at the 1998 Olympics. And no, my son, Brett, is not named after Brett Hull.

That's Doug Weight (*centre*) with Tony Amonte and me at the Nagano Olympics. To this day, I don't know why USA didn't play better that year.

Matt Mallgrave and I have been friends for 30 years. We played hockey together as kids, and he ended up playing for Harvard, as well as the minor leagues. Now he is on Wall Street, making the kind of money I was making in the NHL.

Whenever I threw a party in Arizona, I hired a band called Boogie Nights because they always played music I liked. I knew every word to the songs the band played, so I would go on stage and accompany their lead singer. You aren't surprised, are you?

My former Phoenix teammate Claude Lemieux and I pose at my Arizona going-away party after I signed with Philadelphia. Hanging with the Boogie Nights band, Pepe and I are showing our age. What a great send-off that party was.

Never during my career was I ever at a loss for words. Never did I meet a microphone I didn't like. At the 2002 Olympics, my son, Brett, interviews me on the streets of Salt Lake City for NBC. Throughout my career, I always believed that after I retired I would find a way to stay in front of the camera, and I was correct.

If I wanted to win a hockey game and howl at the moon afterward, Keith Tkachuk (*right*), posing here with me at the 2002 Olympics, is the man I would want leading me. He's the yardstick by which all NHL captains should be judged.

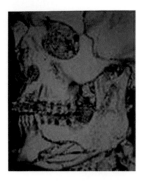

The most vicious hit I took during my career was Derian Hatcher's elbow to my jaw in 1999. Here is the X-ray showing my jaw broken in three places. Eight of my teeth were also broken. Five years later, my jaw was shattered again.

My three seasons in Philadelphia cost me my pretty face. This is how I looked after I healed from having my jaw shattered by a Boris Mironov slapshot in 2004. In addition to the broken jaw, I also ended up with a concussion and post-concussion syndrome. I spent most of that summer with my shades drawn. By the way, I've had many teammates over the years who would swear that Mironov's shot had no impact on my face because I was ugly before and ugly after.

This is me enjoying a quality meal of filet mignon, broccoli and sweet potatoes after Boris Mironov broke my jaw with a booming slap shot in 2004. My wife, Tracy, would make my favourite meals and then just toss them in a blender.

© B. Bennett/Getty Images

I spent much of the 2003–04 season bleeding because of high sticks and Boris Mironov's slap shot to my jaw. In one game against Buffalo, I was cut three times, but even with blood spilling from my mouth, no penalty was called. I was so enraged I threw a water bottle at the ref and vented my frustration to the media, famously saying, "Wake up, NHL, wake up!"

Another Massachusetts player, Marty McInnis (*right*) of the New York Islanders, accompanied Tony Amonte and me on our trip to the Bahamas.

Tracy and I appear here with our close friends Billy and Vicky Jaffe (*centre*), plus Paul and Lisa Rooney, at the Grey Cliff Restaurant in the Bahamas.

Tony Amonte hands me a beer and some Kentucky Fried Chicken as I ski close to shore in the Bahamas. The rest of the story: coming in too fast on my next pass, I slid onto the beach like I was sliding into home plate. The result: I sheared a layer of skin off my backside and leg. The open wound had to be wrapped every day at the infirmary. And for the rest of my vacation, every time I went in the water, my rump felt like I was dipping it in a vat of acid.

I always enjoyed fishing at Sun Valley. We spent six consecutive summers there.

Taking Brett for a spin on Casper, Brandi's first pony. Not going to lie — I'm scared of horses.

Spending time in Sun Valley with Brett at our friends' river-grove farm. It's an amazing place.

Here I am with my prize catch on a vacation in Sun Valley. I spent hours out there fly fishing.

This is me riding a horse in Costa Rica and thinking, "I hate riding a horse." I just don't get how my wife and my daughter, Brandi, get so much enjoyment out of this.

Brandi was 13 when she won her first national dressage championship, riding Pretty Lady. She was the youngest champion in U.S. dressage history.

around the house and moped. I couldn't work out. I tried to golf, but it was a struggle to play 18 holes because of the constant headaches. I usually play golf four times a week in the summer, and I averaged one poor round of golf per week in the summer of 2004. How can you golf when sunlight bothers you? Lights bothered me. My son was eight then, and my daughter was 10, and the regular household noise that my children would make would drive me up the wall. People all around me, including family, friends and even members of the media, were telling me I wasn't acting like myself.

In the eight years since, the NHL has come a long way in terms of how it handles concussions. Given the way that doctors, teams and players now look at concussions, I probably would not have been allowed to play after game four in the 2004 Eastern Conference finals. I had severe headaches the day before I played game five.

This is what I told Philadelphia reporter Tim Panaccio in September of that year: "I was throwing up between periods of that game and didn't play in the third period. I played the next game. Why? Because I'm a hockey player, and I wanted to win a Stanley Cup. Probably a stupid move on my part, but I wanted to win."

To be clear, it didn't matter what the Philadelphia doctors thought about my medical situation after Game 4. It was my decision to play. The doctor would have had to break my leg to prevent me from playing. I was going to do whatever I had to do to win a Stanley Cup, including ignoring health risks. That's just who I was as a player.

My health was a political issue in the fall of 2004 because the NHL locked out players that season, and the only players who would be paid were those who were injured. Since my salary was $7.5 million in the 2004–05 season, the Flyers weren't going to be handing me paycheques without some proof of my concussion.

When the issue was first raised, general manager Bob Clarke's initial response was to point out that I had passed the team's exit physical. Keith Primeau, who eventually retired because of concussion issues, also passed his exit physical. The Flyers knew I was having problems, because I'd told them before I had my physical. I wasn't feeling right, and the headaches hadn't gone away. Clarke and coach Ken Hitchcock both told me that they didn't believe I should try to play in the World Cup of Hockey that was scheduled for August 24. Clarke had told the media in May that he didn't want me, or Primeau, to play in the World Cup. The Flyers were keenly aware that I was injured.

I was still hoping to feel better. It wasn't until July that I officially notified USA Hockey that I wouldn't be able to play in the 2004 World Cup. The Barrow Neurological Institute in Arizona was treating me, and doctors there figured out that my brain stem had been shifted by the force of Mironov's shot. I received treatment, such as deep massages, to help move it back into alignment. Had there been a 2004–05 season, I would not have been ready to play in October.

Although the media accounts made it seem that I was in a heated battle with the Flyers over my money, the organization was quite professional in its dealings with me. I went to see Dr. Karen Johnston in Montreal in October; she was the expert who treated Eric Lindros. A few weeks later, I had an appointment with a doctor in Philadelphia. Once the Flyers read the two doctors' reports, we were able to agree on payment of $1.5 million. The Flyers are a first-class organization, and my take was that the NHL was making sure each team followed a specific protocol when it came to dealing with injured players.

It was probably January before I began to feel better. And when the fog lifted from my brain, I didn't like what I saw in the battle between the NHL and the players over the new collective bargaining agreement. I didn't believe the leadership of the NHL Players' Association was taking us in the right direction. I believe I was one of the first players, if not the first player, to say we should accept a salary cap. I just didn't believe a salary cap was going to blow up our earning potential, and I thought the game needed a way for every team to compete. In my last season in Phoenix, I saw what happened when teams had to dump players for financial reasons. It wasn't a pretty sight.

Whether my moods were being impacted by my concussion or not, I can't say, but I was enraged over the loss of the season and the stubbornness of NHLPA executive director Bob Goodenow. Right from the beginning, I felt as if we were a house cat fighting against a mountain lion.

I started making calls to players, and I ended up talking to about 40 of them, and every one of them was at least willing to discuss accepting a salary cap. My next call was to Ian Pulver, who was one of Goodenow's lieutenants at the NHLPA. I informed him that I had been talking to players who were willing to accept a cap, and this is my recollection of how our conversation went:

"That's not true," he said. "We don't find that at all. We don't find that guys will accept a cap."

I repeated that I had talked to 40 guys, which I considered a reasonable sample of players.

"Don't tell me that guys don't want to do it," I said, my anger starting to show. "I'm telling you the guys would do it."

"We just don't feel that way," Pulver said.

At that point in the conversation, I started to wonder who worked for whom.

There was a players' meeting scheduled for Toronto shortly after my telephone joust with Pulver. And 200 of us showed up to voice our opinions about what was going on. When it was my turn to speak, I stood up, and my first comment was directed at Ian Pulver. I told him never to disrespect me. "I wanted to come through that phone and knock your teeth out," I said.

Pulver said he was sorry I felt that way. I wanted to punch him again. Instead, I said what I had to say about our negotiation stance.

"What are we doing here, guys?" I asked. "The game is changing. Why can't we look at a salary cap, but on our terms?"

I took some heat. Tough guy Tie Domi was adamantly against the salary cap, and he gave me an earful. But there were plenty who agreed with me, including Jarome Iginla.

It was at that time that my relationship with Goodenow broke down. I respected him for what he had done for the NHLPA. Certainly, I benefited from the work Goodenow had done to raise salaries early in my career. When salaries became public under his watch, they escalated dramatically. But somewhere along the line, he seemed to lose track of the reality that he was working for us and not the other way around. He never yelled at me, but I didn't like being around him because of his arrogance. When he answered a question, it always seemed that he was telling you what your opinion should be. He was condescending and made you feel that his word was final. I had the feeling he didn't respect the opinion of any player who didn't agree with him.

It sure seemed to me that there was too much at stake for Goodenow to be as obstinate as he was being. In my mind, the players were risking too much for a war they didn't need to fight. Although agents had negotiated some contracts to reduce the damage of a lost season, every player was losing significantly. Some of the losses were in the millions.

I just didn't believe that a salary cap would hurt us the way Goodenow said it would. I just believed that, even with a salary cap, players would still be paid well. To be honest, I thought the league actually needed a system that would allow more teams to be competitive. I believe that I've been proven correct in my assessment.

When Commissioner Gary Bettman cancelled the season on February 16, we all shared in the blame for letting that happen. The anger consumed me after that, and it probably didn't help that I was still recovering from a severe concussion. It bothered me that players were being looked at as the bad guys in the lost season.

In June 2005, I was golfing in Mario Lemieux's charity golf tournament when I was asked about what had happened in the lost season. My eruption became the news of the day.

"[The NHLPA] could have listened to [its] players," I said. "They could have listened to the players who had an idea of where this thing was going. They could have listened to me; they could have listened to Robert Esche, to Jarome Iginla, to Chris Pronger, and to sign a deal close to what we had in February. . . . Now that we're at this point, I realize I was right. That deal we could have signed in February beats the fuck out of the deal we're going to sign in July."

I wasn't done talking, not by a long shot. "If people are going to sit and chastise professional athletes for being spoiled and being cocky, they need to look at one thing, and that's the deal that we are probably going to end up signing here in the next three weeks," I said. "They'd better understand that pro athletes are not cocky.

Pro athletes care about the game. Everybody out there who calls us spoiled because we play 'a game,' they can all kiss my [ass]. They can all kiss my ass because we have tried so hard to get this game back on the ice."

That sent shock waves around the hockey world. I ended up being interviewed by ESPN's Dan Patrick on *SportsCenter* about what I had said. He came out verbally swinging at me, and we ended up in a heated, emotional sparring match.

It wasn't just good television. It was great television.

After my joust with Patrick, we didn't speak to each other for a long period of time. He didn't invite me on his show, probably because he assumed I wanted to pulverize him for lashing out at me on national television. When we worked on the Stanley Cup final together in 2010, he said, "J.R., I thought you hated me."

I told him I didn't hate him. In fact, I respect his show a great deal. "But I thought you were a dick for coming after me," I said, laughing. "But you thought I was a dick for saying what I did."

Since the clearing of the air, Dan and I have had a great relationship. And it all came out of our heated exchange on television.

In retrospect, my words at Mario's golf tournament probably were among the more stupid comments I've ever made. But I wouldn't take them back. I'm an emotional guy, and I say what I feel at the time. Good or bad, that's who I am.

CHAPTER 17

# Dancing with Probert

When I squared off with Marty McSorley in my first National Hockey League fight, it was a decision born out of ignorance rather than bravery. I had no idea who McSorley was, or what danger I was in, when I knocked him on his rump with a hit during the 1989–90 season. The 220-pound Los Angeles Kings defenceman inexplicably had his head down as he carried the puck near our bench, and I steamrolled him with a solid hit. McSorley was flat on his back, and I stood over him like a triumphant warrior. That was my mistake.

When our eyes met, I sensed that I had just awakened a fire-breathing dragon. Having turned 20 only two weeks before, I honestly didn't appreciate that it was against NHL etiquette to celebrate a heavy check. But after viewing the demonic look on McSorley's face, I instantly understood that I had done something horribly wrong. McSorley quickly was up on his skates, and I felt his long arm of the law grab the back of my neck. Now believing that I had to protect myself, I dropped my gloves. As soon as the first glove came off, I could hear everyone on our bench yell in unison: "Noooooooooooooooooooooo."

Our scrap was akin to a PT boat taking on a destroyer. I was in my first professional fight, and McSorley had already logged more than a hundred fighting majors. He outweighed me by more than 60 pounds. The guys on my bench were screaming for me to get out of there, but it wasn't as if I had a choice. The two-minute instigator penalty McSorley received was well deserved. Within seconds, I became McSorley's personal punching bag. I was in survival mode the instant he jackhammered me with his initial punch. I was flinging my arms as wildly as I could to make it look like I was putting up a good fight, but this was no contest. One of McSorley's punches struck me between the eyes, and I remember my screen went blank. I lost my eyesight for a second or two. It was as if a light switch had been turned off. I could hear everything around me, and I knew what was happening, but there was total blackness.

In retrospect, I wonder whether I sustained a concussion on that McSorley punch. Because it happened more than 20 years ago, I can't remember whether I experienced headaches or any other symptoms that we would associate today with a concussion. Back then, we weren't as aware of concussion symptoms, and I know I stayed in the lineup even when I wasn't feeling quite right.

During my battle with McSorley, I remember thinking I just had to hang on until my teammates could rescue me.

It didn't take me long to realize that if I was going to play the Tasmanian Devil style that Keenan wanted me to play, I was going to have to fight from time to time. I'm proud that I have 40 fighting majors to go with my 513 NHL goals. I also fought Ulf Samuelsson, Garth Butcher, Darcy Tucker and Robyn Regehr, among others.

According to hockeyfights.com, I even had a fight against current

Penguins coach Dan Bylsma when he was playing for Los Angeles, on the day after Christmas in 1999. I don't have any memory of that fight, which didn't last long, according to the Internet. But if I had to theorize as to why I fought Bylsma, I would say it was because I had a general dislike for defensive-style forwards. When I faced a forward whose sole purpose in life seemed to be to prevent me from scoring, my strategy was often to skate toward one of his teammates and chop him on the ankles. The result would be that I would have two opponents trying to deal with me, which usually meant that one of my linemates then had open ice.

The problem with that strategy is that it often meant I had two angered opponents looking to fight me. I don't know for sure if that happened with Bylsma, but it is a reasonable theory. Usually, the people who wanted to fight me believed they had a just provocation.

I wasn't one of those guys who sized up who my opponent was before I decided whether to fight or not. Sometimes it felt like I was a flyweight competing in the heavyweight division. My second fight was against tough guy Craig Berube, and I scrapped twice against the late Bob Probert, who might have been the baddest fighter in NHL history. Whenever I fought someone that Keenan believed was out of my weight class, he would say, "Jeremy, I admire your courage and question your intellect."

It's not as if I enjoyed fighting, because I clearly didn't. But I believed that if I was going to buzz about the ice running into people, then I was going to have to pay a price. Most of my fights came about because I was just an irritating presence. In the 1990s, it was still the tough guys keeping the law and order. When I hit a Detroit Red Wings player, I knew policeman Probert would be looking for me.

The first time I fought Probert, he had come after me because I had caught him with some solid hits. As I recall, he was also mad at me for flattening Shawn Burr. Probert decided he had put up with me long enough, and he began to chase me down. I could hear him calling me out, and inexplicably, I just turned around and dropped the gloves. The whole scene is available on YouTube.

After the game, the big question my teammates had for me was, "What were you thinking?"

What I was thinking is that pain is temporary, while pride is forever. That was my motto in those situations. I would rather be the player who got his ass kicked once in a while than the guy who skated away because he was afraid. My attitude is that as long as I'm going to wake up the next morning, I can accept black eyes, bruises and scars as the cost of doing business in the NHL.

The worst beating I took in an NHL fight probably came from Darcy Tucker when I was playing for Philadelphia. Tucker tattooed me with a couple of hard punches. One of his uppercuts nailed me square on the chin. I think I rose up an inch off the ice.

I had a wild fight against Scott Walker, who is a scrappy, tough customer. The fight, which happened in the first period, started in my zone, and when we finished we were in his zone. It seemed like the fight lasted a minute and a half. When the battle was over, I remember that I was spent. I was totally worthless as a player the rest of the night. I was totally gassed. I couldn't move my fingers or arms very well.

Fights in the NHL often occur because one player is standing up for his teammate or making an opponent pay for unacceptable behaviour on the ice. But even if they occur for those reasons, the primary reason for the fight could be that the players dislike each other. You are always more willing to defend a teammate if the guy you have to fight is someone you can't stand.

Bryan McCabe, then with Chicago, started a fight with me on March 6, 2000, and said after the game that he did so in retaliation for my high stick against Tony Amonte five months before.

"[Roenick] had to be held accountable for what happened," McCabe told the *Chicago Tribune* after the game. "No one forgot about that. We know each other, so we know it is just part of the game. I think he even knew it was coming with the score 6–2 [at the time]. He knows what he did, and I was just trying to keep him honest."

What McCabe didn't say was the truth: that he came after me because he didn't like me. The feeling was mutual. McCabe came after me every time we played. He was a hard-nosed player. We were both cocky. We were always trash-talking. I would tell him how badly I thought he was playing, and he would tell me I was overrated.

The Amonte factor may have been the official reason he attacked me, but it wasn't the only reason. Trust me on that.

I'm guessing that fight didn't go quite the way McCabe thought it would. Remember, I was playing for Phoenix then, meaning I wasn't the hometown boy of the *Chicago Tribune*. But *Tribune* writer K. C. Johnson said, "Roenick held his own against the slightly bigger McCabe, perhaps even squeezing out a close decision in the bout."

My position on fighting is that it is a necessary and entertaining aspect of hockey. I like the tradition of two guys spontaneously throwing down their gloves in the heat of the moment. I respected opponents who came after me when I had wronged them. That's the way it should be done. However, I don't believe we still need players on the roster whose only job is to fight. I hate saying that, because I've known fine men who have played that role for many years.

In all of my years playing in the NHL, I've never had a fighter on my team that I didn't like. Usually, the team's fighter is the most popular guy in the dressing room, and not just because he protects his teammates. Fighters are often the nicest players in the dressing room. I've found fighters' personalities to be a sharp contrast to the image they portray on the ice. When I played against Probert, he seemed like a wild-eyed, vicious thug. But when I played one season with him in Chicago, my attitude about him changed. He seemed like a gentle giant, a pleasant man with a big heart. If you met him in the dressing room, he would strike you as the guy you would want as your neighbour.

There was no one more neighbourly than longtime Chicago tough guy Stu Grimson, who also didn't fit the profile of the typical NHL fighter. Grimson was a born-again Christian who had 234 penalty minutes when the Blackhawks reached the Stanley Cup final in 1991–92. He was a 240-pound enforcer who never flinched against Probert or any of the league's best fighters. He fought hard. But he didn't swear. He didn't carouse. He is the player featured in a television spot for the Foundation for a Better Life, where he receives a call from his daughter in the dressing room and then sings "Itsy-Bitsy Spider" to her between periods. It is a fictional event, but it was certainly a plausible scenario for Grimson. I never had the impression that he loved his role as a fighter, but he cherished his role of being a teammate. And he was a quality teammate. He was a jokester, the kind of guy who tries to lift the spirits of a teammate when he was down.

In newspaper stories, he said he had reconciled his Christian lifestyle with his job as a fighter by viewing himself as a protector.

"Jesus was no wimp," he said once in a newspaper interview, adding, "If there has to be a player in this team environment that sticks up for the smaller man, or the less physical athlete, why wouldn't it be a Christian?"

Grimson said when a teammate was taken advantage of, he felt it was his duty to set things straight.

Religion isn't usually a good fit in an NHL dressing room, where the language is often blue and the jokes off-colour. But it was never an issue with Stu, who never pushed his religious beliefs on anyone. It was hard to find anyone who didn't like Grimson.

Some fighters I've known did fit the stereotype of the wacko guy who became a fighter because he liked being a tough guy. Greg Smyth was a Blackhawks fighter for a while, and he seemed to like the role. He was one of the most entertaining teammates I've ever had. Everyone loved him as well, for different reasons. We called him Bird Dog. We used to say he was crazier than a shithouse rat.

In the early 1990s, the Blackhawks were still flying on commercial flights. We went to the airport, checked in for our flight like everyone else, and then started trading seats with other passengers to get six seats across to facilitate our card game. Most of us would always be mindful of the reality that we were sitting among other paying customers; we tried to keep our voices low and our swearing to a minimum. Smyth didn't care where we were or what we were doing. He was going to be who he was, regardless of the situation. If we were playing cards for money and he lost, he would cuss loudly enough for everyone on the plane to hear.

One time, a passenger in front of us heard one too many curse words from Smyth and turned around and barked at him to "watch your language!"

"No fuckin' way," Smyth screamed back at him.

The passenger sunk in his seat, and we were all stifling our giggles. Smyth wouldn't back down from the league's toughest fighters. He certainly wasn't going to let a civilian tell him what to do.

The men who fight for a living in the NHL are some of the most interesting and likeable men I've ever met. It's hard for me to say NHL tough guys don't deserve the jobs they have today. I don't believe the NHL has outgrown fighting, but I think it has outgrown players whose sole hockey function is to fight.

My confrontation and feud with Berube started because of a battle I was having with his goalie, Ron Hextall. I ran Hextall into the net, and Flyers coach Paul Holmgren blew a gasket. He ordered Berube to go after me. There was no invitation to dance. He just grabbed me and we started fighting. But we didn't throw many punches before we were engulfed in a big scrum involving all of the skaters on the ice. When the linesmen interceded to break up the scuffle, I suddenly realized that Berube was being restrained by officials and I had my right arm free.

Berube was in a vulnerable position. I remember weighing whether I should hold back or launch my best right cross. I opted for the cheap shot. I cold-cocked Berube when he was totally defenceless. Berube was furious, but he couldn't come after me because the linesman had him in a bear hug. That encounter came in 1990, and for the next few years Berube was always looking for his chance to make me pay.

Every time we played Philadelphia, Berube was always trying to get on the ice against me. It didn't happen very often, because I was usually playing against Philadelphia's top players and he was a fourth-liner. But when I was on the ice, I could hear him calling for the winger to cut his shift short to allow him the opportunity to jump on the ice and chase me. If he got on the ice, and I got off, then he would skate quickly to the bench. If he would have caught me, I would have fought him. But I wasn't going to make it easy for him. He chased me for years, but I was always able to elude him. As time marched on and Berube played for other teams, I wondered whether he had forgotten. Could he carry a grudge for a decade? I received my answer in 2003, when Berube was a player/coach for the Philadelphia Phantoms while I was playing for the Flyers.

He came into the Flyers' dressing room, and I said, "Hey, what's up, Chief?"

He responded by hammering me in the fucking mouth with a vicious punch. He knocked me right on my ass.

My teammates were so shocked that the entire room went quiet. Before anyone in the dressing room could even react, Berube had reached down, pulled me up and said, "Now we are even."

He had waited 11 years for his revenge. There was no inclination on my part to further escalate the feud by coming back at him. I rubbed my mouth and said, "I should have known that was coming."

# CHAPTER 18

# To Live and Die in L.A.

When I joined the Los Angeles Kings, the prevailing wisdom seemed to be that I was born to play in Southern California. It was like Elvis moving into Graceland or P.T. Barnum settling into his first big top. I am an entertainer, and L.A. is the entertainment capital of the world. It seemed like the perfect market for me, particularly when you consider that I was kicking around the idea of getting into acting when my NHL career was finished. I like to be a person who knows people, and many of the interesting people to know are located in the zip code 90210.

The Associated Press story on the trade led with the sentence "Jeremy Roenick is going Hollywood."

Since Gretzky left town, the Kings had been seeking a colourful star to help on and off the ice. They thought I was that guy, and I believed I was that guy. After the deal was completed, Kings star Luc Robitaille told the *Los Angeles Times*, "This guy is 'Showtime.' This guy is Magic Johnson."

It wasn't as if I wanted to leave Philadelphia. But the Flyers wanted to pursue unrestricted free agent Peter Forsberg, and they needed to clear space to fit him under a $39 million salary cap. I was the logical choice to move out because my salary was $4.94 million. The problem for the Flyers was that my contract had a no-trade clause.

Bob Clarke, the Flyers general manager at the time, had to call and ask me to waive it. I made it easier for Clarke by telling him that I completely understood why the Flyers wanted Forsberg. I told Clarke I thought it was a great move to bring in Forsberg. He was still one of the world's best players, and he was three and a half years younger than me. I was coming off a concussion. There was no reason for me to stand in the way of the Flyers landing Forsberg.

Throughout my career, even if I didn't agree with decisions that some of my teams have made, I respected their right to run their businesses as they saw fit. The only request I made of Clarke was that he try to trade me to a Western Conference team that was closer to my home in Arizona. He said he would do that.

When he called to say that he had completed a deal with Los Angeles, I was ecstatic. The deal was announced August 4, with the Flyers also giving up a draft pick for what was called "future considerations." In essence, the Flyers were paying a third-round pick to the Kings for taking my $4.94 million salary off their books. The Flyers were paying Forsberg $11.5 million over two seasons.

In my mind, a move to L.A. was the best possible situation for my life and my career. I thought the Kings had potential as a team. They had a skilful, puck-moving defenceman in Lubomir Visnovsky and a tough, hard-nosed defenceman in Mattias Norstrom, plus some talented forward prospects in Michael Cammalleri and Dustin Brown. The team had also signed Pavol Demitra, who was among the league's most productive offensive players for a period in the 1990s.

Demitra and I ended up as roommates, and I loved the guy. Of course, you won't find anyone who didn't like Pavol. He was full of life, and he loved the game. He would do anything for you. He could also be quite funny. When Keith Tkachuk played with Demitra in St. Louis, they were linemates, and I was told they sometimes bickered like an old married couple. Knowing them the way I did, I can imagine that their bickering played like a comedy routine in the St. Louis dressing room.

The truth is that Tkachuk considered Demitra a close friend and often had him over to his house. When you get inside Keith's inner circle, you are a quality person as far as I'm concerned.

Each of us have events in our lives that are overwhelming to the point that we will always remember where we were when we heard the news. One of those events in my life was the 2011 Russian plane crash that killed members of the Lokomotiv Yaroslavl hockey team, including two of my former NHL roommates, Pavol Demitra and Brad McCrimmon.

I had been McCrimmon's roommate when we played together in Phoenix. McCrimmon was nicknamed "Beast" and "Sarge" because of his commanding presence. He wanted to be an NHL coach, and he was in Russia chasing his dream. He figured coaching in the Kontinental Hockey League would be a stepping stone toward being a head coach in the NHL.

The news of the crash came while I was at the clubhouse of the Trump National Golf Club, and I almost dropped my coffee. I started to cry as I heard that Demitra and McCrimmon were among the dead. It's still difficult to accept that they are gone.

\*

I thought my trade to the Kings would be one of the highlights of my career. As it turned out, it was probably the low point of my career. I never would have guessed that I wouldn't be able to deliver offensively.

Off the ice, I delivered immediately for the Kings. They wanted a colourful entertainer, and I gave them one. I arrived in Tinseltown with tinted hair and a silver Porsche. The day after the trade, I threw out the first pitch at a major-league baseball game in Anaheim. I said I liked what our rivals the Mighty Ducks of Anaheim were doing with their team, and then added, "But I still think we will kick their ass."

When *Los Angeles Times* columnist Bill Plaschke gave me a chance to modify that quote, I did by saying, "We're going to kick their ass up and down."

The Kings' public relations vice-president, Mike Altieri, was amazed when I booked my own appearances on *Last Call with Carson Daly* and *The Best Damn Sports Show Period*.

When I wasn't scheduled to play a preseason game, I volunteered to walk the concourse to meet fans. After getting over the initial shock of an athlete wanting to hang out with the masses, the Kings' public relations people had me out there shaking hands, signing autographs and posing for pictures. They viewed me as going above and beyond the call of duty, and I viewed it as me doing what I should be doing to promote my sport.

The running joke that season was that if you couldn't find me, I was in the trainer's room, "icing my tongue" to get ready for my next interview.

If you look back at the stories written about me when I came to Los Angeles, I gave every writer a different perspective, a fresh angle, a unique glimpse of who I really was. Kings general manager Dave Taylor said publicly that he was acquiring me solely for my hockey-playing ability. But to me, that was like saying you buy *Playboy* just to read the articles. If a team acquired me, it would seem logical they wanted the flash *and* the substance.

In an interview with the *Los Angeles Times*, I admitted that I dabbled in poetry. I have been writing poetry since I was at Thayer Academy. One of my first days as a King was spent at the beach writing poetry. "Hey, I'm a metrosexual guy," I told *Times* sportswriter Chris Foster. "I have my hard side and my soft side." Foster wrote that there were more sides to me than on "a Rubik's Cube." That seemed like a fair description.

One of my first purchases in L.A. was a T-shirt that read, "Everyone is an actor." In those first couple of months in Southern California, I did a masterful job of playing myself. It was the role I always wanted. It was the first time in my career that I was totally allowed to explore the entertainment side of being an athlete. I appeared on actress Jenny McCarthy's television show and dressed ballet-dancer style, in a unitard and puffy shirt, for a figure-skating skit. Would Wayne Gretzky have done that for the Kings?

When *Sports Illustrated* writer Michael Farber came out to do a story about me, I took him to the Ivy, a happening restaurant where you constantly run into celebrities.

"They get it here [in Los Angeles]," I told Farber. "They understand the entertainment factor."

On September 24, 2005, I created Internet buzz by dancing on the ice in front of 15,000 fans during the Kings' outdoor preseason game against the Colorado Avalanche in Las Vegas. When a sheet of Plexiglas broke during the game, it was taking forever to fix. The fans and players were becoming restless and bored, and when the Bee Gees' song "You Should Be Dancing" started playing, I began to dance in place by the side boards. When the crowd responded, that was all the encouragement I needed. The spotlight found me and I started ice dancing, disco style, toward centre ice.

It was Las Vegas. It was an exhibition game. It was a game designed to promote the sport of hockey. It just seemed like the thing to do at the time. My teammates were howling, and Colorado centre Joe Sakic told me it was the funniest hockey scene he had ever witnessed.

If you looked at my first five regular-season minutes in a Kings jersey, you would have guessed that my career in Los Angeles was going to be an epic success. On October 6, I scored on my first two shots, helping Los Angeles build a 4–0 first-period lead in Dallas. But this was the "new NHL," with no hooking, holding or obstruction, and teams could no longer go into a defensive shell to preserve a lead. The Stars kept coming, and they beat us 5–4.

I also got cut in the game, and the wound needed five stitches to close. Between the goals and the cut, I felt like I was playing the aggressive way I needed to play to be successful in the NHL. You don't get cut unless you are playing in traffic. After my first game, I thought I was going to thrive in a Los Angeles Kings sweater. I could not have been more wrong.

As it turned out, I was blind to the obstacles that prevented me from succeeding in Los Angeles. When the 2003–04 season ended, I was dealing with a concussion, and I didn't work out at all. As my health started to improve, I still didn't train the way you need to train to properly prepare for a season. Honestly, I was angry over the lockout. I was angry with the league, angry with my union and angry with fans who viewed players as being spoiled. To me, it seemed as if everyone had ruined my game. As the lockout progressed, I found myself not giving a shit.

I was so disenchanted with what was transpiring that I had convinced myself that we might lose another season. The proof of my disillusionment was the fact that I planned a vacation in Italy for late August and early September of 2005. When I should have been skating and working out in preparation for the 2005–06 season, I was feasting on carb-filled pasta and drinking wine in one of the world's most beautiful countries. I bet I gained seven or eight pounds in those 12 days in Italy. I weighed around 220 when I showed up for training camp in Los Angeles. I had to lose about 18 pounds, which took me about a month and a half.

That trip to Italy was probably one of the worst decisions I made in my NHL career. It was a boneheaded move.

Injuries played a role as well. I received my 12th concussion in the preseason when I was decked on a hit by Phoenix Coyotes defenceman Denis Gauthier. I was angry about the hit because I believe every player in the game should understand that big hits shouldn't be delivered in an exhibition game. That's where the respect among players comes into play. When we play in the regular season or playoffs, we all realize that players will be trying to run you through the boards. We don't expect that in an exhibition game. I told Gauthier that in a phone call we had on the subject, and he said he had never looked at a preseason game as being different from a regular-season game. He said I also had to take into account that he was battling to hold his job. Fair enough.

That injury was one of the nagging injuries that slowed me throughout the season. Just before Christmas, I broke my index finger blocking a shot on a penalty kill. That injury occurred in a 4–3 shootout win against Vancouver and sidelined me until early February. I had a goal and an assist in the game, and I helped the Kings come from behind to win it. Coach Andy Murray called it my best game of the season. I was just starting to feel good about my play. The timing could not have been worse.

Maybe I was pressing a bit, too, because I knew some fans looked at me differently after my comments during the summer.

The other issue I had that season was with my skates. This is the issue that I've been criticized over, because fans don't seem to appreciate how fussy I am over my skates. I'm a mental case when it comes to how my skates get sharpened.

Throughout my career, I've had two different radiuses on my skates. I don't know how to do it myself, and I have a hard time explaining the way I like them. But if you ask all my equipment guys through the years, they will verify that I need my skates sharpened to unique specifications.

All of my previous equipment guys figured out how to make them perfect. But Kings assistant equipment manager Rick Garcia couldn't figure it out. It wasn't from a lack of effort. He was a great guy. He called my previous equipment guys in an effort to figure out what I needed. I know the Phoenix Coyotes' head equipment guy, Stan Wilson, spent time on the phone with Rick, trying to explain what I needed. I tried to talk him through how I skated. But nothing worked. He couldn't seem to find the right radius or the correct cut.

Throughout that season, I was never comfortable on my blades. Skating was my game, and when a skater doesn't trust the equipment, then he doesn't play with confidence. I didn't trust my feet to do what I wanted them to do. When you are constantly think-ing about your skates, you suddenly discover you have no hands or head for the game. I felt like if I made a quick cut, my skates were not going to hold. My confidence is tied to my skating.

I suffered a groin injury early in the season. Was that tied to my skates? I just don't know.

I'm not telling this story to suggest that my skates were the only reason why I had a miserable season. I'm telling the story to explain that everything that could go wrong did in 2005–06.

One day at practice, we ended up in a striptease shootout con-test. If you didn't score, you had to take off one item of clothing. I couldn't buy a goal. When it was over, I was skating around in only my jock strap. It was like the ending of the hockey movie *Slap Shot,* when Michael Ontkean skates around in his jock strap. No one else came close to shedding as many items of clothing as I did in that game.

It was simply a weird season. One night, later in the season, when we were fighting for our playoff lives against either Dallas or Anaheim, I had a meltdown in the dressing room between peri-ods because we were playing so poorly. I stormed into the dressing room swinging my stick, destroying an electrical fan and a couple of items that happened to be in the path of my rage. I was a ball of fury, and when I was done swinging my stick like an axe to vent my anger, the blade was shredded. The stick now looked like a danger-ous spear with spikes coming out of the end. I went to whip the last remaining piece of my broken stick into the chalkboard, and it struck the rubber part and catapulted right at our goalie, Mathieu Garon. It nearly decapitated him.

Now, what you should know was that Garon was our best player that night. We were down 2–1, and he was the only reason we were still in the game. And my flying stick caused a cut in his forehead that needed 15 stitches to close. I can't imagine what would have happened if my stick had struck Garon in an eye, or in the throat. That was one of my rants gone very badly. I apologized while he was getting stitches. But nothing I could say summed up the regret I had over that incident.

Despite all of my struggles that season, I still believed I would be named to the 2006 U.S. Olympic team. I had helped the USA win the silver medal at the 2002 Games in Salt Lake City. I was one of the leading goal scorers in American hockey history. In my mind, that was enough to earn me a place on the team. But I was wrong about that. General manager Don Waddell didn't select me, and I'm still upset about that to this day. Shane Doan was struggling that season, and Canada found a spot for him out of respect for his previous performances. USA Hockey officials showed me no such respect.

At this point in my career, I could have used some love from USA Hockey, and what I got was the cold shoulder from Waddell. I felt like I was disrespected.

My bad luck continued the entire season. In late March, I fractured my ankle in a game against the Nashville Predators. When the 2005–06 season mercifully ended, I had 9 goals and 13 assists in 58 games. Los Angeles fans have never forgiven me for that season. My numbers were horrendous, but no one can say I didn't work hard or care greatly about the Kings that season. Even when I wasn't scoring, I tried to be a quality teammate and a cheerleader. As a 600-game NHL player, I qualified for a single hotel room on the road, but I offered to room with young forward Mike

Cammalleri. I told then-rookie George Parros that he could move in with me at my apartment in Manhattan Beach.

In the *Sports Illustrated* article, Kings captain Mattias Norstrom paid me one of the best compliments I ever received. "Every player you play against, you have an assumption," he was quoted as saying. "My picture of J.R. was of a self-centered guy. What a pleasant surprise. When he gets to the rink, it's business. It's about being a team, and he always puts that above his own opinions."

Although the L.A. experience wasn't what I wanted it to be on the ice, I certainly had some memorable moments in my one season of playing hockey in Southern California.

Playing on a team with Luc Robitaille is one of the highlights of my career. He might be the best scoring left wing ever to play the game. Never a strong skater, Robitaille still found a way to be successful. He played smarter than everyone else, and the guy always has a smile on his face. It's a pleasure to be around him because he has such an upbeat personality.

I had many fun moments away from the rink. When I went to L.A., I viewed it as the opportunity to expand my acting career. That happened when producers from the CBS television series *Ghost Whisperer* asked me to play an assistant baseball coach on an episode entitled "Giving Up the Ghost."

My excitement mostly centred on the chance to meet Jennifer Love Hewitt. Although I'm a gentleman who prefers blondes, I've always found Love Hewitt to be irresistible. That attitude didn't change after I was able to work with her. She's a very warm, high-spirited person who likes to joke around and keep her co-workers loose.

In my scene, the pitcher collapses on the mound, and my

character and others race to the mound to help. Jennifer is supposed to come out, revive him, and say something serious and moving. At least, that's what the script called for her to do.

Instead, Jennifer decided to have some fun. She ran out and yelled, "Let me revive you. Look at my breasts. Look at my breasts." Everyone on the set cracked up, and it was challenging to do the scene straight after her playful ad-libbing.

In my year in Los Angeles, I also became better acquainted with actor Cuba Gooding Jr., best known for his uttering of the line "Show me the money" from the movie *Jerry Maguire*. A regular on the celebrity hockey circuit, Gooding has turned himself into a decent player. He knows his share of NHL players, and he is known for his sense of humour and his willingness to zing a guy whenever possible. He did it one night at the Ritz-Carlton, when he was on stage and sang a love ballad to me. I believe it was "You Light Up My Life." It was as hilarious as it sounds. He strolled over to my table and stood beside me as he crooned away and batted his eyes at me. It was delightfully embarrassing for a man who doesn't embarrass easily.

I don't get upstaged very often, but it happened the year I played for the Kings and I appeared on *The Late Late Show with Craig Ferguson*. Just as my interview with Craig started, comedian Chris Rock unexpectedly popped onto the set to surprise Craig. For one of the few times in my life, I was speechless. I had long admired Rock's brand of humour, and I didn't know what to say. I was starstruck. The only issue was that there was no time left for my interview. Wearing my "Money Never Sleeps" T-shirt, I can be heard muttering, "That son of a bitch just ruined my spot."

It was during my season with the Kings that I met actor Vince

Vaughn for the first time. I've always loved the fact that he mentioned my name in director Doug Liman's 1996 movie *Swingers*, which stars Vaughn, Heather Graham and Jon Favreau. That movie seemed to launch Vaughn nationally. In it, Vaughn's character, Trent, uses the Roenick player against his buddy's Wayne Gretzky and the Los Angeles Kings in the NHL '94 Sega Genesis game. "I'm gonna make Gretzky's head bleed for Superfan 99 over here," Trent says. Even people who didn't know anything about me know me because of Vaughn's reference to me in the movie. He made me into a pop icon.

For years, I've been told that I was virtually unstoppable in both the NHLPA Hockey '93 and NHL '94 games. I could shoot from anywhere, and I was always running over opponents and no one could take the puck away from me. I've had guys come up to me and say that they got through college by winning money on video-game bets simply by choosing the Blackhawks because I was on the team. When gamers were savvy, they would ban anyone from using the Blackhawks because I was so dominant.

I've been told by many that I was the greatest video player of all time, and IGN Sports ranked the NHLPA Hockey '93 version of me as the fourth-greatest video athlete of all time. As Trent said in *Swingers* to explain his gaming prowess: "It's not so much me as Roenick. He's good."

So, when I saw Vaughn standing along a wall with his buddies at a Los Angeles bar, I wanted to personally thank him for giving me a shout out in the movie. Much to my surprise, Vaughn seemed as excited to meet me as I was to meet him.

I told him I thought it was the "coolest thing ever" that he mentioned me in that movie.

"Shit, J.R.," he said, "I spent a lot of years watching you play in Chicago. You were the man. I put you in that movie out of respect. You're the best hockey player I ever saw."

Vaughn grew up in Illinois, graduating from Lake Forest High School in 1988, when I was first starting with the Blackhawks.

We've been friends ever since that meeting. In the movie *Wedding Crashers*, Vaughn made sure his character was named Jeremy as a salute to me.

Another night, I was at the Sky Bar and I challenged Justin Timberlake to a dance contest. I was hanging out there with teammates Cammalleri, Sean Avery and a couple of others when I spotted Timberlake with his then-girlfriend Cameron Diaz. We were all well lubricated when I went up to Timberlake and issued the challenge, then demonstrated my best couple of moves.

Timberlake laughed. "J.R., stick to hockey," he said. "The one thing you cannot do is dance."

He then did a step move and a spin and offered: "That's all I got for you. You're done. Get out of here."

We were both laughing. Diaz wasn't as amused as Timberlake was. She looked at me as if I were an annoyance, an idiot or a lunatic, or maybe a combination of the three.

That wasn't the only time I hung out with Avery. I found that I liked Avery. I was amused by his caustic attitude, although he could be irritating at times, even if you liked him.

Avery is always his own worst enemy. He wants to be in the limelight, which doesn't make him unique among athletes, but he has a publicist helping him get there. And he gets so caught up in the pursuit of fame that he makes people forget, or not see, that he is a talented hockey player. This kid can skate, shoot, pass and hit.

All that gets in the way of Avery being a successful player is Avery. He wants to think of himself as a bad boy, so he plays the role of a bad boy.

Once, in the L.A. dressing room, Avery entered and walked past all of us as if we were mannequins.

"Hey, no hello?" Cammalleri asked.

"Why would I say hello to you?" Avery shot back. "I don't even like you."

It would have been funny, if not for the fact that Avery was being serious.

I have no tolerance for teammates who don't have the decency to be cordial in the dressing room. We spend more time with our teammates than our families. In my opinion, it's disrespectful not to say "good morning" to your teammates when you walk into a room. After players retire, they often say that what they miss most is hanging out with the guys. I've always counselled younger players to show respect when you enter the dressing room.

The Kings fired Andy Murray in March, and I felt horrible about that. The only issue I ever had with Murray was his ban on wearing hats in the dressing room. Throughout my career, I wore a hat in the dressing room. Call it my superstition. His ban was the most ridiculous team rule I had ever encountered. But I liked Andy as a person and a coach. When players talk with coaches, the coaches usually do most of the talking. That's not how Andy was with me. The first time we met, I had to keep talking just to keep the conversation rolling.

The more I got to know Andy, the more I liked him. He never made you guess what he was thinking. He told you. If he liked what you were doing, he told you. If he didn't like what you were doing, he told you. He was always straight-up with me. As badly as my season was going, he always treated me with unwavering respect. I felt as if Andy knew that I was always giving my best effort, even though the results were not there. He even tried to be tolerant of my horseplay.

Andy always made it a point that he didn't want any quotes from his players that would inspire the opponents.

"No bulletin-board material," he would say before the media came in. And as he was walking out, I would shout, "The Anaheim Ducks were brutal tonight."

Everyone would laugh, and I believe even Murray would snicker.

On the road, he would slide an information sheet under your door, and then he would quiz you the next day to see if you had read it. He never yelled. He never swore. He would say, "Gosh, darn it, guys." Since most of my NHL coaches had been screamers, Andy's style was unusual. I used to swear all the time around Andy just to get him worked up a bit.

But Murray did coach me the way I wanted to be coached. He coached me honestly. We had 79 points in 70 games when Murray was fired, and we won five of our last 12 games under interim coach John Torchetti. It was certainly not Andy's fault that we missed the playoffs by five points, finishing 10th in the Western Conference. Certainly, I shared the blame for Murray's departure, because it's a team game and therefore all players are at fault. But we had several issues, with our defensive play being chief among them. We gave up 270 goals that season, and no NHL team gave up that many goals and made the playoffs that season.

When the season was over, general manager Dave Taylor also was fired.

As badly as my season in L.A. went, I wanted to return the following season. I had too much pride in my game to want to leave under those circumstances. I wanted to come back and be the player that I should be.

When the Kings hired Dean Lombardi as the team's general manager on April 21, 2006, I thought I had a chance to return. We had known each other for many years. Lombardi was a Boston guy. I believed he might give me a chance to redeem myself. But when I had my meeting with him, it was clear that he wasn't the ally I was hoping he would be.

Lombardi told me that he had been one of my biggest fans, and because of that he was "embarrassed" by my performance level. Even though he hadn't been there during the 2005–06 schedule, he tore apart my season and criticized my attitude and the way I had conducted myself in my one year in Los Angeles. The one moment that seemed to bother him the most was my dance in Las Vegas. He told me I had "disgraced" the game.

I took my beating without complaint because I wanted to come back. I wasn't confrontational. I told Lombardi that if he re-signed me, he was going to be signing the player Dave Taylor thought he was getting when he traded for me. Usually, I don't go down without a battle. But I said nothing because I wanted to stay in Los Angeles. I wanted to prove I could still play. I wanted to win the fans over.

After my meeting with Lombardi, I was scheduled for a meeting with his newly hired coach, Marc Crawford. My interview with Crawford went worse than my meeting with Lombardi. As I sat across from Crawford, I remember thinking that he was among the most arrogant men I had ever met. He seemed to be taking pleasure in reviewing how poorly he thought I had played the previous season.

"Why should we re-sign you?" he asked.

I tried to be as honest as I could be, admitting that I had gone through what I called "an embarrassing season."

"But I want to come back and make amends for that," I said. "I plan to be in the best shape of my life."

"What makes you think you can do that?" Crawford asked.

"Because when I commit to something 100 percent, then it gets done," I said.

Crawford looked across the desk at me and said, "I don't think you can do it."

At that moment, I fully understood how Schoenfeld felt when he wanted to fight me in Phoenix. My thought was to reach across the table and punch Crawford. Until that moment, I thought there was still a chance I could play again for Los Angeles. Crawford made it crystal clear what the new administration felt about me. Crawford was also saying I was mentally weak. When I walked out that door, I was fully committed to spending the summer moulding my body into the best shape it had ever been in.

# CHAPTER 19

# Wayne's World

If it is blasphemy to be mad at Wayne Gretzky, then I was a sinner when I played for Phoenix during the 2006–07 season.

The Great One and I both probably felt like we were in hell for the first couple of months that he coached me. I'm guessing he was as miffed at me as I was at him, but he did a better job of hiding it.

It seemed as though Gretzky and I would be the perfect match when Gretzky called to offer me a contract in the summer of 2006. I was five minutes away from signing with Calgary when my cell phone rang and Gretzky and general manager Mike Barnett offered me a chance to return to Phoenix.

Actually, Barnett told me he would give me a contract if I could get down to "your Chicago playing weight."

"I was 185 pounds when I left," I said. "That's crazy. I can't do that, but I can get in great shape."

There was no doubt in my mind that I was going to have an exceptional season. I was motivated. I was fucking fired up to get myself in awesome shape after Los Angeles' GM, Dean Lombardi, said he did not believe I had the same focus on my hockey career as I did in my younger days. But I was even more fired up when Tracy said she agreed with Lombardi. Nobody knows me like Tracy. If she believed I needed to get my ass in gear, then I did for sure. I spent the summer in California training with T.R. Goodman, who trained many top NHL players, including my buddy Chris Chelios. Goodman worked my fucking tail off. I had accomplished what I had told Crawford I was going to do in my exit interview in Los Angeles. I had worked myself into the best shape of my career. I weighed 198 pounds, 22 pounds less than when I arrived in L.A. the year before. My body was fucking ripped that summer.

When I signed with the Coyotes for $1.2 million, I believed Barnett and Gretzky were going to give me an opportunity to show that I could still be a prominent NHL player. I remember Gretzky talked about how he valued my leadership and energy.

Today, I can see the Coyotes signed me primarily to sell tickets. I had been a popular player in Phoenix for five years, and they were hoping that some of the fans who had stopped coming would return if I was in the lineup.

It was clear to me early that Gretzky never had me in his coaching plans. At some points, I wasn't even a regular on the fourth line. On the coaching board in the dressing room, Gretzky would list his four lines, and I would be the guy written off the side. It was almost embarrassing for me to even be in the dressing room. Because of the way Gretzky handled it, I felt disrespected.

Gretzky knew I was angry because I didn't hide it. Sometimes I would go out for practice and just stand by the side boards, near Gretzky as he coordinated the drills. The four lines would be rolling through the drills, and Gretzky would ask, "J.R, are you going to take any reps with the line?"

"Are you going to put me on a line?" I would answer. When

Gretzky didn't respond, I would add: "Then, nope, I'm staying right here. I'm not on any line. Let the guys who are on lines go."

I was like a child who'd had his lollipop taken away. I pouted. Clearly, that wasn't the best way to handle the situation, but my anger sometimes seizes command of my brain. Respect is an important issue with me. As a veteran player nearing 500 NHL goals, I felt as if I deserved more respect than I was receiving from Gretzky. My belief was that, as a nine-time All-Star, I had earned the right to always know where I stood with regard to playing time. If I wasn't playing, I wanted to know before I started my game preparation ritual at the morning skate. Right or wrong, that's how I felt. If coaches have already made up their minds that I'm not playing that night, then tell me before I start getting mentally ready to play. All that I ask is that my coach communicates with me. I don't like surprises when it comes to these situations. If you told me before the morning skate I wasn't playing, I was fine. If you told me later than that, then I felt disrespected.

At one point in the season, my anger reached the point where I started hatching my own conspiracy theories about Gretzky's decisions regarding my playing time. I didn't believe that Gretzky was anti-American, but I started to wonder how he would have treated me if I had been a Canadian star trying to reach his 500th goal. Gretzky is a very proud Canadian. If I had played for his gold medal–winning Olympic team, instead of the silver medal–winning Americans, at Salt Lake in 2002, would he have taken the same approach in dealing with me?

At the 2002 Winter Games in Salt Lake City, Gretzky was the executive director of the Canadian hockey team, and he went on a rant against the American media, European hockey officials and everyone who wasn't supporting Canada. The Canadians were struggling at the time, and he was clearly trying to take the pressure off his team by saying everyone in the world hated Canada.

My response was to say that Gretzky should get an endorsement deal with Kleenex because of all of the crying he was doing. I did regret that remark as soon as I said it, because Gretzky had spent his entire career trying to do the right thing. That was probably disrespectful on my part. He deserved his right to stand up for his team. As it turned out, Gretzky's rant was the right fix for the Canadian team. As the media took shots at Gretzky's bizarre speech, his players rallied. They came together and beat us in the gold-medal game.

Even as I wondered whether Gretzky would treat me differently if I was a Canadian, I'm not sure I ever supported my own thought process. I was just looking to lay blame for my situation. I was trying to make myself feel better. I wanted to believe I was being discriminated against because it's easier to accept than the idea that my coach didn't believe I was good enough to play. But an athlete has to be emotional to play this sport well. Hockey players boil over when their playing time is slashed or when they feel they have no opportunity to redeem themselves. Today, when I look back objectively at what happened that season, I see there was a 13-game span from late October to late November where Gretzky gave me my opportunity. I played 17 minutes or more in 10 of those games. I didn't score a single goal. That's when Gretzky gave up on me. At that point, my ice time began to dwindle and I started to feel like the 13th forward.

From November 25 until January 31, I never had 15 minutes of playing time in a game. That's the period when I felt disrespected, the time when I wondered whether Gretzky could have picked me up rather than keeping me down.

Gretzky would probably argue that I was my own worst enemy at that point. He would be right. My boiling anger scalded Phoenix assistant coach Barry Smith one day when he didn't deserve it.

Once, at a morning skate, I was leaving the ice when Smith yelled at me to come back on the ice.

"Where are you going? You need to skate," Smith said.

"Why?" I asked.

"Because you aren't playing tonight," he said.

This was the first I had heard about that decision. Gretzky hadn't said anything to me about it. My anger was boiling over at this point.

"I'm not skating," I said, adding expletives for emphasis.

"You *are* skating," Smith said, "because you need to do some extra work."

What it all boiled down to is that I didn't feel I was playing poorly enough to warrant the disrespect I was feeling. As mad as I was, I did skate over to the goal line, although not with any degree of urgency. When Smith blew the whistle, I did skate, but it was at a leisurely, holding-hands-with-your-girlfriend pace and not a professional athlete's pace. I took my time skating down the ice and then meandered back.

Smith asked me what the heck I was doing. I told him I was skating, and then we both turned up the volume on the yelling.

"I've been around a long time and I don't deserve this treatment," I said.

He said something to the effect that he had been around a long time as well and didn't deserve to take grief from me.

"I've won a Stanley Cup," Smith added.

"Yeah, as an assistant coach," I said, making it sound like an insult.

I can't remember every word that was uttered after that, but I can tell you that I said some unkind remarks to a man I respected quite a bit He said some hurtful words, and then I added more. It was ugly.

"Get off the ice," Smith finally screamed at me.

"That's exactly what I've been trying to do," I said.

I've always regretted what I said to Barry that day. Although I didn't believe I was being treated respectfully, there was no justification for my taking out my anger on him. I liked Barry, and I certainly respected the work he did as an assistant coach. He had been one of Scotty Bowman's assistants in Detroit, and Bowman is the greatest coach in NHL history. Barry deserved better than I gave him at that moment in my life. Whenever I became angry that season, it seemed I immediately escalated to Defcon 1.

My relationship with Gretzky boiled over when the Coyotes were playing in Vancouver on December 12. I had suffered back spasms in the previous game, but I told Gretzky I was healthy enough to play. At 5 p.m., Gretzky told me I wasn't playing. I was miffed, to say the least. Ed Jovanovski was coming back to Vancouver. It felt like a big game. I wanted to play. Gretzky said he was scratching me because of my injury, but I was definitely a healthy scratch as far as I was concerned.

No question I was mad. After Gretzky told me I wasn't playing, I rode the stationary bike for a while. Then I wished the boys luck, and then I left General Motors Place. I decided to go to the Keg Steakhouse for dinner. I ended up meeting my old Chicago teammate and roommate Mike Hudson. We ate and watched the game on television. I certainly didn't want to be in the press box, where the media could ask me about Gretzky's decision to leave me out of the game.

As mad as I was, I didn't leave the building out of anger. This wasn't a premeditated protest against Gretzky or the team. If I wasn't going to play, then I was going to eat. I was hungry. I intended to watch the game at the restaurant. It became an issue only because someone saw me at the restaurant and called a local radio station. The guys on the air began talking about me being in the restaurant while my team was playing. The radio guys made it seem as if I had committed a crime against humanity. It was blown way out of proportion.

After the game, I rejoined my teammates. We stayed over that night, and I hung out with them right after the game. There was certainly no attempt on my part to abandon my team.

To say I was stunned by the media attention my dinner at the Keg received would be an understatement. It's not as if I punched anyone, or cussed anyone out, or said I didn't want to wear the Coyotes sweater ever again. I ate a steak and watched my team play on television. That was my despicable act.

Gretzky called me into his office the next day and said he didn't think it was a big deal that I left, but it was an unwritten rule that players should be in the press box if they are scratched.

Unwritten rule? I can't recall exactly what I said to Gretzky, but it was something like "Fuck unwritten rules."

I wasn't always inclined to follow all of the rules that were down on paper. I certainly wasn't going to be good at following rules I didn't know existed. At that point, I had been in the NHL for 18 years, and I certainly didn't know there was a rule against leaving the building if you were a healthy scratch. My impression was that coaches didn't like having veterans hanging around if they were scratched. They didn't want them poisoning the well with their anger.

"What, do you give your support from the press box? Give support with pom-poms from the press box?" I said to the media after the incident. "There's nothing that a player who isn't playing can do. If anything, [coaches] want players that are not playing away because it's a distraction."

Even when the media treated my dinner as if it were a federal crime, I didn't regret my action.

"I don't think there is anything wrong with going and having a nice dinner, having a beer and watching the hockey game," I said.

I don't believe Gretzky wanted to do anything beyond giving me a stern talk, but the media made such a major deal of it that I think he felt obligated to suspend/sit me for one more game. He even told me that Vancouver was simply the "wrong place" for me to be out in public while my team was playing. The implication was that, had I done it in a place like Tampa, Carolina or Nashville, it would not have been an issue. But Vancouver is a hockey town. Gretzky also said he didn't appreciate that it put him in an awkward position.

The entire incident bothered me then, and it bothers me today. I have made remarks, or committed acts, that deservedly caused me trouble. But c'mon, going out to dinner?

"I treat players like men and they should act like men," Gretzky told reporters the day after it happened. "J.R., all in all, has been pretty positive. But the reality is, last night he made a mistake."

He said he wasn't disappointed, because he viewed me as "a very emotional young man and a good person." But he added, "But what he did wasn't right."

Totally frustrated by what had happened in Vancouver, I told the *East Valley Tribune* that I would probably retire at the end of the season.

"The way it seems to be going right now," I said. "I don't think anybody would want to give me another chance, to tell you the truth."

Controversy has never bothered me. Thick skin is a requirement if you are going to say what you feel, like I always have. I have rhino skin. But Gretzky has always tried to avoid controversy and criticism. It bothered him to have to deal with this. He kept insisting that he had benched me because I was hurt, and I kept saying I was healthy enough to play against the Canucks.

"He was legitimately hurt," Gretzky told the *Tribune*. "He could hardly get through the game in San Jose. If he were 21 years old and had 25 goals, then yeah, you throw him in the lineup. Reality is—and nobody likes to face it—he's not 21 years old and he doesn't have 30 goals right now, so I was giving him a break and a night off to rest his back, to regroup and come back."

That's not how I saw it. But Gretzky was certainly not the first, or the last, coach I ever disagreed with on the interpretation of how I was playing, or how I should be playing.

There was no question that I struggled over the first two months of that season. I only had one goal in 28 games. But I thought I had worked my tail off, and that's what I told the media when this situation developed. I admitted that I was frustrated by my diminishing role on the team. This is hardly a new player–coach disagreement. The coach tells a player that he will get more playing time if he plays better, and the player insists that, if given more playing time, he will play better and be more productive.

ESPN.com had a story headlined "Roenick benched, future uncertain." The lead sentence of the story was "Jeremy Roenick wants to retire at the end of the year, but he may not have to wait that long." The clear implication was that the Coyotes might dump me. Gretzky killed that speculation.

"I'm never going to tell him to do anything [regarding his career]," Gretzky said. "I have too much respect for what he's done for the game and how much he loves the game. He was the face of this team when it came here, and I want him to enjoy this year. And I want him to love playing here again and living in this city again. As I said to him, down the road here we'd like to have him [as] part of our organization."

Gretzky and I made our peace on the Vancouver issue, but my situation in Phoenix deteriorated, even as I was getting more productive. At the time that Gretzky scratched me in Vancouver, I had played 28 of the team's 29 games, averaging 15:24. After missing the Vancouver game and the next one, against Columbus, I appeared in 42 of 51 games, averaging just under 13 minutes of ice time but scoring 10 more goals. So, my second half of the season actually wasn't all that bad, given the reduced ice time.

Another reason why playing time became less of an issue for me was that my daughter, Brandi, became ill with a serious kidney ailment called IgA nephropathy around the Christmas holiday. She was 12 at the time, and she was one of the country's best equestrian riders. She was hospitalized for seven days, and she only had about 30 percent kidney function. It was an extremely scary time in my life, and it certainly put my complaints about Gretzky into perspective. Not surprisingly, Gretzky was as helpful as he could be during my family crisis. He told me to take a home game off to go to the hospital, and he cleared me to miss a road trip. "The most important thing is the health of J.R.'s child," Gretzky told the media. "That's more important than what we've got going on right now."

Later in the month, Gretzky scratched me. But I was far less hostile than I would have been a month before. As I explained to writer David Vest, "I'm in such a good place right now mentally, especially with everything that I've gone through the last week and a half with my daughter, that I'm just not going to let things bother me. I'm just going to try to enjoy myself and help the young guys develop, be a good role model and a good teacher and a good cheerleader. That's what I do best, use my mouth. I might as well use it."

After Brandi became sick, I was a kinder, gentler J.R. To this day, we have to worry that if she contracts an infection, it could attack her kidneys. Certainly, anyone who has ever dealt with a child's serious illness understands that it changes you.

In late March, when Gretzky scratched me one night against Chicago, I went upstairs and went suite by suite, thanking our season-ticket holders for supporting us. I made up my mind that I was going to contribute, even if I wasn't going to be on the ice.

Looking back now at that season, it's not as if I didn't admire, or like, Wayne, because I liked him then and I still like him today. It wasn't that I didn't respect Wayne, because how can you not respect Gretzky for what he accomplished and how he conducted himself over the years? We just didn't get along as player and coach. I believed he never really provided me the opportunity to be an effective player. That season, I averaged under 14 minutes of ice time per game and totalled 11 goals and 18 assists.

I'm clearly not the only hockey guy who didn't believe Gretzky had the same magic as a coach he had possessed as a player, but I may be among the few who believe it truly wasn't his fault. My observation is that Gretzky already had a full-time job being

Wayne Gretzky, and he didn't have the time it required to become a successful coach. He's a great guy, a phenomenal ambassador for Canada and the sport of hockey. He didn't have any time left to learn to be a first-rate coach.

He was a once-in-a-century player, and that doesn't mean he could be a great coach without putting in the time. Just because someone is a master carpenter doesn't mean he knows how to build a house. You can't teach a player to be Wayne Gretzky, even if you are Wayne Gretzky.

Coaching in today's NHL is time-intensive. Gretzky had so much going on in his life that he had to leave too much of the work to his assistants. He had endorsement deals, business obligations, and he couldn't walk down the street in any Canadian city without being hounded for an autograph. You have to be hands-on to be a great coach. As a general rule, icons don't make great coaches because their days are full just being icons.

Also, it's really difficult to know how good Gretzky was as a bench coach because, let's face it, the Coyotes were a low-budget, below-average team when he was their coach.

As I've stated many times, you can't ever evaluate how I feel personally about a coach by whether or not we had issues when I played for him. Mike Keenan and I argued ferociously all of the time, and today he and I are the best of friends. When you watch us working together as NBC analysts, I think that's quite clear. Jim Schoenfeld and I almost came to blows when I played for him, but I like him as a person. Ken Hitchcock and I didn't always mesh as coach and player, but I think he's a tremendous hockey guy.

The same is true for Wayne Gretzky. I have nothing but respect for the Great One, especially for the person he is. I've said publicly that he was the smartest player I played against. He thought about the game differently than the rest of us. If I were to see him now, I would greet him as a friend, not a coach that once ticked me off.

Over the last couple of months of that 2006–07 season, I repeated my intention to retire, even though I believed I could still play.

For the final five games of the season, I played on a line with Owen Nolan and Shane Doan. We clicked, and I generated three goals and three assists in those five games. My ice time was over 17 minutes for each of the last three games. I hadn't played that much over a three-game span since November. In my final game in a Phoenix uniform, I scored into an empty net to preserve a 3–1 victory. It was my 495th NHL goal. I needed five more to join the 500-goal club, and I told members of the media after the game that I might have to accept the fact that I might not get there, although privately I was hoping there was a chance I might play again.

On July 1, the first official day of free agency, my phone did not ring. It didn't ring the next day, either. Over the Fourth of July holiday weekend, I was in a resort in Coeur d'Alene, Idaho, hanging out in Bruce Willis's bar. The actor was actually there, performing with one of his bands. I was drinking and having a great time with my friends and Tracy when I decided to catch up with *Philadelphia Inquirer* reporter Tim Panaccio. My text to him was: "I'm retiring; is that still news?"

Panaccio called my father to get confirmation, and his response was that if I had texted it, then it was probably true. The *Inquirer* dutifully reported my retirement, and it was picked up by various news organizations. My agent and the Coyotes couldn't confirm my decision, and I didn't return any phone calls. I didn't really want to talk to anyone.

Mostly, my text to Panaccio was meant to be funny, but I really did believe my career was over. I didn't believe anyone still had faith in my ability. But I was wrong in that assessment.

CHAPTER 20

# Reprieve

When I was a young player, Doug Wilson was the Chicago veteran who showed me the ropes. When I was an older player, it was Wilson who threw me a lifeline to help rescue my career.

Mentally, I was not ready to retire in the summer of 2007. But I did nothing to help myself. I didn't spend the summer with T.R. Goodman to send a message to teams that I was serious about returning. I wasn't working out at all. That's why I was surprised when Wilson, my first NHL roommate, now the general manager of the San Jose Sharks, called me on August 10 and asked me to fly to San Jose to meet him.

As soon as Wilson picked me up at the airport, he was probably thinking he had made a mistake, because I was grossly overweight, probably weighing as much as, or more than, I did when I went to Los Angeles. At that point, I had to weigh at least 220 pounds.

Wilson took me golfing, and before we left I stocked the cart with a couple of beers for each of us. Once we were alone in the golf cart, it was clear that Doug didn't bring me to San Jose to drink with him. We had one of the most serious talks I ever had in my career. He didn't pull his punches.

"J.R., what are you doing?" he said. "Your career has been too good to go out the way you are going out now."

I explained the messiness of the Los Angeles and Phoenix situations, but none of my words offered insight into why I hadn't readied myself over the summer to play again.

"What if I give you another shot?" Wilson said.

"You would do that for me?" I asked.

Wilson said he would if I would accept a contract on his terms. He would pay me the league minimum of $500,000. He wanted my head, my heart and my wheels. He didn't want my mouth. "No media," he said. "I want you to come in and only be a hockey player. You are going to keep your mouth shut and just play hockey."

Wilson said he would tell the PR department to keep my interviews to the bare minimum.

"And you can't have one drop of alcohol the entire season," Wilson said. "Not one beer."

When he made that demand of me, I was starting to sip a Bud Light. I stopped the can at my lips and quickly poured the beverage onto the fairway.

"You just saw me have my last drink," I said.

"Do you think you can do this?" he asked.

"I don't *think* I can do it," I said. "I know I can do it. You give me this opportunity and I won't waste it."

At this point in my life, I was ready to make this level of commitment. The month before, Tracy's father, Richard, had died suddenly. I was devastated. I don't think I realized how much I relied on him for support. His death changed me. It made me realize how precious life is, and how important it is to make your life count for those around you.

Tracy called her father's death "the biggest bitch-slap" I ever received. She was right.

After the funeral, I told Tracy that my goal was to be the best husband I could ever be to her. I wanted to take care of her like her dad would have wanted me to take care of me.

Tracy says that she saw instant change. I started to confront my issues head on, instead of ignoring them as I had done in the past. I didn't want to hide from my problems anymore. I let go of friendships that weren't good for me. I finally turned gambling into a non-issue. I embraced what was good in my life, like being a good husband and father. And I threw out the rest of the baggage.

It was easy for me to tell Wilson that I wouldn't drink because I was a man in the midst of major change in my life. And although I've admitted that I had a gambling problem during my NHL career, I don't believe I had a drinking problem. I can see why people could think otherwise, because I have what seems to be a long list of drinking stories. But don't forget that I played two decades in the NHL.

It wasn't as if I was drinking every night I was on the road. There were periods during my career when I didn't drink much alcohol at all. To me, Wilson's demand that I quit drinking was a way of gauging the level of commitment I had to being the best player I could be. I was an older player, and Wilson wanted to make sure that I wasn't accepting a contract just to be one of the guys. He wanted to be sure I wanted to play because I was still hungry to compete.

The Sharks had won 51 games the previous season and then lost to Detroit in the Western Conference semifinals. Doug Wilson was looking for a gritty third-line centre, and he believed I could fill that role. He was trying to push his team to the next level.

The previous June, I had watched Teemu Selanne, who had been selected right after me in the 1988 NHL draft, finally win his Stanley Cup while playing for Anaheim. In 2006, Rod Brind'Amour, drafted before me in 1988, won his Stanley Cup with the Carolina Hurricanes. Maybe it was my turn to win a Stanley Cup. It felt as if Wilson was going to help fulfill my destiny.

Ron Wilson, no relation to Doug, was the team's coach, and I knew him well. We had mixed well when he was Team USA's 1998 Olympic coach. Wilson is tough, but he's a funny man. As long as you are working hard, you can joke around with him.

With only a month to get in shape before training camp, I went home to Arizona and lived in the gym. I lost 15 pounds in three weeks. A couple of weeks later, I called Wilson and told him I wanted to wear number 27, the number I wore in Chicago. To me, 27 was symbolic of my commitment to be a hockey player and not a sports personality. When I wore number 97, as I did in Phoenix, Philadelphia and L.A., I felt like I needed to be more than just a player.

"That's funny," Wilson said, "because I was thinking yesterday that I was going to ask you to change your number back to 27."

The deal was announced on September 5, and no one was writing that Wilson was a genius for signing me. There were probably snickers around the NHL. The general perception seemed to be that I didn't have anything left in the tank. But I knew Doug Wilson believed I could help the team, and I was determined to reward his faith in me. I didn't consume any alcohol the entire season. My weight dropped to 187, and I felt better than I had in years. I scored 15 goals playing on the third and fourth line. I kept my promise to Wilson. I kept my mouth shut. I had fun with the fans. I didn't create any controversy.

I was on my best behaviour all season. I tried to be the league's best third-line centre. Doug didn't want me to be the centre of attention, and I respected his wishes. I tried to be a leader without stepping on the toes of the team's established leaders, such as captain Patrick Marleau and veteran Joe Thornton.

My respect for Thornton was instantaneous. He is an incredible playmaker, and I discovered immediately that he was a good man. He wanted to win. It was clear to me that he was part of the solution in San Jose, not part of the problem. I didn't have the same good vibe about Marleau. I thought he was one of the most talented players I ever had on my team, but he didn't seem to have the level of emotion that I believe you need to be a great player. What was more frustrating, he didn't seem to want to acquire that emotion. He disappointed me with his unwillingness to accept the idea that he needed to make changes in his approach. As someone who understood what it takes to be a great captain because I played alongside Keith Tkachuk and Chris Chelios, I can tell you Marleau didn't have those qualities. Disappointed with Marleau's leadership, I tried to do what I could to be a leader behind the scenes in 2007–08.

One of the more enjoyable aspects of being an older player was having younger players look up to you. Tracy and I pretty much adopted Devin Setoguchi and Torrey Mitchell. They were always at our home. Setoguchi lived with us for a while, and after he moved out he still brought his laundry over to our house. I had serious discussions with those two about what it takes to have a successful NHL career. And I also had some hilarious moments with the players who were almost half my age.

One night, my cell phone rang at three o'clock in the morning. It was Setoguchi and Mitchell. They told me to go to my front door.

No one was there. I left the door ajar and started toward the kitchen for some water. Suddenly, the door burst open and it's Setoguchi and Mitchell, out of breath, wearing nothing but running shoes. They were giggling like elementary-school girls. Obviously, many bottles of beer had been killed in the making of this story. Setoguchi and Mitchell had run naked from their apartment to my house. It was more than a mile. Tracy, sound asleep, heard the noise of their arrival. She came downstairs to discover my two teammates standing naked in our living room. Having been a hockey wife for almost two decades, nothing surprises Tracy. So she said simply, "Why don't you have any clothes on?"

"Because we are having naked races," Mitchell said matter-of-factly.

"Well, put some clothes on, because my daughter is sleeping upstairs," Tracy said. "If she wakes up and sees you guys, she could be traumatized for life."

"We'll do that," Setoguchi said. "But can you answer one question first?" Setoguchi put his arm around Mitchell, and they turned around together. "Can you tell us which one of us has the nicest ass?" Setoguchi said.

Tracy rolled her eyes and went off to bed, comforted in the knowledge that her two "Sharks kids" were simply under the influence of a very high blood alcohol content.

One of my favourite practical jokes occurred during my two years in San Jose. It involved my efforts to achieve payback against Ryane Clowe for a joke he pulled on me.

We were on the road, and I decided to pull the time-honoured hockey prank of removing all of the furniture from his hotel room. That joke became harder to pull off as the years went by because hotel security has improved considerably. These days, if your ID doesn't say you are in the room, you don't get a key. To get around that issue, I dressed in a bathing suit and went down to the front desk and put all of my acting ability on display. I explained that I had gone down for a swim and I had forgotten my key. I didn't have any ID to show them. This was an elaborate fucking ruse to say the least. They balked at first, but I turned on the charm. Before long, I had secured Clowe's key. Minutes later, I had put together a crew to remove every item from his room. We reassembled it in the area by the elevator. It was exactly the same; we even remade Clowe's bed.

What makes this story funnier was Clowe's reaction. When Clowe found his room empty and his bed in the hallway, he decided he was too tired to put it all back the way it was. So he said, "Fuck it," climbed into his bed and slept in the hallway all night.

Honestly, I believe that I was playing at a higher level in my last two seasons than I was playing in my last two seasons in Philadelphia. Whether you want to believe it was fate or coincidence, my second game in a San Jose jersey was in Vancouver, where, the previous season, I had triggered a controversy by going out to dinner at the Keg when I was a healthy scratch.

Do you think I was pumped up to play that game? In my new role as a checking-line centre with linemates Milan Michalek and Torrey Mitchell, I played 13 minutes and scored two first-period goals on three shots in a 3–2 win against the Canucks. When the game was over, Wilson came into the dressing room and shouted that "J.R. needs to take everyone to the Keg for a steak dinner . . . or at least the coaches."

The local media wanted to turn my production into an atonement story, and I obliged. They asked me which was more satisfying: my night at the Keg or the two goals.

"I don't know," I said, playing along with the storyline. "That steak at the Keg was really good. They serve a really good steak. There's no question about that. But I will take two goals instead."

The *Vancouver Sun* story read: "Why couldn't Jeremy Roenick have done the honourable thing and just spent Friday night at Keg Caesars? The Canucks certainly would have been happy to pick up the bar tab." Given all the publicity I provided the Keg over a two-year period, I probably should eat there free for life.

I met some special people and had some special moments in San Jose, such as scoring my 500th career NHL goal on November 10. At the time, that put me in the company of Mike Modano and Joe Mullen as the only American-born 500-goal scorers. Since then, Tkachuk has joined the club. I mentioned to people that I didn't want to score my 500th into an empty net. I probably should have said I didn't want to score my 500th because of a strange bounce, because that's what happened.

In a game against the Phoenix Coyotes, I fired the puck into the offensive zone and Coyotes goalie Alex Auld basically deflected it into his own net. The puck hit the glass, the net and then Auld's stick before it slid into the net from a strange angle. At least I was playing well when I scored that goal. The goal came in the midst of a five-game point-scoring streak and a run during which I had at least one point in nine out of 10 games.

It seemed fitting that I would score the 500th against Phoenix, where I had played for five seasons. My 50th goal had come in my hometown Boston Garden, and my 100th in Chicago Stadium.

After the game, I carried my son, Brett, on my back as I skated around for a victory lap. I also told the media that I was thrilled to score the goal in San Jose because "a lot of people threw me to the dogs after last year, and this team gave me a chance."

After the game, I presented the 500th-goal puck to Doug Wilson as a token of my appreciation for the opportunity he had given me. Had he not called me, I probably would have been forever stuck at 495.

It was my coach, Ron Wilson, who had the nicest comment after the game: "It was an emotional moment," he said. "J.R. plays with a lot of passion. To see that joy is inspirational. Our team sees that it's okay to be passionate in the way you play the game."

Although I liked playing for Ron, it wasn't always a smooth ride for the two of us. During the 2008 playoffs, we played the Calgary Flames in the first round and we weren't at the top of our game. We were all on edge, and Ron screamed at me during game five because he believed I had taken a long shift. I screamed back, using my full arsenal of expletives, because he was fucking wrong in his assessment. I had only been out there 25 seconds or so because the centre before was late coming off.

Between periods, I went into his office and told him I didn't fucking appreciate the way he screamed at me on the bench when I was innocent of the fucking charge. Then I unleashed a string of foul language that would have made a prison guard blush. Ron didn't budge an inch and told me profanely that I had no right to speak to him like that. He climbed into the gutter with me, and we pounded each other with foul language and insults. What happened next probably is what earned me a benching. Ron is a memorabilia collector, and his office contained several historically significant artifacts he had picked up during his career.

Among them was a game-used stick he had been given by New Jersey Devils goalie Martin Brodeur. I grabbed the stick and flung it against the wall. At that point, I believe Ron may have momentarily lost his mind when he saw the Brodeur stick airborne.

It's never easy to explain how I could lose control of my emotions in those situations. Unquestionably, I was frustrated because I hadn't been playing poorly in that series. But you also have to take into account that, even after 19 years, I still played hockey with molten passion. I was still flying around the ice, breathing fire and looking for prey. It's not easy to turn off the passion between periods. When I'm in my battle mode, I'm not going to take kindly to a coach wrongly second-guessing something I did, or didn't, do.

When I'm fired up, it's not in me to say, "Geez, Ronny, you may have a point there about the shift length. I will try to work on that." It's not going to happen that way. When I'm in my competitive mode, my mouth is a flamethrower and I fire at will.

Luckily, the Brodeur stick wasn't broken, but I felt terrible after it happened. Ron loved his items, and I had shown disrespect to a coach I liked and admired.

Considering that I didn't have a single point in the first five games of the series, Ron might have already been thinking he was going to scratch me for game six in Calgary. But I certainly gave him another reason to take me out of the lineup. Like the professional he is, Ron brought me in to tell me I was sitting out the game. He said he didn't have to give me a reason. "But I think you know why you are sitting out," he said.

Leaving his office, I remember thinking I was either getting benched because he was pissed off that I threw his Brodeur stick or because I was brutal. Probably, I was scratched for both reasons.

If Wilson hoped to motivate me with the benching, it definitely worked. When we lost game six in Calgary, I made up my mind that I would be a difference-maker in game seven if given the chance. On the morning of that game, in San Jose, Ron sent me a text predicting I was going to have a big game. At the morning skate, Ron gathered everyone around and said none of us should worry because we were going to be carried that night by a player who had netted more game-seven goals than most players in NHL history.

He was talking about me. At that time, I had scored four goals in game sevens. As it turned out, Ron was accurate in his forecast, because I had one of the best playoff performances of my career, netting two goals and two assists in San Jose's 5–3 win.

With San Jose trailing 2–1, I fired a low shot through Setoguchi's screen to beat Calgary goalie Miikka Kiprusoff to tie the game. We'd been struggling on the power play (4-for-27) through the first six games of the series, and Wilson rewarded my goal by putting me on the power-play unit. Three minutes after my first goal, I found some open ice and blistered a high shot past Kiprusoff to give us a 3–2 lead.

At the time, only Glenn Anderson (with seven) had scored more goals in seventh games of playoff series than my six. Although I played only 12 minutes in the game, my four points tied the Sharks' team record for points in a playoff game.

I thought our response to that game-seven challenge against the Flames would launch us on a successful playoff run. It did not. Inexplicably, we lost the first three games of the second-round series against Dallas. We showed some mental toughness by winning games four and five, but we were unlucky in game six, losing in the fourth overtime on Brenden Morrow's goal.

The problem the Sharks have is that they are judged solely on how they perform in the playoffs. It's almost as if anything less than the franchise's first Stanley Cup championship is considered a failure. A second-round playoff exit cost Ron Wilson his job. People always want to know why the Sharks can't get over the hump, and there seems to be no real answer for that except that we weren't on a roll at the right time.

The disappointing finish didn't reduce my enthusiasm for continuing my career in Northern California. I still believed this team could win the Stanley Cup, and I still believed I could contribute to that cause. Doug Wilson offered me another one-year contract, this time for a million dollars. Wilson's willingness to double my salary felt like a true compliment. Frankly, I would have come back for the same salary.

My second season in San Jose didn't go as well as my first, simply because of injuries.

In mid-December, we were playing the Anaheim Ducks, and defenceman Brett Festerling cross-checked me from behind. I tried to stop myself, and my elbow hit the boards. I felt my shoulder pop out. I played the next two periods, even though I suspected I would be out the next couple of weeks.

But I was shocked when the MRI showed that I needed my shoulder rebuilt. I missed 28 games and wasn't able to return until February.

When I returned to the lineup, I was playing on the fourth line with Claude Lemieux and Jody Shelley. We combined for 115 years on the planet. At age 33, Shelley was the baby of the unit.

As a team, we seemed even more ready than we were the previous season. We won the President's Trophy with 53 wins. We only lost five times in regulation at home. First-year head coach Todd McLellan had brought a fresh sense of urgency. But in the play-offs, we lost our first two games at home against Anaheim, and we never recovered. We were knocked out in six games. It was certainly among the most disappointing playoff exits of my career. I believed the Sharks had enough quality players to win the Stanley Cup.

Again, we just didn't seem to be the gritty team that could get on a roll. I'm not sure that there is anyone in the organization who is more at fault than any other. Doug Wilson is a quality general manager, and Todd McLellan knows what he is doing. You can't say the players weren't good enough. We just couldn't peak at the right time.

I would probably be a mess today if Wilson had not provided me with the opportunity to end my career with a positive experience. After two seasons in San Jose, I did consider playing another season.

It's said that athletes are the last to know when it's time to retire. But really it's the friends, fans and family members of an athlete who may be the last to know that it is time for him to retire. In the spirit of supporting an athlete, they sometimes are enablers when it comes to athletes playing beyond their expiration date. Everyone I knew, including teammates, was telling me to play another season. What I needed was a friend who could set aside emotion before giving me advice. Again, it was Doug Wilson who filled that role.

When I went to meet with Doug for the season-ending meeting, I told him I was considering playing another season.

"As a friend, not as a general manager, I'm telling you it's time to hang them up," Doug told me.

He told me I had enjoyed a great career, scored more than 500 goals and proved in San Jose that I could still play. In my two seasons in San Jose, my number 27 jersey was the hottest-selling Sharks jersey. I had done what he asked me to do, and now it was time to walk away. He told me he was worried that the next concussion I suffered might be the one that caused permanent damage.

When Wilson said he believed it was time for me to retire, it felt as if the weight of the world had been lifted from my shoulders. My next breath was the easiest one I ever took. I needed someone to tell me it was time to quit playing, and Doug Wilson was the friend who gave it to me straight. That was more than appropriate. When I first entered the NHL, I was in a room with Doug Wilson as my teammate. When I realized my NHL career was over, I was in a room with Doug Wilson.

Being the class act that he is, Wilson implied that there was a job in the organization if I wanted it. The Chicago Blackhawks also seemed interested in bringing me on as an ambassador.

At a very emotional retirement press conference, I almost broke down several times. Asked what advice I would give a younger player, I said: "Be yourself, enjoy what you're doing. Don't be afraid to open your mouth. Don't be afraid to say what you feel. Be different. Don't be afraid to rock the boat every once in a while. But do it with respect. Enjoy what you do, work hard and love your teammates."

That's really the gospel according to J.R.

My buddies Chris Chelios, Keith Tkachuk and Mike Modano all either called in or checked in with video greetings. Amazingly, Chelios, who is eight years older than me, was still a year away from his own retirement. "I always thought you'd retire with me," Chelios said. "Actually, I might be retired. I just don't know it yet."

Chelios brought up the fact that my mouth had gotten him in trouble on more than one occasion—like the spring before, when I went on the radio in Chicago and said Red Wings coach Mike Babcock, a proud Canadian, wasn't playing Chelios because he was anti-American. Although he said that radio interview was "entertaining," Chelios added: "You put me through hell with the press for a couple days. It's nothing that I'm not used to . . . always answering for you."

There were many moments when I had to fight back the tears, such as when Chelios said no one had been a greater ambassador for USA Hockey or the NHL than I had been for years. That meant a lot coming from the man I call Captain America.

Tkachuk received the biggest laugh of the press conference. When reporters asked me what I was planning to do in retirement, Tkachuk interrupted and said I should go on the television show *Dancing with the Stars*. What he didn't know is that I had already been approached about that possibility.

I've done a couple of rounds of interviews with the producers, and I was offered a chance to participate in the winter of 2011 when David Arquette, Chaz Bono, Nancy Grace and Hope Solo were among the contestants. I had to decline the invitation because I had just signed a five-year contract with NBC, a rival network, as a hockey analyst.

Too bad I never got my chance, because I would have won that competition. I am an excellent dancer. Just ask Justin Timberlake.

# CHAPTER 21

# When the Cheering Stops

When you play for a National Hockey League team, you always have an identity, a schedule and a purpose. You know who you are and what you are about. You wear your allegiance on the front of your jersey, and you have teammates who will be as close to you as brothers and a fan base that usually treats you like royalty.

Your mission is always to win the Stanley Cup. Always, there are workouts to be completed, games to be played, passes to be made, bodychecks to be delivered, goals to be scored, road trips to be taken, team dinners to be eaten, beer to be consumed, autographs to be signed, applause to be heard, people to be met and bows to be taken. It's like living in an adventure movie. Every day, your job is invigorating, exciting and emotional. On some days, it's exhilarating. Then one day you wake up and your career is over. The dream is no more.

Your body is too battered. Your stride is too slow. Your instincts aren't as sharp as they once were. Your sparkle has lost its lustre. A press release is issued announcing your retirement, and then, for the first time since you were five or six years old, you have no team to call your own.

On a Wednesday, you are a million-dollar athlete, and then on Thursday you are fucking unemployed.

I tell you this not to suggest that anyone should feel sorry for a retiring National Hockey League player. In today's game, most athletes who have been wise with their money don't face financial hardship. It's not like the situation of the loyal workers who log 20 years on the job with one company and then unexpectedly find themselves pink-slipped with kids still in college and a mortgage to pay. Those are the folks who deserve our empathy, not an athlete who has made millions of dollars in his career. I tell you this simply to show that no matter how you try to fool yourself into believing you will be ready when retirement comes, it's still an overwhelming psychological event when it happens. Many athletes will tell you that the hardest aspect of retiring from the game is not knowing what to do next. You may have money, but you don't know how you will occupy your time. You have this nagging sense that you don't belong anywhere. Teammates, who seemed like family to you the day before, are moving forward without you; you are being left behind, a casualty of growing older.

Even if you know it's the right decision, you feel adrift, not knowing whether you will drown in sadness or find yourself in paradise. "I'm nervous only because I don't know what I'm going to do in the future," I admitted to Sharks general manager Doug Wilson after we had decided it was time for me to retire. When I first came to the Chicago Blackhawks, my roommate Wilson taught me how to navigate the NHL rink. Now, two decades later, Wilson was telling me how to sail away from my sport. "I've been through it," Wilson told me. "I know how it goes. And with your personality and resumé, you will have plenty of opportunities. You will get to pick and choose." We talked for about 30 minutes, and he advised me to be patient. He told me to go home, let my body heal, and not decide to do anything for five or six months.

Even though I wasn't sure whether I shared Doug's optimistic assessment of my future employment possibilities, I trusted his instincts. He's an honest man, and he would not have said what he did unless he believed it.

While I had no specific "retirement plan," I did have a vague idea that I wanted to find a job where my personality could be viewed as the most important qualification on my resumé. In essence, I wanted to be paid to be Jeremy Roenick. I wanted a job that could spotlight my ability to keep a party going. For years, I had been saying that my objective after hockey was "to try to figure out how to stay in front of the camera."

My former youth hockey teammate Justin Duberman, now an NHL player agent, once said about me: "Jeremy Roenick is an expert on the most meaningless things in life. He can't tell you what our president's foreign policy is, but he knows the words to every song. He knows every magic trick, every dice game, and the rules to every drinking game. Anything in life that is insignificant, Roenick is great at."

Duberman calls me "a vacation from reality." "If you need a break from the reality of real life, Jeremy is the perfect guy to be with," Duberman said.

He forgot to mention that I know more than my fair share of lines from movies, and I'm willing to fully expose myself in the name of giving everyone a good laugh, such as the time I lip-synced Enrique Iglesias's song "Hero" on Michael Landsberg's show on TSN, *Off the Record*.

When I retired, Yahoo.com listed my top 10 pop-culture

moments, and the *Hockey News*'s website listed my top 10 quotes. How many NHL players have had enough colourful moments, or spouted enough interesting words, to spawn those kinds of lists when they retire?

No one can say I didn't try to make it interesting when I played. One night, I had NHL referee Kerry Fraser busting out with laughter after I tongue-lashed him for missing what seemed to be an obvious penalty against an opponent for pulling me to the ice.

"How can you not fucking call that?" I said.

"Because you fell down," Fraser said.

"Do you think I would just fall down?" I screamed at him. "I'm the best skater in the league."

Fraser just laughed at me. From that point on, any time I ended up on the ice, Kerry would yell in my direction: "J.R., you can't fall down because you are the best skater in the world." It was a tough loss for the league when Fraser had to retire, because he was an exceptional referee and a quality guy.

Another time, at Toronto's Air Canada Centre, the Kiss Cam scanned the Flyers' bench and settled on me. Seizing the comedic moment, I leaned over and kissed teammate Mark Recchi on the cheek.

Probably the most famous verbal sparring match of my career involved my 1996 Western Conference semifinals encounter with Colorado goalie Patrick Roy. In game three, I had a breakaway and beat Roy on a slick fucking move that tied the game 3–3. We ended up winning the game in overtime. In game four, I ended up on another breakaway in overtime. On this play, I was hauled down from behind just as I was about to shoot. No penalty was called on the play. If you look at the replay, it was clearly a penalty. But in that era, nothing less than assault and battery was called in overtime.

Roy told the media that it wouldn't have mattered because "I don't think [Roenick] would have beaten me."

When the media came back to me for my reply, I said: "It should have been a penalty shot, there's no doubt about it. I like Patrick's quote that he would've stopped me. I'd just want to know where he was in game three—probably getting his jock out of the rafters in the United Center maybe."

Roy was allowed to have the last word, and he uttered the words that probably defined him as a personality: "I can't really hear what Jeremy says, because I've got my two Stanley Cup rings plugging my ears."

As we got to know each other through the years, I told Roy that was the funniest line I had heard in my career.

My exchange with Roy was really playful, but there was more anger involved when I locked horns verbally with goalie Garth Snow while he was playing for the New York Islanders and I was with the Flyers in 2002.

Snow and I were always giving it to each other during games. We are both ultra-competitive. I felt as if there was respect between us. But the trash talk between us was always R-rated and constant.

One night, after a 3–1 loss to the Islanders, I was upset with referee Don Van Massenhoven because he waved off two of our goals. One of the penalties was a goalie-interference call that came about because Snow was guilty of embellishment. It wasn't even a quality acting job. It was obvious he was trying to sell the call.

"He should be worried about playing the game, not innovating it," Snow told the media. "He thinks he's Brett Hull or something. You should remind him that he didn't go to college. He's a junior guy. So he's not that bright."

Snow graduated from the University of Maine before signing his first NHL contract. He was 23 when he played his first NHL game. I barely made it through high school, played some junior games, but was in the NHL at 18.

When I read what Snow said, I was angry enough to summon Panaccio to offer my rebuttal argument.

"We have to analyze the situation here," I said. "It's not my fault [Snow] didn't have any other options coming out of high school. Second of all, if going to college gets you a career backup-goaltender job, and my route gets you a thousand points and a thousand games, and when you compare the two contracts, it doesn't take a rocket scientist to figure out whose decision was better."

Ten years later, I hear Snow has a master's of business administration (MBA). I still don't have a single college credit. He also is general manager of the New York Islanders. I'm an NBC analyst. If you go to a website called HockeyZonePlus.com, it analyzes career earnings of NHL players, and it says Snow earned about eight-and-a-half million dollars in his NHL career. My career take was roughly $60 million.

Maybe now that Snow has an MBA, he can see that I made the smart fucking decision not to go to college. I don't need an economics degree to know that $60 million is greater than $8 million.

We can still have some fun with this—can't we, Garth?

\* \* \*

As a seven-year-old, I watched Gordie Howe play to the crowd in the warmup, and I never forgot that lesson. Hockey is part of the entertainment business, and I believe players have never paid enough homage to that reality.

Every time I was in the All-Star Game, I had to be talked out of playing without my helmet. I always had to give in because of safety issues.

At least I was able to throw a hit in an All-Star Game—a rare occurrence. I hit Alexei Zhitnik twice.

"Why do you always fucking hit me?" he said.

"Because you are fucking easy to hit," I said.

Always, I tried to be glib in interviews with reporters. My words are usually unfiltered. When I was playing in San Jose, I was asked once why the team was playing better on the road than at home.

"Because our wives and girlfriends are not with us on the road," I replied.

Political correctness isn't always in me.

Fortunately, I've always been a people person, and the entertainment side came naturally to me. I liked having some fun with the crowd during the pre game warmups. Just as Mr. Hockey made my day by dumping ice on my head, I've tried to play with the children in the crowd. I've reached through the photographer's hole in the Plexiglas and grabbed a kid's fries and eaten them. I've snatched baseball caps, worn them in warmups, and then returned them.

When people brought signs mentioning me, I've told them that I liked them. When they made signs I didn't like, I've told them that as well.

One fat lady in Phoenix would always show me a sign that read,

"You suck." My response was to create my own sign that read, "Go eat another hot dog."

Like I said, no one will ever accuse me of being fucking politically correct.

In Columbus, there was an older gentleman who always brought signs to the rink riding me about being in the twilight of my career. When I was playing with San Jose, he would tell me, through the clever use of signage, that I was old and over-the-hill to the point that I should be playing in the senior league.

One time, I prepared for my game in Columbus by making my own sign that read, "Congratulations on still being alive." I pinned it to my chest and went out for the warmup. I skated over to the older Blue Jackets fan and pushed my chest against the glass so he could read the sign.

He started laughing so hard that I thought he might have a cardiac arrest. As it turned out, he knew my then-Sharks teammate Jody Shelley, and he sent word through Shelley that he appreciated my willingness to engage him. He said he wanted to make a contribution to my charitable foundation. Not long after, I received a cheque from him.

Handing out pucks during warmups was a regular part of my routine. When I played with the Coyotes, I would give away 10 or 15 before every game, home or away. To this day, I have people who come up and tell me how it meant the world to them a decade ago when I tossed them a puck or handed their child a puck.

The great Bobby Hull was always known as an athlete who signed every autograph, and I always tried to follow his example. The Phoenix Coyotes hosted a carnival when I was there, and the line for my autograph was out the door. Everyone seemed surprised that I stayed the extra hour or two to make sure everyone received their autograph. To me, that wasn't extra effort. That's the effort we *should* be putting into taking care of hockey's fans. We are selling the sport as entertainment. We should be treating all fans like they are our best customers.

Much to my teammates' chagrin, I even signed multiple items for the adults who flock outside the team hotel, knowing full well these fellows would resell them. I was respectful of my teammates who don't appreciate their autograph being peddled for profit. But my attitude was that if someone can make some money off my signature, good for him. I don't pretend to know anything about the autograph economy, but if I can help someone make a living by signing a trading card, I'm happy to do it as long as the person is reasonable in his request and I'm not pressed for time.

One of my favourite autograph stories involves my random meeting of a Toronto fan named Darcy Walsh who has become a lifelong friend.

In my second NHL season in 1989–90, I showed up at Maple Leaf Gardens for a morning skate, and there was a mob of autograph hounds waiting for us. If you signed everyone's autograph, you could be there half an hour or longer. That's how many fans were waiting for you. I was moving through the line that morning, signing as many as I could, when I came upon a young man who asked me to sign five hockey cards.

I signed three of them and asked him if they were all for him. He didn't say a word. I knew the answer anyway. Dealers pay kids to get the autographs because players were more likely to sign for kids than adults. But the kid was very polite, so I signed all five.

After the morning skate, I knew there would be another mob outside wanting more autographs, and I wanted to get something to eat before my game-day nap. I didn't have time for a lengthy signing session. I found a side door and walked out. But the autograph hounds are highly organized, and they had a lookout on the corner who yelled, "Roenick is on the side of the building."

When I looked up, I saw everyone running toward me. Then I saw the polite kid I had talked to two hours before, getting into a car parked several feet in front of me.

I jumped into the back seat of the car and yelled, "Go. Go. Go." As we pulled away, I told the driver and the kid, "Sorry I jumped in, but I just didn't have time to sign everyone's autograph."

The kid told me his name, and it turned out that it was his friend who had picked him up. They offered to drive me back to the Westin Harbour Castle. When I got out of the car at the hotel, I told young Darcy: "Don't go down and hang out with those autograph hounds anymore. The next time I come to town, just call me at the Westin Harbour Castle. You and I will go to breakfast and then I will take you to the rink."

The next time I came to Toronto, there was a message on my phone. "Mr. Roenick, this is Darcy."

I called him, took him to breakfast and brought him with me to the rink. You can imagine what those autograph hounds thought when they watched Darcy climb out of the cab with me. I brought him into the dressing room, got him tickets. I met with him almost every time I played in Toronto, and we remain friends to this day.

Darcy has seen some nutty shit hanging out with me through the years. He was with me one cold fucking day outside the Air Canada Centre, when a crowd of about 75 people broke into spontaneous applause because I stayed 30 minutes and signed autographs for everyone there. I think it was minus-20 that day.

Another time in Toronto, Darcy and I were driving on Lawrence Avenue, trying to merge onto the Allen Expressway, when we were held up by a driver who stopped to shout at someone in another car. I started yelling at the guy. He yelled back. Expletives escalated, and I decided to get out of the car. Not sure what the fuck I was intending to do. He exited his car and started coming toward me, and he was a big fucking man, probably weighing 220 pounds. He looked like he was ready to fight me. Can't say for sure what I would have done had he started swinging at me.

When he was close enough to see me, he recognized me and said, "Sorry, Jeremy, didn't know it was you."

He immediately backed off. We both retreated to our cars. I was grateful that I hadn't gotten myself into trouble. My would-be sparring partner apparently had other feelings. Just before he sped off, he yelled: "Fuck you, Roenick, I never did like you."

We still laugh about that.

It seems as if I've had several memorable moments in Toronto, like the time in 2004 when I received a flower delivery at the Royal York hotel at five o'clock in the morning.

When I heard the knock at the door and looked at the clock, I suspected something was up. Toronto radio stations were well known for pulling pranks on opposing players when they came to town. Usually, these involved wake-up calls in the wee hours of the morning or a prank designed to prevent a player from getting a good night's sleep.

As I walked to the door, I could actually hear the man through the door, talking to the radio hosts back at the studio.

"Who's there?" I asked, deciding to play along.

"Delivery for Mr. Roenick," he said in his best professional voice.

"At five o'clock in the morning?" I asked.

He mumbled some explanation, but I didn't hear it because I was already headed to the bathroom. I grabbed the wastepaper basket and filled it with water. I walked back to the door, opened it, and threw the bucket of water at the guy.

"Looked like the flowers needed water," I said, before slamming the door.

Fifteen minutes later, there was another knock. When I opened the door, the drenched man was standing there. "This is really pushing it, I know," he said, "but the guys at the studio want to talk to you."

Much to his surprise, I took the phone and talked for 10 minutes with the guys, who were laughing nonstop about their buddy getting soaked. They thought I was the coolest guy for adding my own touch to their gag. To me, it was always fun during the playoffs to also be sparring with the other team's media and fans.

To say I'm spontaneous is an understatement. If I get myself into trouble, it's usually because I do something crazy just for laughs.

I've had my share of wild-ass moments, like the time in the summer of 2010 when I removed all of my clothes on the 13th hole of the Atlantic City Country Club. Playing with my former teammate Rick Tocchet, I badly hooked my second shot and the ball plunked in the middle of a water hazard.

Irate over my horseshit shot, I attempted to fling my Nike 3-wood down the course as if I were competing in a track-and-field hammer throw. The problem was that I held onto it just a second too long. I hooked my throw, and my club followed my ball into the water.

Tocchet thought the entire scene was hilarious, particularly when I started to remove my clothes.

"What the fuck are you doing?" he asked.

"I'm going in the water to get my club," I said.

"Buy a new fucking club," he said.

"I like the club and I have five holes to go," I said. "I'm getting that club out of the fucking water."

Picture me standing bare-assed on the fairway, arguing with Tocchet, and imagine what people were thinking as they arrived at the tee box behind us.

Tocchet's laughter was out of control as I tiptoed into the water to find my club.

My club landed in water that was seven or eight feet deep, and it was the murkiest, foulest water you can imagine. I almost threw up when I came up from my first dive attempt. If I had opened my eyes in that water, I think I would have gone blind. Luckily, I knew where the club had entered the water and I found it on my second dive. Tocchet has a photo of me standing buck naked in the water, holding up my club.

I may be 42 years old, but I can still act like a teenager from time to time.

Although it sounds silly saying it, I thought I could make another living by being me. What I didn't know, exactly, was how to do it. I had dabbled in acting, appearing on the television shows *Heist*,

*Hack, Arli$$, Leverage, Ghost Whisperer* and *Being Frank*. I had talked about trying to land my own talk show, figuring my expansive knowledge of useless shit could serve me well if I were trying to conduct an interview or carry on a conversation with a celebrity from Hollywood or the sports world.

But the most logical career path for me was to go into television as a hockey analyst.

Wilson was right when he said offers would come. I had some phone calls from teams, and there were several opportunities in Canada. One of the calls came from the producers of the CBC television show *Battle of the Blades,* which featured former hockey players serving as partners for elite figure skaters in a competition similar in approach to *Dancing with the Stars.*

Originally, the producers wanted me to be a competitor in season two. My answer was a quick, "No, thank you." I had no interest in wearing skates again. As soon as I announced my retirement, it was like I had an instant hatred of skating. The idea of putting on my skates again, for any reason, is revolting. I don't want to lace 'em up to skate on a pond. I'm not going to play in a beer league for fun. If I'm not playing at the highest level, I'm not wearing skates.

But my reaction was different when producers offered me the opportunity to be a judge on season two of *Battle of the Blades.* They wanted me to replace the famed U.S. figure skater, Olympic gold medallist Dick Button, who left after the first season. What they were asking me to do was to appear on television and offer commentary and opinion about pairs figure skating, a sport I know nothing about. As my former coach Ken Hitchcock always said, I have an opinion about everything. It seemed like a perfect role for me. Producers wanted me to be me, and I play that role reasonably well. I accepted their three-year contract offer.

My role was to assess how the skating pairs were progressing while flirting with the female competitors and poking fun at the ex-NHL players. I did both with equal enthusiasm. The first time former NHL tough guy Georges Laraque appeared on the show, I said he owned the biggest ass I've ever seen on a figure skater. When former first-overall NHL draft pick Bryan Berard showed up with his tattoos, long hair and generally scruffy appearance, I said, "It's nice of the Hell's Angels to let Bryan come and do the show with us."

Mostly, I was in awe of how hard the players and professional figure skaters worked on this show. Former St. Louis Blues player Kelly Chase lost 45 pounds while competing on the show. They have competed through injuries. They have treated the show like an important competition.

The most awkward figure skater was probably Laraque, who happens to be one of my friends. He was such an extra-large athlete that there was concern that the blades were going to break off his skates. As an NHL player, he was all-muscle, all-powerful, all-fuck-you. That doesn't work in figure skating, but Georges gave it all he had.

Berard shocked me the most because he almost won the event. He was always an exceptional skater in the NHL, and he worked at the figure skating more than I expected he would.

The difficult aspect of the job was actually voting people off the show. I know all of the players, and it was hard to cut someone. As competitors, these guys aren't happy when they are told they are gone. Todd Simpson was particularly mad at me when he was eliminated.

The best NHL player in the competition was Valeri Bure. He is such a graceful skater and athlete. He and partner Katia Gordeeva looked like a professional team when they were done.

One of my favourite moments on the show was the night figure-skating legend Katarina Witt was a guest judge on our Halloween show. Katarina is simply gorgeous, and I felt it was my job to remind everyone how sexy she is. We were all wearing devil costumes, complete with horns on our heads. As the show started, I offered that "I'm feeling horny tonight." It was my job to come up with bawdy lines like that. I wasn't on the show for my figure-skating expertise.

Early in the summer, after I retired in 2009, I received a call from an agent named Mark Lepselter who said he wanted to talk to me about my potential in the broadcasting world. He had an idea of what I should be doing with my life after hockey. We agreed to meet in Chicago in July.

This was not a suit-and-tie type of meeting. I wore a T-shirt and flip-flops. He dressed casually. It was 10:30 in the morning when we met in the lobby.

He looked at me, and I looked at him. "Want to get a drink?" I asked.

"Sure," he said.

A minute later, we were standing at the hotel bar. "What'll you have?" I asked.

"Tequila," he said.

I looked at him, laughed and said, "Fuck it—make it two."

Lepselter describes our first meeting as "love at first sight."

After an hour of shots, I suggested we move the meeting to Carmine's, where they always take care of me. For the next six-

and-a-half hours, we drank and talked. I don't think there was a five-minute interval when we didn't have a drink in our hand. He's my kind of guy. I'm his kind of guy. No forced conversation. No awkward pauses. We talked about everything and anything. It was a business meeting, but we weren't talking about business. It was a gorgeous day, and people were stopping by to say hello. I may be retired, but I still have fans in Chicago. Time slipped away, and suddenly it was 6:30. I had a car picking me up to take me to the airport to meet Tracy and my son, Brett.

"We'll kick it back at about nine o'clock," I said before I departed.

A few hours later, we were back at a rooftop bar, joined by my wife and another couple. We gabbed until closing time. As we were walking out, Lepselter remembered he was a businessman and I was a potential client. He asked how much time I would need to make a decision about his proposal to represent me.

"Dude, are we cool?" he says

"Send me the contract," I said. "It's done."

That's the way business should be transacted. Get to know the man. Figure out who he is. Make sure your wife is there to offer a second opinion. If it feels right, go with your instincts.

Lepselter says it was one of the best days he ever had in his business. "At our first meeting, it was like we had known each other for 20 years," he says.

That fall, Lepselter began to pitch my availability to national entities such as NBC and ESPN, and NBC producer Sam Flood was interested. He liked my name, my personality, and that I was a Boston guy. "I will keep Roenick in mind," he told Lepselter.

Oddly, my break at NBC came about because John Stevens was fired as coach of the Philadelphia Flyers on December 4, 2009.

That started dominos falling, to my benefit. To replace him, the Flyers hired Peter Laviolette. NBC had hired Laviolette to be an analyst for their coverage of the 2010 Winter Olympic Games. Now, with an unexpected hole in his broadcast team two months before the Olympics, Flood called Lepselter. Suddenly, I had a career that seems perfect for me. I think being an analyst is about trying to connect with fans and help them understand and enjoy the game.

For me, the most difficult aspect of retirement was losing the dressing room. I miss hanging out with the guys. I miss the horseplay. I miss the cutting humour. I miss the practical jokes.

When you enter an NHL dressing room, it's like living in Peter Pan's Never Never Land. Outside of that room, you have to be a mature adult. But inside that room, you never have to grow up. You are free to talk about anything, including the size of a man's dick.

At one of my NHL stops, penis talk was a frequent occurrence because one of our teammates was shockingly well-endowed. He contributed significantly to our on-ice performance, but if you ask any of his teammates what made this player stand out, they would all say he had the largest cock they had ever seen.

In the dressing room, you would catch yourself staring at it and have to remind yourself not to look. Guys would refer to it as the "Louisville Slugger." Somebody said it looked like a baby's arm, and we laughed at that comment for two weeks.

If this story bothers you, I apologize, but athletes in an NHL dressing room aren't talking about global warming or the size of the national debt. Talk in an NHL dressing room is usually about sex, or cars, or sports. If you listened to 10 minutes of conversation in an NHL locker room, you might think you were back in high school. And if a player is endowed with a rocket-size penis, we are going to talk and joke about it.

It was such an amazing spectacle that I told my wife about it. That's only important because of what happened one year at the team party I held at my home. The guys were all gathered with me downstairs, drinking much more than we should. In an alcohol-induced moment of hilarity, I convinced my well-endowed team-mate to haul out the Louisville Slugger and hang it out of his pants as my wife, Tracy, was descending down the stairs on the way to the wine cellar. Tracy had to walk past us to reach her destination. Considering she was talking to us as she came down, I wondered if she would even notice. But I should have known that you can't miss the Louisville Slugger. She took a step away from the stairs, shrieked "Oh my God" and headed back up the stairs. Meanwhile, we were all laughing our tails off.

I'm not sure she has forgiven me for that humorous moment, and mentioning it in this book probably won't help. I don't believe Tracy has ever recovered.

In the dressing room, there is always something going on that keeps the boys loose. On one of the teams I played on, there was a contest held to see which player could jerk off the most times on a road trip. True story. But I'm not going to reveal the team or the players. The contest was called "The Knuckle Cup." The plan was hatched as we boarded a flight to begin a trip. The rules were laid out as our plane was hitting cruising altitude. Obviously, it would be the honour system of counting. Everyone had a good laugh. The contest was forgotten for a couple of minutes, until one of the most popular veterans exited the airplane bathroom and yelled, "One."

Every fucking guy on the team was rolling in the aisle.

One of my teammates claimed to have scored a 13 on one day of the competition. His explanation: "I was a healthy scratch—what can I say?"

# CHAPTER 22

# Friends and Enemies

When Norelco officials hired me to act in a humorous commercial involving NHL playoff beards in 2012, they also asked me to pick a former NHL star to appear alongside me. My first choice was Mike Modano.

People always assumed that I hated Modano because I viewed him as my biggest rival. But the truth is I liked Modano, even in the days when it was my personal mission to staple his ass to the boards.

As we were filming the commercial and telling war stories about playing in the NHL, Modano's take was always, "J.R. was always trying to kill me." Maybe I was. There's no question that I was envious of his talent. He was the most effortless, graceful skater I ever saw. He was like a fucking eagle. He just flew over the ice. He had great hands, and he seemed fucking flawless when he was stickhandling pucks, receiving pucks, passing pucks or shooting pucks. He made everything look easy. The man could rip a 100-mile-an-hour slapshot and make it seem as if he was barely breaking a sweat.

As great as Wayne Gretzky was in terms of offensive production, he never looked as magnificent as Modano did when he was skating up ice.

Since Modano and I were 10 years old, I've measured myself against him. I wanted to outperform him. For 14 years, I believe I was able to do that. But in the end, he caught and passed me. In comparing our careers, he was the better player. He won our competition.

Can't recall exactly when I accepted that reality. But very late in my career, when I was playing in San Jose, I had Modano lined up in the corner. I had him locked in. I was going to run him. But as I started to skate toward him, I opened my mouth and these words tumbled out: "Mike, look out behind, here I come." Instead of drilling him, I just rode him into the boards with a bear hug.

As we both started chasing the play back up ice, Modano yelled, "Fuck, J.R., you have changed."

Maybe I had. Somewhere along the line, my envy of Modano had simply morphed into respect and admiration. By the time I aborted that hit, Modano and I had played on two Olympic teams together. We had been in All-Star Games together. Although we had not really talked about it, we had become old friends.

It was like Larry Bird vs. Magic Johnson in the NBA. Bird has said many times that every morning, he would look in the newspaper to see what Johnson had done the night before. He didn't want to like Johnson. He just wanted to compete with him. That was how I was about Modano. I always knew how Modano was doing. I wanted to compete with him. Over time, Bird started to realize that he liked Johnson. Over time, I realized that I should be grateful that I had Modano in the league to be my measuring stick. My competition with him forced me to be a better player, and I'm sure our rivalry pushed him as well. If nothing else, my two-decade pursuit of Modano proved that an athlete with some fire and determination can compete with a more talented player.

I believe Modano is the greatest American-born player of all time. At worst, he's in the top three with Chris Chelios and Pat LaFontaine.

## My 10 Favourite Opponents

There's no question that Modano is number one on my list of all-time favourite opponents. Here are the others on my Top 10 list:

2. STEVE YZERMAN. He represented everything I thought a captain and leader should be. He was so fucking talented that he always brought the best out of me. I always felt like I matched up well with Yzerman, even in his best scoring seasons.

3. SERGEI FEDOROV. He was a horse, bigger than you'd think he was. He could skate, handle the puck like a magician and check you until you hated him. You didn't get a break when you played centre against Detroit in those days, because you would end up facing Yzerman, and then you got Fedorov the next shift. That's like meeting the bear after you fought the fucking lion.

4. PAVEL BURE. He was always just one stride away from being on a breakaway. He was jet-propelled. I loved playing against the Russian players because they tested you with their speed. I respected their speed, but I wasn't intimidated by it.

5. ALEXANDER MOGILNY. Today we talk about Evgeni Malkin and Alex Ovechkin, but neither of those guys could skate with Mogilny or Fedorov or Bure. Mogilny also had a great sense of where to be in the offensive zone. It's easy to forget that Mogilny scored 76 goals for Buffalo in 1992–93. Regardless of what era we are talking about, that is a lot of goals.

6. PETER FORSBERG. He always impressed me because he was such a complete player. He was powerful on his skates, and you couldn't intimidate him with physical play. He once threw an elbow at the late Bob Probert because Probert had elbowed him. How many NHL stars would trade elbows with Bob Fucking Probert? Bob said after the game that he respected Forsberg for doing that.

7. MARK MESSIER. Playing against Mark Messier was what it must have been like to play against Gordie Howe in the 1950s. You just always knew that Messier would do whatever he had to do to win a hockey game. He was fucking ruthless.

8. PATRICK ROY. Although I know it's not true, it always felt as if I scored every time I played against Roy. I loved the passion he brought to the game. It always seemed like he enjoyed himself on the ice. He was a serious competitor who didn't forget that hockey is supposed to be entertainment.

9. BRIAN LEETCH. One of the best puck-moving defencemen in NHL history. He's among the top five players in American hockey history. And I was playing against him when he was a little shit playing prep school hockey in Connecticut.

10. TEEMU SELANNE. He is probably the nicest player I ever competed against, and certainly one of the most intelligent athletes in NHL history. That's why he is still playing. He understands the game at an advanced fucking level. He is also unpredictable. You have no idea what he is going to do next.

## *My 10 Favourite Arenas*

1. CHICAGO STADIUM. This is where I developed into an NHL player. I still believe that that old barn, demolished in 1995, was louder than the current United Center.

2. MAPLE LEAF GARDENS. I had more points against the Toronto Maple Leafs than any other team. I liked being in a rink where fans were on top of you. When I sat on the bench, I could have reached over and grabbed a handful of popcorn from fans. When I sat on the bench, my sweat poured on fans.

3. BOSTON GARDEN. Where I grew up, it was home ice. It was where I used to watch Rick Middleton play. It was where I dreamed about becoming an NHL player. It felt like Original Six hockey in that building. Plus, the arena had rats the size of raccoons.

4. MONTREAL FORUM. The building had an aura to it. The minute you walked into the Forum, you immediately sensed all the history that had happened there. It was fun to realize you were skating on the same fucking rink where Rocket Richard used to dominate the league.

5. MADISON SQUARE GARDEN. Muhammad Ali fought Joe Frazier at the Garden. The Rolling Stones played there. John Lennon sang there. Many famous people got to perform there, and I feel honoured to have played there.

6. THE SPECTRUM IN PHILADELPHIA. Loved to play there because the fans there do more name-calling than in any other NHL city. Must have been a bitch to play there when the Broad Street Bullies were roaming the ice.

7. SAN JOSE'S SHARK TANK. This arena is the NHL's best-kept secret. It's just a neat atmosphere, with smart, passionate fans.

8. L.A. FORUM. It was the coolest thing to see celebrities coming out to see us play. It was just fun to see Sylvester Stallone, or the late John Candy, or Goldie Hawn with Kurt Russell sitting along the glass.

9. LE COLISÉE IN QUEBEC CITY. That arena tied my youth and adult careers together, because I played in the peewee tournament there and then I played against the NHL Nordiques.

10. JOE LOUIS ARENA. Detroit is Hockeytown, and I feel like I helped contribute to the creation of that image because I played there so often. It was always a highly competitive game when the Blackhawks went into Joe Louis. They had some tough teams when Probert and Joey Kocur played there.

## *Five Goalies Who Gave Me the Most Trouble*

1. MARTY BRODEUR. He was the fucking king in the Eastern Conference.

2. DOMINIK HASEK. Hasek's acrobatic style was so crazy and un-fucking-predictable that I had no clue as to how to approach him with a shot. As a shooter, I had no book on him. You would shoot high, and he would throw up a glove or pad and stop you. Go low, and it seemed like he had boarded up the net.

3. CURTIS JOSEPH. I played against him a lot, and I never had as much success against him as I thought I should.

4. KIRK McLEAN. When he was playing in Vancouver, I thought he was the most technically sound goalie I played against. To me, it seemed like he was always in position. You couldn't get him out of position.

5. MIKE RICHTER. He was as competitive in the net as I was on the ice. He was a battler, and I respected him for that. He never gave up on a shot.

## *My Five Toughest Teammates*

1. BOB PROBERT. He was a teddy bear off the ice and a fucking animal on the ice.

2. DONALD BRASHEAR. Would not want to meet him in a dark alley. He was big, strong and ferocious.

3. GEORGES LARAQUE. I don't believe Georges loved being an enforcer, even though he was scary good in that role.

4. STU GRIMSON. He would pound the hell out of someone and then apologize for it later. Deeply religious, Grimson struggled to reconcile his faith with his profession.

5. MIKE PELUSO. He was tough as shit, but he had a sentimental side. When he was playing for the Devils, and they were winning the Stanley Cup, the TV camera caught him crying on the bench with two minutes to go. He was so happy to win the Stanley Cup. I was so happy for him that I started crying watching him.

## My All-Time Favourite Teammates

1. CHRIS CHELIOS (CHICAGO). He's the player every coach wants on his team. He's the ultimate competitor, a player who put his team first every day of his career. He liked to howl at the moon at night, but was always ready to play the next day. If you went to war, you'd want Chelios in your squad. He reminds me of a fucking drill sergeant.

2. TONY AMONTE (CHICAGO AND PHILADELPHIA). He was my linemate at Thayer Academy, and he ended up playing with me in the NHL. I view him as a brother.

3. KEITH "WALT" TKACHUK (PHOENIX). Everything I said about Chelios, I can also say about Tkachuk. I admired the way he took care of everyone on the team. You won't find too many players who didn't like Big Walt.

4. RICK TOCCHET (PHOENIX AND PHILADELPHIA). Great competitor, good friend, good guy, fun to be around. And he scored 440 NHL goals. He was a 40-goal scorer three times. You forgot about that, didn't you?

5. BRYAN MARCHMENT (CHICAGO). He was a total team guy. He blocked shots, fought for his teammates, played hard every shift, never wanted any personal accolades. He was all about the team. And he was a mean motherfucker when he hit you.

6. MICHEL GOULET AND STEVE LARMER (CHICAGO). Can't separate these two players because they were my first long-term linemates and they helped me become the player I was.

7. JOE THORNTON (SAN JOSE). He's just one of the NHL's great guys, always fun to be around, always very positive. And he's one of the best playmaking centres I've seen.

8. MARK RECCHI (PHILADELPHIA). He was a small player with a big heart and plenty of grit. You don't think of him as a Hall of Famer, and yet he netted 577 goals. He had a true love for the game.

9. STÉPHANE MATTEAU (CHICAGO). I played with him in junior and in the NHL, and he always kept me laughing. One night when we were playing for Chicago, Stéphane and I were in a redneck bar where a couple of locals challenged us to a game of pool for twenty dollars. When we shot pool, we always divided the balls into "stripes" or "solids." But our opponents that night used the terms "highs" and "lows." After the break, Stéphane was confused and

shot the 3-ball into the pocket when we actually had stripes. One of our opponents pointed out Stéphane's error by saying simply, "You are high." "No, I'm just a little drunk," Stéphane replied. Thought that was hilarious two decades ago and still think it's funny today.

10. TRAVIS GREEN (PHOENIX). He and I were the same guy in terms of the way we viewed life. We had similar personalities, and we had the same interests. We both liked to gamble. We both liked to enjoy ourselves away from the rink. Probably had as much fun hanging with Travis as I did hanging with any other teammate I ever had.

## Five Players I Hated During My Career

1. ROB RAY. I didn't like Ray as a player because he took trash-talking too far. When I was going through a difficult time in my life, he went way over the line with what he said to me in a game. Based on what he said to me, I lost all fucking respect for him as an NHL player and a person.

2. PATRICK MARLEAU. He had all of the skill in the world but not nearly enough desire to take advantage of that talent. I should have had his skill, and he should have had my heart.

3. STEVE OTT. The funny aspect of Ott appearing on this list is that I like him as a person and hate him as a player. He is a prick on the ice. He is always chirping at you to try to get you off your game. He's always in your face. He's like a gnat that you can't seem to swat away. No one likes playing against him, and yet his teammates always like him. It's like he's two different people, or that he has an

on-off switch. He seems like a quality person until the game starts, and then he makes you want to punch him in the face.

4. ROMAN CECHMANEK. He would look good in the regular season, and then the playoffs would start and suddenly he was giving up bad goals. In 2000–01, he had a 2.01 goals-against average and .920 save percentage in the regular season. Then, his playoff numbers were 3.11 and .896. The way he performed in the playoffs made me believe he had come to the NHL just for the money and not to play with world's best players and win the Stanley Cup. To me, he seemed like a phony, a true fraud. I had no use for him.

5. OLEG TVERDOVSKY. He always thought he was more skilled than he really was, and he put no effort into making himself a better player. That's why I had to kick his ass twice in practice.

## My All-Time Favourite Games

1. THE 1991 NHL ALL-STAR GAME IN CHICAGO. It was my first All-Star Game, it was in my home rink, and it came days after the Gulf War had been launched. When the fans sang the national anthem before the game, it was the most emotional crowd I've ever seen at a hockey arena. The rendition was loud and animated. There were people crying in the arena and in homes across North America.

2. THE 2002 OLYMPIC GOLD-MEDAL GAME IN SALT LAKE CITY. Although we lost that game to Canada, I still view it fondly. I have the silver medal hanging in my home in Arizona. How many athletes can say they won an Olympic medal?

3. CHICAGO BLACKHAWKS AT ST. LOUIS BLUES, NORRIS DIVISION FINAL, GAME FIVE, APRIL 26, 1989. That's the game where Glen Featherstone knocked out my teeth, and I came back to score the series-clinching goal. I was 19 at the time, and I think that's the night I informed the hockey world what kind of player I was going to be.

4. MY FIRST CANADA CUP GAME AGAINST CANADA, SEPTEMBER 2, 1991, IN HAMILTON, ONTARIO. We lost that game 6–3, but I remember it was just a thrill to be playing against that level of competition. Four years earlier, I had watched Mario Lemieux and Wayne Gretzky play for Canada in their dramatic win over the Soviets, and now I was on the ice against the great Canadian team.

5. THAYER ACADEMY VS. AVON OLD FARMS, 1986 CHAMPIONSHIP GAME. This was the prep school championship game in which Tony Amonte and Jeremy Roenick realized we could measure up to Brian Leetch's greatness. Amonte and I both had big games to down Leetch's Old Farms.

6. FIRST BANTAM CHAMPIONSHIP, 1983. My Jersey Rockets had trouble beating the Chicago Americans. We could only beat them in big tournaments, like in the 1983 national bantam championship game, which we won in the fourth overtime. Even after playing 1,363 NHL regular-season games and 154 playoff games, I still remember that bantam championship game as if it happened yesterday. You play to win championships, and I remember that one.

7. CHICAGO BLACKHAWKS AT MINNESOTA NORTH STARS, FEBRUARY 14, 1989. It felt like I was playing a scene from the movie *Planes, Trains and Automobiles* as I was delayed by everything from a traffic accident to bad weather between Hull, Quebec, and Bloomington, Minnesota. When I arrived, I didn't even receive a jersey with my name on it. But I did get my first NHL goal (against Kari Takko), assisted by Brian Noonan, with whom I'd played summer league hockey in Boston.

8. PHILADELPHIA FLYERS AT TORONTO MAPLE LEAFS, EASTERN CONFERENCE SEMIFINAL, GAME SIX, MAY 4, 2004. I scored the overtime game-winner against my friend Eddie Belfour to clinch the series for the Flyers. Was this the biggest goal of my career? Many of my fans believe it is.

9. CHICAGO BLACKHAWKS VS. EDMONTON OILERS, CAMPBELL CONFERENCE FINAL, 1990. This was game four, where Mark Messier decided his Edmonton Oilers were going to win the Stanley Cup. He cut a few Blackhawks in this game, including me. He was breathing fire that night. I couldn't even look him in the eye. That's generally considered the turning point in the Oilers' run for the Stanley Cup. That's the game where I learned what it means to carry a team.

10. CHICAGO BLACKHAWKS AT PITTSBURGH PENGUINS, STANLEY CUP FINAL, GAME ONE, MAY 26, 1992. Many of my favourite games didn't go my way, and this was one of them. We came into this game on a roll and built a 4–1 lead against Mario Lemieux's Pittsburgh Penguins but ended up losing 5–4.

# CHAPTER 23

# Who I Am

The late comedian George Carlin had a famous routine in which he listed the seven words you can't say on television. On May 8, 2011, I came up with the eighth. The word is "gutless."

That was the word I used on a live broadcast on the Versus network to describe the performance of Patrick Marleau of the San Jose Sharks in game five of the Western Conference final against the Detroit Red Wings. Although my job as a hockey analyst for Versus was to critique player performance, my use of the word "gutless" created a shitstorm of protests, debate and comments about what I should, or should not, say on television.

At the time of my verbal blast, Marleau had no points in the series. My criticism came with the score tied 3–3, after he allowed Detroit's Pavel Datsyuk to steal the puck from him along the boards in the San Jose zone. Marleau then made a feeble fucking effort to check Datsyuk, who was able to feed the puck to Nicklas Lidstrom, whose shot was tipped in by Tomas Holmstrom for the game-winner with 6:08 remaining in regulation.

During the postgame show, I said Marleau had turned in "an

My children, Brell and Brandi, make me the filling of a kiss sandwich. Love this photo.

Tracy snapped this beautiful photo of me with our children, and then she had a painting made of it. The portrait hangs by our bed.

I played with a great bunch of guys at the Olympics in Salt Lake City. Here I am with (*left to right*) Doug Weight, Brian Leetch, Chris Chelios, Mike Richter, Mike York and Brian Rolston.

Posing at the 2004 All-Star Game in Minnesota with my friend Bill Deacon (*centre*) and Hall of Famer Mark Messier. In the early days, Messier scared me to death. He had a mean, intimidating look that could make you tremble.

The U.S. Air Force gave me the ride of my life. I was allowed to be the backseater for an experienced pilot of an F-16 fighter jet. That aircraft pulls nine g's, and the pilot did what he could to make me puke. But I kept my cookies. I felt so sick afterward, however, that I cancelled my dinner plans.

One of my closest friends is John Whitehead (*far right*) from Chicago. We met in Las Vegas when he came up to me and asked if anyone had ever told me I looked like Jeremy Roenick. I told him no one ever had. When he discovered who I was, he called me a derogatory name. I've loved him ever since. Here he is with his wife, Julie (*second from the right*), Tracy and me.

Long-time friends Darcy Walsh (*centre*) and Bill Deacon pose with me. Early in my career, I met Darcy when he was a young kid seeking an autograph in Toronto. Over the years, Bill has been my buddy and my business associate, as well as my caddy when I played in the celebrity golf tournament at Lake Tahoe.

When I moved to Arizona, Bob and Ruth Lavinia were my neighbours. Bob became a father figure to me, and we are still close. Wonderful people.

The night before the Blackhawks held a heritage night in my honour, Tracy had this sick cake made for a surprise party she threw for me. The party, held at The Underground, lasted until the wee hours of the morning. The ceremony was fantastic—with video clips and signs, it felt like a retirement celebration. Fans received Roenick memorabilia. The Blackhawks did everything but raise my number to the rafters.

When Los Angeles Kings general manager Dave Taylor acquired me from Philadelphia before the 2005–06 season, he told me he wanted me for my hockey ability and not my marketing value. But I knew better. This is an example of the photos that ran with the many stories published about my arrival in Southern California.

Tracy, Brett and I celebrate my 500th NHL goal, inside the San Jose Sharks' dressing room. The milestone came November 11, 2007, during a game against the Phoenix Coyotes—19 years after my first NHL goal. Doug Wilson was my first roommate on the Blackhawks, and he was my general manager in San Jose when I scored the goal.

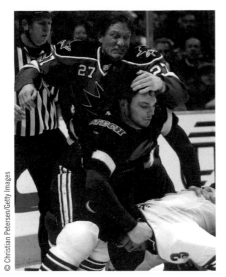

Although I wouldn't consider myself a fighter, I did my share of scrapping. Here, I'm going after Phoenix forward Daniel Carcillo, who was trying to help one of his teammates during a game in 2007–08. That's Phoenix defenceman Keith Yandle on the ice. I don't much care for staged fights, but I don't mind when players defend themselves when the action boils over.

Derian Hatcher (*left*) and I played together for the Philadelphia Flyers alumni in the Winter Classic. After looking at this photo, people have jokingly asked me whether I was trying to figure out how to hit my own teammate.

I'm spontaneous to say the least. After I "accidentally" threw my Nike 3-wood into a water hazard at the Atlantic Country Club, I completely stripped down on the 13th fairway, dove into the water and retrieved my club. That's me, buck naked, after successfully completing my club-saving mission.

What you see here is the pride of Thayer Academy hockey. That's me posing with Tony Amonte and our coach Arthur Valicenti (*centre*) at my U.S. Hockey Hall of Fame induction ceremony in Buffalo. In our last season playing for Coach Valicenti, Tony and I combined for 64 goals and 88 assists. I played 24 games and Amonte played 28.

My family was with me on February 11, 2012, when the Coyotes made me the seventh player inducted into their Ring of Honor. My close friend Craig Conley and I pose with his fiancée, Jessica Bright.

Brett and I ham it up for a picture during my tenure in San Jose.

Rick Tocchet and I in the Flyers alumni dressing room before taking the ice for an old-timers' game at the 2012 Winter Classic. Even with our playing days finished, Rick and I remain good friends.

Here, the Roenick family gathers together for my induction into the Coyotes' ring of honour.

The summer this book was being prepared for publication, Tracy and I celebrated our 20th wedding anniversary.

unbelievable poor effort . . . a gutless, gutless performance . . . zero points in the series, and he has a game like that."

Later, on the *Hockey Central* show, fellow Versus analyst Keith Jones asked whether I believed Marleau was injured.

"He's hurt, all right," I said, pointing to my heart. "Right here, he's hurt."

My Twitter account was overrun by haters, as well as by others who thanked me for calling out Marleau for not doing his job in a crucial playoff game. Some Sharks fans were upset with me, saying I had turned on the team after they had supported me during my time in San Jose. The biggest shock to me about the episode was the surprise that people expressed that I would call out a player, especially a former teammate.

When I was a player, I was more than willing to get into a teammate's face in the name of getting him to play better. Why wouldn't I confront a player when I'm an analyst? Isn't that my job?

Whether I'm an NHL player or working as an analyst in a television studio, I can't be a perimeter player. That's not my personality. It's safe when you play on the outside. You don't get hurt. But I don't play safe. Never have. Never will. That's not who I am. I thought everyone understood that about me. Diplomacy is not my thing.

I often challenged teammates because I cared more about winning than any other aspect of competition. Chris Chelios and I were friends, but Chris never had an issue getting in my face if he didn't like something I was doing. Keith Tkachuk and I had the same kind of relationship.

When I thought a player could be giving more on the ice, I fucking told him. Nothing infuriates me more than players who act as if they don't give a shit. When you play for a team, it's more than a fucking job. The vast majority of NHL players put their heart into winning. But sometimes you temporarily have a mental lapse for a few moments or a game, and you need a teammate or a coach to snap you back into focus.

In my career, I only ran into a few teammates whom I considered lost causes. I couldn't stand playing with goalie Roman Cechmanek in Philadelphia because I felt like he had one foot back in the Czech Republic the minute the regular season was over. He didn't seem to be as serious about the NHL playoffs as the rest of us were. It made me wonder whether he would have preferred playing for his country in the World Championships rather than the Stanley Cup playoffs. Players only get paid in the regular season, not the playoffs. It didn't seem like a coincidence to me that when the paycheques stopped coming, Cechmanek's performance level went downhill. I remember telling teammates after the 2001–02 season that if he was in Philadelphia's net the following fall, I wasn't fucking coming back.

Robert Reichel and I played together in Phoenix in 1998–99, and trainers told me that Reichel had asked to have his post-season physical before we played game seven of our first-round playoff series. That made me believe that Reichel mentally had his bags packed for a trip home to the Czech Republic.

If you think that didn't fucking irritate his teammates, you don't understand the mentality of an NHL player. I have no respect for players who have their minds someplace else when there is a game to be played. I've had my share of off-ice issues, but I'm fairly confident that my former teammates would say that when it came time to play the game, I was all in. When you are fully committed, it also means you are not timid about telling a teammate he needs to amp up his effort.

It was amusing to read people say that I wouldn't have told Marleau to his face that I thought his performance was gutless. I played two seasons with Marleau as my captain in San Jose, and I never had a problem telling him we needed more from him. One night, I even went to his home to discuss the struggles he was going through. It was around Thanksgiving. I was with my family at home. But I couldn't stop thinking about the team, and how dominant the Sharks could be if Marleau would realize his potential. After thinking about it all day, I couldn't take it anymore. I left my family, climbed into my car and drove to Marleau's house. My intention wasn't to yell at him. I wanted to inspire him, to let him know that his teammates were behind him. I went there to tell him that I believed he could be one of league's very best players if he just altered his game slightly. He needed to play with more of an edge. He needed to show some bigger balls when the game was on the line.

What no one seems to understand is that I believe Marleau is a special talent. He's an amazing player, with great skating ability. I am in awe of how he can play the game, but I'm totally frustrated by the lack of desire he shows. I see him as a player who should dominate. He could be like Sidney Crosby or Steven Stamkos. Marleau frustrated me when I played with him because I wanted more from him. He was earning $6.9 million per season, and I just didn't believe he brought the superstar effort that you would expect from that calibre of player.

I tried to tell him that that night, but I could tell 10 minutes into our conversation that I was wasting my time. He considered my arrival at his house as an intrusion. He listened to me, but he never did anything to change the way he was.

Probably, I will never understand Marleau. He will always

boast good offensive numbers, but he could be so much more than numbers.

When Marleau lost his captaincy on August 17, 2009, it certainly wasn't a surprise to those of us who played with him. No matter how big the game was, Marleau's face was always the same. We just didn't see any true passion from him. Win or lose, he was the same.

I wasn't the first, nor will I be the last, analyst to call out Marleau. In 2008, Mike Milbury, now my NBC colleague, said Marleau did a "double flamingo" to get out of the way of a shot from Mike Modano in a playoff game against Dallas. If you are going to be a leader in the NHL, you have to block a shot and you have to show emotion. When I was playing for the Blackhawks in a game at St. Louis years ago, we gave up two goals in the last minute and I fucking snapped. I destroyed three electric fans with my hockey stick. The Blues made me pay a few hundred dollars for the fans. But it was worth every penny, because I sent a message to my teammates that playing that poorly in the final minutes was inexcusable. We never saw Marleau in one of those moments when I was in San Jose. What we got from him was the same temperament. It was like he was punching a time clock every day—punch in, punch out, like he had an ordinary job.

On the night that I ripped Marleau on Versus, I received calls from three Sharks players upset over Marleau's lack of effort on that play.

"You obviously have not heard what I said about Marleau," I said to them.

People ask me whether I have spoken to Marleau about my criticism. As of the writing of this book, I have not. Frankly, I don't give a shit whether he likes me or not. There was a sign that Marleau didn't like me before I blasted him on the air. After I retired, I came back for San Jose's first game. After the game, Tracy and I were downstairs waiting for the guys to come out of the locker room. Marleau and his wife walked right past us without even acknowledging that we were there. But the bottom line is this: NBC doesn't pay me to be polite. They pay me to analyze hockey games, and it's part of my job to say on live television whether a player is performing well or not. When the game was on the line, Marleau was dreadful.

You can like Marleau because he's a good father, or because he's polite and soft-spoken. You can like him because he's good-looking. I'm not analyzing those aspects of his life. But being good-looking doesn't earn you a Stanley Cup championship.

During my playing career, I ran into some people who accepted mediocrity. That was okay for them; it's not okay for me. One reason our society is messed up these days is the acceptance of mediocrity. We haven't demanded greatness from ourselves.

NBC didn't hire me to spoon-feed sugar-coated analysis to the viewers. I was hired to bring passion to the broadcast. Sometimes, my passion boils over into outrage or confrontation, like what happened on February 29, 2012, when fellow NBC analyst Mike Milbury and I became involved in a heated argument over Dallas forward Eric Nystrom's hit on Pittsburgh defenceman Kris Letang. What viewers saw on television was the PG version of an R-rated argument that Milbury and I had had earlier that evening.

I wasn't scheduled to be involved in the post-game coverage, but I was watching that game in the green room as I prepared for my time on the air later that night. I saw the hit and loved the hit live and on the replay. When I watched Milbury and Keith Jones analyze the hit during the intermission, I was stunned when they agreed it was a dirty hit and that Nystrom should be suspended.

"Are you fucking kidding me?" I screamed at my television.

When they were off the air, I marched into the studio. "Mike, are you fucking nuts?" I asked. "Jonesy . . . What's wrong with you? Are you going fucking soft on me? It was a great hit, a beautiful hit."

Milbury told me to fuck off. "It was a brutal hit, a chickenshit hit," Milbury said.

"You're calling this a chickenshit hit, the same guy who went into the stands and beat a guy with a shoe?" I said.

In 1979, Milbury picked up the nickname "Mad Mike" Milbury after he climbed into the stands to help teammates Terry O'Reilly and Peter McNab, who were battling with fans at Madison Square Garden. In the heat of the battle, Milbury grabbed a fan's leg and the fan's shoe came off. Milbury then whacked the fan with the shoe before throwing it on the ice.

Now Mad Mike is going all Greenpeace on me because he believes Nystrom nicked Letang's jaw. "Look at his head snap back," Milbury yelled.

"Your head would snap back if I hit you in the chest, too," I said.

"It's a new game, J.R. This is exactly what we are trying to get rid of," Milbury said.

"Fuck that," I said.

Jones sat out the argument, but I dragged him in. "Why don't you be controversial for one time in your fucking TV life?" I said.

"Get out of here. You're fucking crazy," Milbury said.

NBC producer Sam Flood immediately stepped into the studio and told me to get out of there. He then informed me that he wanted me on the post-game show to continue this debate.

Mike and I were slightly more professional on camera, meaning there were no F-bombs and I didn't call him a "pussy," as I had in our earlier argument. But our on-air battle was still intense. The news accounts of it said it looked like we almost came to blows. That wasn't true, but the passion was genuine.

Milbury's position was that Nystrom had tried to "decapitate" Letang rather than play the puck, and I said Letang had put himself in a vulnerable position. Jones tried to compare the hit to the big hit Raffi Torres of Vancouver had laid on Brent Seabrook of Chicago in the 2011 playoffs. He clearly thought it was a cheap shot.

"We should just take hitting out of the game," I said sarcastically.

Milbury's point was that the objective of the new rules "is to change the mindset" from not hurting players when they are in a vulnerable position. To me, if a player puts himself in a vulnerable position, that's his fault and he may have to pay the consequences. I never expected the rules to protect me when I was on the ice. I learned to keep my head up.

When our debate was winding down, Milbury told me on live television to get out of the studio. "Don't let the door hit you on the way out," he said.

My final shot was to say that I was going to order Milbury a Shirley Temple drink.

It was great television. Flood loved the passion and the give-and-take. He used social media to make sure everyone watched our confrontation. Television works best when two analysts have differing opinions, because fan opinions usually vary widely.

Personally, I had nothing against Letang. He is an excellent player. He plays at full speed all of the time. I admire the way he plays. But my analysis of the hit had nothing to do with how I felt about him. I never want to see a player get hurt. I identify with players—especially someone who suffers a concussion, because I had so many in my career. But hockey is a contact sport, and you accept some risk when you decide to play. By lowering his head in an effort to stretch for the puck, Letang made himself more vulnerable. I don't believe Nystrom was targeting Letang's head.

Obviously, Brendan Shanahan, the NHL's director of player safety, agreed with me, because Nystrom was not suspended.

After I defended the Nystrom hit, Pittsburgh fans came after me viciously on Twitter. As this book is being written, I have more than a hundred thousand Twitter followers, and I enjoy interacting with everyone. But I have to say that there is a small group of sick, twisted Pittsburgh fans whose priorities are seriously fucked up. The shit they say makes me believe that karma is going to fuck these people up someday, and I would like to be there to see it.

I appreciate people with passion, but there are lines that shouldn't ever be crossed, and some people cross those lines with no remorse. They are pussies, cowards who hide behind the anonymity of a computer screen. I'm not going to say anything on Twitter, or on the television airwaves, that I wouldn't say to your face. That's who I am.

About the time the Letang situation was going on, I had flown to Minnesota with Tracy to visit Jack Jablonski, the high school player who was paralyzed by a hit from behind during a game. After reading the story about him, I felt like I wanted to do something to help. He followed me on Twitter, and I felt I wanted to meet him. If he wanted someone to listen, I could do that. If he wanted someone to tell stories to help take his mind off his medical issues for a few hours, I could do that. If he needed someone to help raise awareness for the cause of eliminating hits from behind, I could do that. If he needed help raising money for that cause, I could do that. It was an inspiring four-hour visit with a remarkable young man. We are still in touch today.

But even my tweet about Jablonski couldn't be left alone by this small group of faceless idiot Pittsburgh fans on Twitter. Still mad over my comments about the Letang hit, some said they were glad Jablonski was paralyzed and hoped I would end up paralyzed as well.

Some of the most disgusting words I've ever seen in print came from Pittsburgh fans angry over my take on the Letang hit. There were a couple of comments from two college students from Villanova that made me think that I should go down there and snap photos of them, to expose them as the pussies they really are. Wouldn't they just shit themselves if I showed up at their door with a camera? These kind of people try to stay faceless and anonymous, but it didn't take me long to figure out what high school they attended.

Please note that I'm talking about a small group of Pittsburgh fans here. Mostly, I enjoy Twitter because it allows me to connect with fans. I've always enjoyed interacting with fans, although I don't think some fans truly understand what I'm about.

When the Blackhawks won the Stanley Cup in 2010, I teared up on the air as I talked about Chicago winning the championship for the first time since 1961. It was emotional for me to see Blackhawks carrying the Stanley Cup. I had worn the Chicago jersey proudly, and the Blackhawks' triumph reminded me how my teammates and I had reached the Stanley Cup final in 1992, only to fall short against Pittsburgh.

I was happy for the city of Chicago, where I had always been treated well. I was happy for the Wirtz family. Although I'd had my differences with the late Mr. Wirtz over the contract, I still had a soft spot for him, and I was glad the Wirtz name was engraved on the Cup.

Those were the feelings I had. Based on how my Twitter account fucking blew up, you would have thought my emotions were satanic in origin. Philadelphia fans crucified me for being happy for the Blackhawks. The amount of hatred that came my way was staggering.

What people don't seem to grasp is that I would have been equally teary-eyed had the Flyers won the Cup. I loved my time in Philadelphia. Fans in Philly appreciate gritty players. I was born to play for the Flyers.

Philly is a lunchpail-and-hardhat town. The Broad Street Bullies, who won back-to-back Stanley Cup championships in 1974 and 1975, are still worshipped like gods in Philadelphia. It's been 37 years since Philadelphia has had a Stanley Cup parade, and fans deserve another one. I would have been just as thrilled to see players wearing the orange and black hoisting the Stanley Cup.

To be honest, every Stanley Cup on-ice celebration leaves me a little misty. Ever since I watched Eruzione celebrate with his American teammates on Lake Placid ice, I wanted to know the joy that he was feeling at that moment.

Some players don't like to watch the Stanley Cup final after their team is eliminated, but I always made a point of watching the celebration because I wanted the mob scene on the ice to be another motivation for me.

I remember in 2001 I was at a nice restaurant, Cowboy Ciao's in Scottsdale, Arizona, with some friends on the night of game seven of the Stanley Cup final between the Colorado Avalanche and the New Jersey Devils. That was the year the Avalanche rallied around 40-year-old Ray Bourque to win a Cup for him. The Colorado team had erased a 3–2 series lead to force a seventh game against the defending Stanley Cup champion Devils.

At that time, I was 31. I was beginning to wonder whether I would ever have another chance at winning the Stanley Cup. It had been nine years since I reached the final, and at that point, I had not won a playoff series in five years. It was important to me to see Bourque win his Stanley Cup. Unfortunately, I had plans that night, and Cowboy Ciao's is not a big-screen-TV-style restaurant. The closest bar with televisions showing the game was Madison's Restaurant and Bar, located four blocks away.

I was the only person in my party who had any interest in seeing the game. Three times, I excused myself from the table and hauled my ass down to check on Bourque's progress. The timing of my last trip was perfect. I arrived at Madison's not long before the Avalanche had completed a 3–1 triumph and Colorado captain Joe Sakic handed the Cup to Bourque, who had tears streaming down his cheeks.

As I stood in the bar and watched Bourque raise the Cup, I was just as emotional as I was on the air the night when the Blackhawks won in 2010.

Winning a Stanley Cup was the one goal I didn't achieve in my NHL career. But it doesn't keep me up at night. That statement will piss off my haters on Twitter because they love to give me shit about my lack of a championship. Pittsburgh fans seem to take particular delight in pointing that out.

"Sidney Crosby has a Cup, and you don't," they will write.

It makes me laugh, because I think they believe that reading those words will put me over the edge. It doesn't, really. It was an awesome experience to wear an NHL uniform, to score 50 goals in a season, to be an All-Star, to hang out in the dressing room with the guys. It's impossible to describe how close you become with your teammates. I had high moments and low moments in my career, but most of my low moments resulted from my mouth. I have nothing but fond memories about my results on the ice. I feel as if my career was a huge success.

I don't believe the lack of a championship defines my career, because I know I put my heart and soul into accomplishing that goal. I just wasn't in the right city at the right time. I believed my Philadelphia teams were good enough to win. In real terms, my best chance came in 1992, when the Blackhawks reached the Stanley Cup final. But history has shown that the Penguins team that beat us was much better than we realized.

However, the true missed opportunity may have come just one month after Bourque won his Stanley Cup, when I was an unrestricted free agent and chose to sign with Philadelphia over Detroit. I believed both teams had an excellent chance to win the championship. As I've said, while it was Rick Tocchet who finally convinced me to choose Philadelphia, a major factor in my decision was my belief that the Philadelphia area offered the best possibility for my wife, Tracy, and daughter, Brandi, to pursue their interest in competitive horse riding. For most of my career, I hadn't paid enough attention to my family concerns; I had realized that I needed better balance in my life. I wanted to think more about my family.

What I didn't know when I declined Detroit's offer is that, 11 months later, the Red Wings would win the Stanley Cup championship.

I loved my time with the Flyers; playing in Philadelphia is one of the highlights of my career. But I often think about what might have been had I gone to Detroit.

Because it was the best decision for my family, it would be nice for me to tell you that I would still make the same decision today if I had a do-over. But that wouldn't do justice to how badly I wanted a championship ring.

The truth is that if I would have known Detroit would win a Stanley Cup in 2002, I would have said, "Fuck the horses."

# Acknowledgements

Book publishing is like hockey: it's a team sport. This is my book, but creating it was a collaborative effort. Make no mistake about that. It's funny that most of the same people who were major contributors in my hockey career also gave me a boost in my first literary endeavour. My player agent, Neil Abbott, along with my most important coach, Mike Keenan, and my great teammate Keith Tkachuk, provided considerable insight and stories for the book, as did long time friends Matt Mallgrave, Justin Duberman and Darcy Walsh. I also have to thank my parents, Wally and Jo, as well as my brother, Trevor, for all the memories, many of which I recall in the first chapter.

Kevin Allen and I spent many hours talking about the book and Kevin spent many more hours than that crafting my story into the book you have in your hand. I thank him for his hard work and for listening to my many stories over the past 18 months. He truly made a difference in bringing this project together.

Thanks to Mike Modano for the competition. Those years of using you as the yardstick by which to measure myself provided plenty of stories for this book. And I offer my appreciation to

293

everyone else who gave me one of the great anecdotes or kernels of information that help fill in these pages.

It has been great to work with publishing companies that truly understand hockey. HarperCollins Canada has an all-star team that includes my affable editor, Jim Gifford, and the others who helped pull everything together: Iris Tupholme, Noelle Zitzer, Brad Wilson, Alan Jones, Kelly Hope and Jason Pratt, as well as our proofreader, Patricia MacDonald, and our superb copy editor, Lloyd Davis. That man knows the sport. In the U.S., Triumph Books is another publisher with plenty of experience in hockey books. My thanks go to the Triumph staff, including Mitch Rogatz, Tom Bast, Adam Motin and others.

I also want to thank my fans, many of whom have been with me since I showed up in Chicago as a skinny teenager who had no idea what life in the NHL was all about. You should know that I've always appreciated and cherished your support. Thanks for shelling out your hard-earned money to read about my life in hockey.

Also, I would like to thank my current agent, Mark Lepselter of Maxx Sports Entertainment, who knew I wanted to write a book before I did. I wasn't sure, but he said it was a great idea. And as usual, he was right. It was a fantastic idea. I can't wait to do another.

Finally, I need to thank my family, especially my children, Brandi and Brett, and my wife, Tracy, who is my strongest rock, my friend and my life partner. I love you guys very much. Thanks for allowing me to lead the most tremendous life I could ever imagine.

# Index

# Index

Graham, Dirk, 2, 50, 78, 84, 91–92
Green, Travis, 274
Gretzky, Wayne ("The Great One"), 7, 21, 83, 152, 265–66
  as coach of Phoenix Coyotes, 216–27
  injured by Gary Suter, 164–65
Grimson, Stu, 85, 194–95, 272
Guts (game), 117, 120–21

Harney, James, 157
Harper, Ron, 76
Hart, Gordon, 126
Hasek, Dominik, 57–58, 152, 271
Hatcher, Derian, 125–29, 170
Hay, Don, 110
Henry, Charlie, 101
Hewitt, Jennifer Love, 208, 209
Hextall, Ron, 196
Hitchcock, Ken, 147–49, 153, 154, 176–77, 181, 184, 227, 258
*Hockey Central*, 279
*Hockey News, The*, 29–30
Holmgren, Paul, 196
Howe, Gordie, 3–4
Hudson, Mike, 221
Hull, Bobby, 78–79, 252
Hull, Brett, 97
Hull Olympiques, 21, 44–47, 101

Islanders. *See* New York Islanders

Jablonski, Jack, 286–87
Jagr, Jaromir, 84
Janney, Craig, 102, 103, 105, 123–24
Joe Louis Arena, 270
Johnson, K.C., 193
Johnson, Magic, 266
Johnston, Eddie, 21–22
Johnston, Karen, 176, 184
Jones, Keith, 284
Joseph, Curtis, 271

Kapanen, Sami, 178
Keenan, Mike ("Iron Mike"), 33, 50, 54–59, 62, 84–85, 87–88. *See also specific topics*
  Blackhawks' firing of, 88–89, 98
  coaching strategies, 56, 58
  Dave Manson and, 52–53, 62
  early encounters with J.R., 18–19, 33–34
  interactions with J.R., 43–44, 51, 59, 70, 73, 79, 87, 94, 136, 227
  influence on J.R., 3, 4, 45, 73, 190
  Steve Larmer and, 82
  as St. Louis Blues' general manager, 97
  tactics and philosophy, 56, 58–59, 68, 85–86, 94, 131
  Team Canada coached by, 82–83, 88
  Tracy Roenick and, 69, 89, 136
  Trent Yawney and, 55, 59

299

# Index

# Index

# Index